THE OUTDOOR CLASSROOM

Integrating Learning and Adventure

Edited by

James R. Jelmberg, PhD
University of New Hampshire

Greg S. Goodman, EdD
Clarion University of Pennsylvania

HAMPTON PRESS, INC.
CRESSKILL, NEW JERSEY

Printed in the United States of America

Library of Congress Cataloging-in-Publication Data

The outdoor classroom : integrating learning and adventure / edited by
James R. Jelmberg, Greg S. Goodman
     p. cm.
   Includes bibliographic references and index.
   ISBN 978-1-57273-798-3 (hardbound) -- ISBN 978-1-57273-799-0 (pbk.)
1. Outdoor education. 2. Experiential learning. 3. Adventure education. 4. Critical
pedagogy. I. Jelmberg, James. R. II. Goodman, Greg S., 1949-
   LC1047.O938 2008
   371.3'84--dc22
                        2007041001

Hampton Press, Inc.
23 Broadway
Cresskill, NJ 07626

This book is dedicated to two outstanding mentors from the education department at The University of New Hampshire . Professor Michael Andrew is the founder and Director of the groundbreaking Five Year Teacher Education Program at the University of New Hampshire. This innovative and integrated, undergraduate/graduate program features an early exploring teaching course and a full year internship with a master's degree option. In addition to his considerable administrative responsibilities, Mike has been a prolific author, an inspiring professor, and a visionary educational leader. Fortunately for me, he found time to be my mentor. I have been privileged to have taught courses, conducted research, and published articles with him. He also finds time to manage his 20-acre horse farm and to coach and play the unusually challenging sport of polo. It gives me great pleasure to dedicate this book to Professor and Director Mike Andrew, a man for all seasons.

Dwight Webb has been an inspiration and a visionary leader in New Hampshire's outdoor education community for over 30 years. As a professor of counselor education at the University of New Hampshire, Dwight has had the opportunity to lend direction to hundreds of students. For me, Dwight's openness and generosity of spirit was a lighthouse during dark days of my early career explorations. Dwight supported my Outward Bound (O.B.) ventures and validated my early work adapting O.B. for public school use. He taught me how to yodel, and he has continued to support my growth in every regard. Much of this book is a reflection of Dwight's legacy and love of the outdoors.

CONTENTS

PART III
MYTHS AND LEGENDS

PREFACE

The Outdoor Classroom is a series of love stories. Like love, it is relationship-based and empirical in nature. In examples and strategies, we are led into a world of teaching and learning that is fueled by environmental connection. The relationships represented, whether between teacher and student, peer and mentor, are not in the magical "do this and it will change everything" category. Rather, it is an earthy love based on trial and error, observation, reflection and integration. The education of the outdoor teacher is based on that person's experience over time. As Greg Goodman says, after returning from a "perfect" day on the rockface with a group of alternative school students "fairly humming with joy along the trail, my high from the success of the day's activity was quickly returned to earth's floor by the hanging scent of marijuana on the trail's corridor." His high was not the same as that of his students. Here was a turning point. Would he say, "I'm never, ever going to take those kids outside the school again!" I have heard teachers say that. Or would he seek counsel and try to learn what was going on, both with his students and with himself? We are better for his taking the latter course.

The value of the book is found in the truthful nature of the reflections, and the stories by Jelmberg, Goodman, and other knowledgeable outdoor educators who have labored long in these vineyards. As a foundation we have Paulo Freire's seminal work on "critical pedagogy." The author's choice of Freire speaks to the desire to take outdoor education from the rarefied world of privilege and connect it to the "foundations of multicultural education, postmodernism, and social justice." With the Freire reference, there is also the implied warning that this book is not about a magical transformation that takes place simply because a person skis down a hill or climbs a mountain.

Next, Jelmberg and Goodman establish what is an essential fact. By focusing on the mind-body connection instead of the Cartesian split, they go to the heart of learning through experience. Mind-body relationships are formed through feeling the tines of a sea urchin on a rocky shore, the sandpaper texture of a skate in an aquarium touch tank, the struggle toward conflict resolution when it is getting dark and everyone is hungry or the experience of fear and trust while being belayed on a challenge course. We become connected to the subject. This resonates with my work and what my colleague Richard Maizell calls the "ABC Triangle": Affect, Behavior, and Cognition working in concert with each other.

Part Two, "Outdoor Education Praxis," takes us through several "cuts" or "angles" on outdoor experience. Backpacking and overnight work is differentiated from the day trip to a woodland; rock climbing and initiative problem-solving has its own section; and the water environments of oceans, streams, and ponds are presented. Practical information is presented in the form of activities, required equipment, and strategies. This section is significantly balanced with a look at college and university learning as it relates to outdoor education. Dating back to the Dartmouth Outing Club, we see an evolution toward connection with physical education classes, Adventure-Based Counseling, classroom adventure activities and ultimately toward the highly evolved graduate and undergraduate programs at Prescott College. *The Outdoor Classroom* will be extremely useful for the college student searching for a learning and career path.

In "Myths and Legends," Tim Churchard speaks of his love for his mentor Keith King, the pioneer outdoor educator from Keene State College, and of the therapeutic and socially responsive connections his friend Bill Cuff has given to him. He weaves that passion and skill into his work with youth at the Rochester Alternative School. The shared instinct toward good people and their practices ensure that Jim Jelmberg and Greg Goodman know what they are talking about.

Jim Schoel

Coordinator of Experiential Education
SEEM Special Needs Collaborative
Stoneham, MA

ACKNOWLEDGEMENTS

Many people have contributed to the creation of this book. It is with great appreciation for their thoughts, commitment, and writing that we recognize their contributions. First and foremost, our wives, Johanne Jelmberg and Andy Goodman, have been our greatest supporters. Their love, patience, and understanding have helped us during the months of deliberation when we were impatient, discouraged, or stuck deciding what would stay and what we would cut. When we conceived of writing this book, we were aboard Peter Ordway's sailboat, Pelorus Jack, in the middle of Casco Bay. From that vantage point, all that lay ahead looked fortuitous.

The heroes and heroines of this text are the teachers and administrators who have lead the trips and shouldered the responsibilities related to making all of these adventures successful. Thank you Jim Dodge, Al Rocci, Marcia Ross, Chris Pollet, Anne Heisey, Joe Hadam, Tom Bonoccorsi, Todd Allen, Stephanie Ward, Linda Mengers, Sue Bissell, Cathy Dawson, Linda Reif, Paula Ickeringill, Beth Doran, Al Stuart, Al Lofgren, Holly Pirtle, Sheila Johnson, Lynn Ellsworth, Michelle McInnis, and Debra Shaw. We are particularly grateful to John Parsons, John MacArthur, Linda Becker, Sue Williams, and Katie Firczuk from the Phoenix Team for contributing their updated Seacoast curriculum and for keeping the Oyster River Middle School Program filled with adventure. We thank all of the Middle School staff who have helped to keep making this dynamic venture successful.

All of the Myths and Legends contributors have made this book fun to compile. Jed Williamson, Dan Garvey, Deborah Freed, Gene Rose, Gary Sells, and Tim Churchard have been legendary leaders in outdoor education for many years. Their love of the outdoors has been contagious, and it is impossible to say how many lives have been changed by the interaction of these folks and those who were new to outdoor learning. We would like to thank outdoor education legend, Jim Schoel, Director of Project Adventure and co-author of *Islands of Healing* who has contributed greatly with his preface to this book. We also thank Professor Jo Laird for her geology expertise and Professors Dick Weyrick and James Barrett for their forestry expertise. Also, we thank Pam McPhee and the Browne Center staff for their support. Evelyn Browne was an early supporter of our work, and the legacy she has left on the Dame Road is a tribute to all of the early outdoor education friends. Mark Yacovone, Barbara Locke, and Doug Prince were instrumental to our progress with their computer photography expertise and willingness to do what we thought could not be done. Richard Knight, Jannik and Toshi Jelmberg and Pete Hartle also contributed greatly to the photography.

We would like to also thank our critical readers and reviewers, Bruce Smith, Paul Beare, and Michael Peters. Lastly, we thank Barbara Morton for her dedication to editorial excellence. This book is visually distinguished by her intelligence and attention to detail.

INTRODUCTION

The Outdoor Classroom is designed to be an inspirational instructional guide for teachers and other educational professionals working with students in grades 4 through the college years. This book is also written to serve as a text for college instructors teaching courses in experiential education (EE), outdoor education, recreation, and curriculum methods. In our work within public schools as well as in our roles as university teachers, we strive to incorporate experiential learning process and interdisciplinary learning methodology as best practices to increase motivation and to maximize student learning.

As a textbook, *The Outdoor Classroom* is unique within the field of EE because it breaks new ground by linking critical pedagogy with adventure learning. Pedagogy is defined as the philosophical foundation of education. One's pedagogy represents the belief system that connects the daily processes of instruction with a sense of purpose. Critical pedagogy, the foundation for this book, is a pedagogy based on a love of humanity and a belief that all people are created equal and are deserving of an education that furthers their ability to achieve socially just opportunities (Freire, 1970). As we describe in depth throughout this book, critical pedagogy can provide multiple pathways for engaging learners in meaningful educational experience. The notion of critical pedagogy is the contribution of one of education's premier mentors, Paulo Freire (McLaren, 2000). Freire was an early and courageous proponent of true democracy: the concept that women, the poor, and the politically oppressed or underrepresented were deserving of equal opportunities to access health care, adequate housing, and proper nutrition. Freire (1970) believed that one of the keys to breaking out of the oppression of ignorance was through education. His contribution, critical pedagogy, has been a large part of the foundations of multicultural education, postmodernism, and social justice education. Although several writers have previously presented links between multicultural education and EE (Roberts & Rodriguez, 1999), this is the one of the first books to place these values among the top of EE's purposes.

The Outdoor Classroom is divided into three parts. In part I, Outdoor Education and Critical Pedagogy, we articulate the role of critical pedagogy within EE. The values of multicultural education are also strongly reinforced. The second part of the book focused on the praxis of experiential education. Praxis is the term Freire (1970) developed to describe the application of critical pedagogy within the classroom. Because our classroom is located in the outdoors, we position praxis within all of the settings selected by our authors: the mountains, woods, rivers, rock faces, and oceans that are our "classrooms." This section of the book provides clear, "how-to" instructions for planning, organizing, conducting, and evaluating outdoor education or EE as a methodology for improving student achievement.

Part III, the Myths and Legends, represents the soul of outdoor education. During our many years of work in and around EE, we have been fortunate to know and accompany many of the important contributors to this dynamic enterprise called experiential learning. For your edification and inspiration, we have asked several of these individuals to pen or speak their response to why they became connected to EE and what they have received for their efforts. Although all of the stories have unique, personal attributes, the writers' overarching common denominators are the call of nature's wonder and the awakening of healthy and powerful spirits within ourselves and others. What we do, this teaching and learning and re-learning and re-teaching, is the process of discovery learning, reflective teaching, and EE that is the quintessence of the outdoor classroom. Always growing, questioning, and challenging life in the present is the Tao of outdoor educators. As you will read in this section, the lure and calling of the outdoors is the stuff of legends.

REFERENCES

Freire, P. (1970). *Pedagogy of the oppressed*. New York: Continuum.
McLaren, P. (2000). *Che Guevara, Paulo Freire, and the pedagogy of revolution*. Lanham, MD: Rowman and Littlefield.
Roberts, N., & Rodriguez, D. (1999). *Multicultural issues in outdoor education*. ERIC Document: ED438151.

ABOUT THE AUTHORS

Mary Breunig has been involved in outdoor and experiential education for 18 years. She has spent 7 of those years leading outdoor wilderness trips year-round. Mary is currently an assistant professor in the Department of Recreation and Leisure Studies at Brock University in St. Catharines, Ontario, Canada. Mary's teaching and research focuses on issues of social and environmental justice in outdoor and experiential education. She is co-editor of the *Journal of Experiential Education*.

Greg S. Goodman is an assistant professor in the Education Department at Clarion University in Pennsylvania. Since completing a 26-day Outward Bound course in the Colorado Rockies in 1970, he has been a self-described, "born-again" outdoor education disciple. His previous books include: *Alternatives in Education* (Lang, 1999), *Reducing Hate Crimes and Violence among American Youth* (Lang, 2001), *Critical Multicultural Conversations* (Hampton Press, 2004), and *The Hiker's Guide to the Central Sierra* (Hergenroeder, 2004).

James R. Jelmberg started a school-wide outdoor education program over 30 years ago at the Oyster River Middle School in Durham, New Hampshire. He directed the program and led wilderness expeditions for over 10 years while teaching seminars on outdoor education at Brandeis University and the University of New Hampshire. Jim has been a consultant in middle school education for colleges in New Hampshire and schools in South Africa. His research publications include such topics as college-based teacher education program versus state-sponsored alternative certification programs, and comparing student perceptions of instruction in teacher education and other college courses. Jim is on the education department faculty at the University of New Hampshire.

Jon McLaren designed and directed the University of Maryland's Outdoor Education Program for 10 years. He currently works for the City of Tacoma

Park, Maryland, where he enjoys delivering community programs. When not at work, he enjoys skateboarding, rock climbing, home renovating, and being with his wife Julie, daughter Aubrey, and son Ian. He got his start in the outdoors at Camp Minikani in Hubertus, Wisconsin.

I

OUTDOOR EDUCATION
AND CRITICAL PEDAGOGY

1

THE OUTDOOR CLASSROOM

Greg S. Goodman

James R. Jelmberg

You do not have to be good.
You do not have to walk on your knees
For a hundred miles through the desert, repenting.
You only have to let the soft animal of your body
Love what it loves.

—Oliver (1986)

The goal of creating an exciting learning environment has been pre-eminent in outdoor education philosophy since its inception more than 50 years ago. In our current application of outdoor education theory, none of the adventure lore is lost. In fact, as our society continues to advance technologically and scientifically, traditional outdoor approaches to learning become even more meaningful and relevant. Using many of the techniques and exercises adopted and adapted from Outward Bound, the National Outdoor Leadership School, and other dynamic experiential learning organizations, outdoor education teachers can create lessons that inspire student achievement in their own locales—urban or rural. Although many lessons in this text take the reader to forests and seashores, moral or metaphorical equivalents of our most beautiful natural areas can be found in many outdoor locations from urban parks to riverfronts. The city abounds with outdoor learning possibilities.

These authors come to outdoor education seeking robust intellectual stimulation, increased sense of personal agency, and positive psychosocial identification. Our concern for the environment is only surpassed by our love of humanity and a perceived need for greater connectedness between the diverse constituencies living within our communities. The combination of environmental and humanitarian crisis we face both locally and globally requires the implementation of rigorous and relevant educational practices. Real problems such as poverty, urban decay, racism, global warming, and the achievement gap demand active, socially just, and meaningful educational approaches. Because these requirements are so compelling and dynamic, outdoor education's experiential learning method is perfectly suited for these community and educational challenges. In the early days of Outward Bound, Willie Unsoeld would speak of moral equivalents. His point was that modern society was "damn confusing," and educators needed to create character building activities through metaphors of courage. A metaphor that can be created by rappelling down a rock face could relate to the moral equivalent of overcoming fear of succumbing to personal failure resulting from poor choices. For example, the courage applied to complete a difficult rappel could have a moral equivalent of finding the requisite resolve for refusing to join a gang or staying away from drugs. In our society, we need to provide more examples of the value of courage and inner strength for our youth's healthy development. This is especially true in inner-city and closely related urban areas. In places where there is not an easy connection to natural exposure to healthy adventure, the use of metaphors and moral equivalents are an essential component of a good teacher's pedagogy and praxis.

CRITICAL PEDAGOGY

The Outdoor Classroom breaks new ground by linking traditional outdoor educational philosophy with critical pedagogy. Critical pedagogy is the contribution of the mentor Paulo Freire (1970). Freire, a Brazilian schooling and social visionary, appealed to the world's educators to consider the provision of social justice as the pre-eminent mission for all teachers. Social justice in Freire's eyes meant giving citizens the ability to read and, therefore, the key to learning how to break away from the oppressive domination of poverty and social inequality (McLaren, 2000). Throughout all of his life, Freire championed concern for the poor, illiterate, and underrepresented citizens by developing literacy circles and calling for the education of all, not just an elite few. Out of his love of the people and a desire to provide education for the empowerment of all, Freire inspired educators interested in social justice to adopt critical pedagogy as essential to the development of meaningful educational practice (McLaren, 2000).

For all students, but especially for those attending urban schools, critical pedagogy has wide applicability in our educational community. As our national educational system continues to confront a crisis of relevance and is challenged in all areas for improvements, the need for educational reform is most critical in urban settings where unemployment and underemployment is pervasive and alienation from successful role models predominates. For most urban youth, large-scale efforts to provide equal opportunity appear to be economically and socially unsupported. In response to the need to bring excitement and relevance back to the schools, *The Outdoor Classroom* is written to help teachers support and teach underrepresented individuals and groups.

In today's confusing culture, it may be fair to add that almost all youth require authentic activities to build connection to real-world meaning for the value of one another and the need to protect our environment. Often lost in a make-believe world of video games and a mass-marketed culture of violence and escapism, today's youth need mentoring to guide them to the world of authentic experience and personal connectedness. We believe Freire, were he still alive, would approve of these efforts to create more robust learning environments and curricula, especially ones that represent and reinforce policies of social justice and environmental education.

Freire's work has ignited a new political revolution in American educational dialogue (Goodman, 1999; Kincheloe & Steinberg, 1997; McLaren, 1997). Informed by Freire's thought and word, educators for social justice are inspired to have hope for the future through Freire's critical pedagogy: the pedagogy of love. In Freire's eyes, love was a love for humanity. This love is not a romantic love, but a compassion and connectedness with all people to create successful communities. Successful communities, in Freire's eyes, were ones in which all citizens could read, develop personal agency, and leave poverty and injustice behind. To actually do this work, one must engage in an educational process that produces direct, observable results. Building on critical pedagogy's essential mission, *The Outdoor Classroom* helps educators improve their schools and communities by having students connect with one another and through creating an awareness of environmental concerns. In successful outdoor programs, antiracist teaching and recycling programs run hand in hand with experientially delivered social studies and science curriculum.

The Outdoor Classroom includes specific curriculum and instructional strategies one can adapt and apply in one's own setting. Many lessons are integrated. An example of integrated instruction could be that the math is applied in measurement to determine how many miles one will walk. If this walk happens to travel through a salt marsh, the math is integrated with lessons of biology (what animals abound?) or hydrology (what is the salinity of the water?) or botany (which plants live in this habitat?). Students get multiple entreaties to learning as they slog through the marsh.

The Outdoor Classroom also includes organizational advice, orientation materials for parents/guardians, and a host of protocols germane to program safety and operation. The goals of outdoor education are simple, but their accomplishment is profound. When we re-read the assessments our students contribute in debriefing, we are inspired to continue our work in this adventure-filled domain. We trust the reader will find these lessons inspiring and enjoyable, too.

WHY THE OUTDOOR CLASSROOM?

There are many compelling reasons why the outdoor classroom is an ideal learning environment. Being in the outdoors is highly motivating because it is filled with so many natural opportunities for stimulation. In an outdoor setting, all of our senses are aroused. Hearing the sound of the wind, bird calls, and other natural noises (or silence) all comprise integral parts of the sensory stimulation. Also, the fresh air, rain or blue sky, and other environmental stimuli can help to create an excitement in the senses. The combined effect of visual, auditory, and kinesthetic stimulations can afford multimodality invitations for learning. The mind is fully engaged with the compelling call of holistic, multimodality instruction (Watson-Gegeo & Gegeo, 2004). The sense of holistic integration is well-articulated by Watson-Gegeo and Gegeo:

> We now realize from research that we human beings understand the world the way that we do because of the kinds of bodies and the potential for neuronal development that we have (Regier, 1995, 1996). As feminists have also argued (Grosz, 1993), ours is an embodied mind, and therefore the Cartesian split between body and mind constitutes a fundamental error in Western philosophy. Until now it has been assumed that the higher cognitive functions are independent of other mental processes, such as feelings, intuition, and so forth—in fact, that they must be kept separate from the latter, less rational mental processes. However, research has shown that emotion, for instance, is essential to making logical, rational judgments, including moral decisions (Damasio, 1994), and that emotion "links closely with cognition to shape action,

thought, and long-term development" (Fischer, Kennedy, and Cheng, 1998, pp. 22-23). Howard Gardner (1983, 1989) has demonstrated that human beings develop "multiple intelligences," including many forms of intelligence and knowing that lie outside the "cognitive skills" emphasized or even recognized in schools as important. (p. 243)

The outdoor classroom is also liberating. Being able to freely move one's body can be joyous. Exerting oneself to accomplish a task is fulfilling. Long walks, paddles, or ski adventures open one up to the beauty of the world and the possibilities that may be there for one to enjoy individually and collectively. Being able to learn how we can respect and preserve nature for the future is connected to our ability to participate and enjoy the environment at the moment (Hampton & Cole, 1995). Like the irony of a Zen koan, people in our advanced technological society have become alienated from their environment, nature, and simple pleasures of life. Urban youth more frequently access the world vicariously through film rather than authentically with their whole body.

THE TEACHABLE MOMENT

In outdoor education, we seek opportunities for learning that we call "the teachable moment." This phenomenon is identified as a specific and significant moment in time when the student's interest is peaked. In experiential education, the achievement of the teachable moment is the quintessence of the pedagogy. The work of this school of education is to achieve a vivid, unforgettable learning experience. In a meaningful context, students grasp concepts and facts that can be lost in less lively or pedantic presentations. Through the creation of a perfectly teachable moment, outdoor learning has a tendency to remain embedded in the student's memory. Lessons learned in exciting contexts have a way of crystallizing in one's memory. For example, teaching the definition of courage as the ability to overcome fear is completely clear to a student who just completed a 200-foot rappel. As Jed Williamson taught about Jack London, the real significance of learning to build a fire with three matches is clearer when the student has been outside and personally experienced wet wood, gusting winds, and biting cold.

In re-reading the student writing we have collected over the past 30 years, recurrent themes emerge. The deeply personal connection that the students achieve with the lesson objectives inspires us to include examples for the reader's edification. The writing we have received is rich with a robust student voice. The debriefing process we employ is inspired by Dewey's (1944) admonition not to just do but to seriously consider our experience's value and meaning. Learning, according to Dewey, was the process of thinking about our experiences. In a culture that is experience-wealthy (as in quantity not quality) and critically thinking poor, learning how to apply the Dewey learning method is enriching. As we re-read our student's writing and take our own advice to consider this work's meaning, we find this process creates a reinforcing loop (Senge, 1990).

HOW TO USE THIS BOOK

The purpose of this book is to situate the discipline of outdoor education as an instrument for teaching social justice and environmental education and to provide specific examples of successful outdoor classroom curriculum activities—praxis that includes an adventure component. Because of the large number of alternative and charter schools including outdoor education within their programs, this book has reached beyond the traditional public school. Whichever environment one teaches in, however, know that these activities have been accomplished with literally thousands of students covering the complete span of educational and age levels from mid-primary years through college. All of the activities presented here are clearly defined and articulated. One can easily use this book as a field guide or a lesson planner.

Representing a total experience of more than 100 years, these authors have worked with every conceivable population from special needs to at-risk, and from gifted and talented to average students. Our experience has yielded highly positive responses from students, parents, teachers, and administrators. Each of the units has been field-tested and is valid for the population we recommend. As we demonstrate in Part II, Outdoor Educational Praxis, the learning and conclusions of participants provides compelling evidence of program effectiveness.

WHAT WILL BE LEARNED

This book provides detailed examples of activities that were actually given to our outdoor education participants. These include orientation materials for students, parents, teachers, and administrators, successful curriculum units and assignments, and evaluative feedback or assessment instruments such as student journals, interviews, letters from parents and administrators, published article citations from professional authors, and news clippings from local newspapers.

These adventure curriculum examples are easily adaptable to one's specific circumstances, curriculum requirements, and environmental surroundings. For many of the examples, we use an outdoor program with more than 30 years of history and experience, The Oyster River Middle School outdoor program. Additional examples abound from the University of Maryland outdoor program, a New Hampshire alternative educational program for at-risk youth, and some general outdoor program components from the Appalachian Mountain Club and the University of New Hampshire Department of Forestry.

The middle school outdoor education program began as a series of science expeditions with ecology, geology, weather, and mathematics activities. As the program evolved through the years, teachers involved in the program began to add curriculum activities from social studies and language arts. The inclusion of all subjects greatly enriched the learning experiences for each of the students. As we hope readers will discover here, the program activities in this book are easily adaptable to different grade levels and locales.

Originally an outdoor component of the science curriculum, the middle school program combined science with self-concept activities in an expeditions approach. Overnight and day programs included backpacking, rappelling, and cross-country skiing as initiative adventures that challenged students to trek to various natural habitats from New England's seacoast to the White Mountains. This program was able to gain tremendous support from all of the school's shareholders and has continued to be an important part of the school's curriculum.

The outdoor program at the Winnacunnet Alternative School was successful at turning many of the mainstream high school's potential dropouts into high school graduates. Using canoeing, rock climbing, hiking, skiing, and other excursions for methodology, students were surprised into learning that they were capable of having fun and being successful. This phenomenal discovery needed to occur before they could reconnect to discovery and learning. Years of drug use and abuse stalled development and arrested learning. Alternative education students had been thrown out of school so many times, that their sense of self-efficacy in academics was completely diminished. As is explored in Chapter 4, outdoor education curriculum and methods are powerful tools for turning at-risk students into advocates for their own success and agency.

GOALS

We believe that effective outdoor classrooms are based on two primary goals. First, a successful outdoor classroom seeks to increase academic achievement with highly motivating activities. By providing opportunities to interact in a robust, adventuresome environment, outdoor educators help students to develop academic competency through healthy connections with their teachers as they work together in the outdoor classroom. Connecting students and their teachers in an atmosphere of mutual enhancement builds respect for everyone and opens possibilities for new identifications with learning (Miller, 2003). All students, including those who have experienced repeated failure and who have felt put down in traditional school settings, can see and be viewed as equal participants in a learning and discovery process. Instruction in the outdoor classroom is designed to experientially integrate science, language arts, math, art, music, and social studies activities. Students are prepared with background information before each trip, observations recorded during the expedition, and conclusions compiled, written, and discussed afterward. All aspects of learning are linked to the experience as a personal and collective discovery within a spirit of adventure (Rief, 1984).

The element of adventure abounds whenever students hike, ski or rappel within wilderness or other outdoor settings. These adventure initiatives often instill confidence, trust, and teamwork; but more than anything else, these experiences make learning fun. Through outdoor education, positive school identifications are created for students. The characteristics of joy and trust are essential to students who face subtle and/or obvious academic challenges. To increase student academic achievement, few activities are more effective than outdoor education.

Additional benefits of adventure-based academic connectedness include the following: (a) improving engagement in learning with multiple opportunities and choices for involvement, and (b) creating a space to develop mutual understanding between diverse groups of students. Being placed in the woods or beside a body of water, students' senses are aroused and their natural instincts for interaction within these environments are engaged. The element of mutual understanding can be achieved when students, teachers, parents, and administrators work together to achieve common goals. While hiking, cooking, and investigating their natural environment, the whole person becomes observable as roles are less fixed. These activities always seem to lead to increased mutual understanding. Student's groups, formed randomly from all sections of a grade level, were gender-balanced, and assigned to teachers and parent leaders. These smaller groups work together as a team in all problem-solving situations, from scaling rock faces, and mending broken equipment, to preparing meals. Cooperation, sharing, and mutual help become essential for successful completion as students would experience different curriculum, habitats, seasons, and initiatives. Because parents can also be involved, all of the working together serves to strengthen relationships not only among peers but also between community and school.

The second goal of successful outdoor classrooms includes the development of academic and social competency through self-efficacy (Bandura, 1997). *Self-efficacy* is defined as "beliefs in one's capacity to organize and execute the courses of action required to produce given attainments" (p. 3). Self-efficacy in outdoor education is characterized by the following elements: (a) giving students multiple opportunities for success and failure, (b) developing experiential scaffolds for student knowledge and skill acquisition (Vygotsky, 1978), and (c) believing that the only true failure is a non-attempt or nonparticipation. As we articulate further in Chapter 7 on rock climbing, for some students simply being at the edge of a rock face is a display of great courage. By expanding our conceptualization of the student's agency, the way in which students exercise control over their lives, accomplishment of a learning outcome can have multiple opportunities for success. Success ranges from an approximation of activity completion to acts exceeding lesson-outcome expectations. An example of surpassing lesson expectations may include expressions of compassionate understanding of a peer's personal encounter with the challenge of the day. The trust that emerges from caring about one another may signal a profound personal breakthrough (Schoel, Prouty, & Radcliff, 1989).

Right from the first moment, as students learn to experience success, their sense of self-efficacy is enhanced (Bandura, 1997). Self-efficacy stems from actual engagement with specific activities. The sense of self-efficacy leads toward improved attitudes about their environment and the classroom (Bandura, 1997). Knowing that improved self-efficacy is related to academic progress, we can clearly seek its accomplishment in the outdoor classroom. Increase in self-efficacy improves academic progress and this can become a reinforcing loop (Senge, 1990). Any student who rappels a rock face, backpacks several miles, or cross-country skis within natural habitats may gain self-efficacy, which when applied, can help with other academic challenges. The metaphor here is that when one takes the initiative, academic or otherwise, self-efficacy is enhanced. Successful climbs and academic success are achieved one step at a time. How metaphors work to sustain images of success can be discussed with students before, during, and after each experience.

Although the goals and elements of the outdoor classroom can be consistent regardless of school population and diversity of communities, the types of activities each program establishes are determined by the students and their individual needs. A fourth grade science class will utilize vastly different activities than a high school alternative school. No matter what setting teachers find themselves in, they will be well served as they implement outdoor techniques to motivate students to achieve academic and social success through increased academic connectedness (Miller, 2003) and enhanced self-efficacy (Bandura, 1997).

HOW TO TEACH OUTDOORS

Although skills specific to rock climbing, hiking, and back-packing are covered in individual chapters further on in this book, there are several pedagogical practices unique to outdoor education that teachers and students need to address. The foremost of these concepts is how to act with respect for the environment. What must be considered when bringing a group out into the environment for an experience in the outdoor classroom?

The most important consideration for teachers, parents, and students is safety. Although each activity carries its own inherent risk factors, group size and supervision can be considered fairly constant. From our experience, groups of 8 to 10 students with 2 adults are an ideal pairing. When things are going along perfectly, as in some ideal scenario, one adult could lead a group of eight with ease. However, with a group of at-risk youth, an extra set of eyes and ears can help to keep the activity safe and well supervised.

For many students, outdoor education is the first time they have an opportunity to experience being with their peers outside of the classroom's boundaries. This sensation of freedom can be equated as a license to act without regard to school rules. Most famous among this infraction is alternative school students trying to smoke cigarettes or other substances. They may also smoke or use drugs in school; however, the safety risk and consequences are generally not as critical. Starting a fire or causing an accident are real, negative consequences of getting high or smoking in the outdoors.

Obviously, each group will have its own specific requirements concerning supervision. How the organization of the program addresses these issues will be critical in determining outcomes. As a general rule, we believe that smaller is better not only for safety, but in the provision of quality and quantity of attention the students receive. One of the best outcomes of outdoor education is the opportunity for teachers and students to see each other apart from the classroom's role constraints. The quality of the student–teacher relationship is very often enhanced from sharing time and conversation outdoors.

PROTECTING THE ENVIRONMENT

When we bring students to the outdoors, we have a responsibility to protect not only the students but the environment into which they have been delivered. The protective practice is best summarized as Leave No Trace (LNT) (Hampton & Cole, 1995). LNT rules include the following:

1. Plan ahead and prepare
2. Camp and travel in durable areas
3. Pack it in, pack it out
4. Properly dispose of what you cannot pack out
5. Leave what you find
6. Minimize use and impact of fire (Hampton & Cole, 1995, p. 4)

Considering Rule 1, preparing students for the outdoors readies them for essential questions like, "Where is the bathroom?" A trip to the state park can spare you the need for elaborate explanations of waste removal procedures. A climb up Mt. Shasta or on any other glacier requires more detailed preparation. Glaciers are not a place to leave any human waste, and appropriate systems for waste removal are essential. Leaders' anticipation of personal needs can make the day better for the participants as well as for the environment.

For day trips, prior knowledge of toilet facilities and contingencies for the lack of them is the best practice. Needing to use the outdoors for relief can be problematic. LNT requires burying waste in solid ground or removal. Urine is generally not a problem away from trails and streams; however, waste paper needs to be removed, burned, or buried. Local areas will dictate protocol. Obviously, on beaches or in well-used parks, the protocol will be different than it is on a remote backpacking trip.

Pack it in, pack it out has been in effect for more than 40 years. This rule eliminates litter, and it includes biodegradable items such as orange and banana peels. Although these items degrade with time, the next hiker may be minutes behind you, and they won't share your opinion about composting in nature. Nature is best appreciated in its pure, natural state.

Finally, leave nature intact for the next person. Do not take flowers, rocks, or other items out of the forests. All of the things we find are for viewing, drawing, painting, or photographing. Leaving these items intact for the next person respects nature's beauty and protects its delicate balance. The same general rule applies to animals. Respecting the animal's home and not interfering with their habitat protects these beings for future progenetiveness and other survival behaviors. We are safer and they are happier if we leave them alone.

ETHICS

Best practices in outdoor education require the consideration of ethical use of nature and concern for our fellow humans as we travel on life's paths. First choice in ethical decision making is not to act in any manner that would place our students at risk. Working in the wild, it is impossible to remove all risk; however, there are best practices that are clearly delineated from their inverse.

Knowing the trails and routes, having solid skills in the field, and responsibly leading one's group with regard to weather are all part of ethical best practices. In psychology, scope of practice and scope of competence are the guiding ethical principles. They also have a place in outdoor education. Guide only that which you know and maintain proper decision-making and leadership skills.

Three characteristics of outdoor success are having the right equipment, knowing what one is doing, and making the correct decisions. Integrating these three components is the key to every successful outdoor experience. Of course, nature and people are not predictable. However, being prepared for changes in weather, anticipating medical emergencies, and knowing how to adjust direction can make all the difference between disaster and success. Defining success in a way that is consistent with protecting the environment and the participants is the finest example of best practices. Your school's attorney and administration will concur with our definition. Leaders who have returned to report serious injury or fatalities know that caution is good judgment. Nature has inherent risks that our use of best practices can only mitigate.

REFERENCES

Bandura, A. (1997). *Self-efficacy: The exercise of control.* New York: Freeman.

Damasio, A. (1994). *Descartes' error: Emotion, reason, and the human brain.* New York: Grosset/Dunlap.

Dewey, J. (1944). *Democracy and education.* Toronto, Ontario: Collier-Macmillan.

Fischer, K.W., Kennedy, B., & Cheng, C-L. (1998). Culture and biology in emotional development. *New Directions for Child Development, 81,* 21-43.

Freire, P. (1970). *Pedagogy of the oppressed.* New York: Continuum.

Gardner, H. (1983). *Frames of mind: The theory of multiple intelligences.* New York: Basic Books.

Goodman, G. (1999). *Alternatives in education: Critical pedagogy for disaffected youth.* New York: Peter Lang.

Grosz, E. (1993). Bodies and knowledge: Feminism and the crisis of reason. In L. Alcoff & E. Potter (Eds.), *Feminist epistemologies* (pp. 187-216). New York: Routledge.

Hampton, B., & Cole, D. (1995). *Soft paths.* Mechanicsburg, PA: Stockdale Press.

Kincheloe, J., & Steinberg, S. (1997). *Changing multiculturalism.* Buckingham, England: Open University Press.

McLaren, P. (1997). *Revolutionary multiculturalism: Pedagogies of dissent for the new millennium.* Boulder, CO: Westview.

McLaren, P. (2000). *Che Guevara, Paulo Freire, and the pedagogy of revolution.* Lanham, MD: Rowman & Littlefield.

Miller, J. B. (2003). Telling the truth about power. *Research and Action Report, 25*(1).

Oliver, M. (1986). *Dream work.* New York: Atlantic Monthly Press.

Regier, T. (1995). A model of the human capacity for categorizing spatial relations. *Cognitive Linguistics, 6,* 63-88.

Regier, T. (1996). *The human semantic potential: Spatial language and constrained connectionism.* Cambridge, MA: MIT Press.

Rief, L. (1984, September). Writing and rappelling. *Learning Magazine,* pp. 73-76.

Roberts, N., & Rodriguez, D. (1999). *Multicultural issues in outdoor education.* ERIC Digest: ED438151.

Schoel, J., Prouty, D., & Radcliff, P. (1989). *Islands of healing: A guide to adventure based counseling.* Hamilton, MA: Project Adventure.

Senge, P.M. (1990). *The fifth discipline: The art and practice of the learning organization.* New York: Doubleday.

Vygotsky, L.S. (1978). *Mind in society: The development of higher psychological processes* (M. Cole, V. John-Steiner, S. Scribner, & E. Souberman, Eds.). Cambridge, MA: Harvard University Press.

Watson-Gegeo, K., & Gegeo, D. W. (2004). Deep culture: Pushing the epistemological boundaries of multicultural education. In G. Goodman & K. Carey (Eds.), *Critical multicultural conversations* (pp. 235-256). Cresskill, NJ: Hampton Press.

2

OUTDOOR EDUCATION PHILOSOPHY

Greg S. Goodman

"Next morning I started squishing along, first telling myself that it could not rain any harder. Then I tried the opposite approach. "Cheer up," I said, "it could be worse." So I cheered up, and sure enough it got worse. A few days later I reached the summit on hands and knees in a heroic crawl through the blast of a typhoon.

—Blanchard (1985, p. 289)

Tracking the foundations of outdoor education philosophy can be intellectually stimulating and exciting. From Zen to existentialism, one can find links to connect metaphysical wonder to physical experience (Smith, Roland, Havens, & Hoyt, 1992). Because this base is so broad, outdoor educational philosophies often lead one to a myriad of pedagogical paths: teaching at-risk youth, guiding fourth graders on a forest field trip, conducting substance abuse recovery groups, facilitating teacher preparation programs at the university, or providing corporate leadership training. No matter which philosophical foundation best relates to your leadership position, your choice can still end up working to provide solid footing for the outdoor education you apply. As we discuss many of the philosophic roots of outdoor education, we attempt to follow these foundations from a historic perspective and try to link today's practices to the thinking that has preceded us. The point is that no matter which philosophic position one selects to ascribe to, there is ample room for connecting outdoor education's dynamic experience and one's development of a rationale for pursuing a particular path.

Outdoor education's philosophy connects to the 18th-century contributions of the Romantic movement as exemplified by writer/philosopher Jean Jacques Rousseau (1712-1778) and later Thoreau, Emerson, Hawthorne, and poets Coleridge, Wordsworth, Shelly, Blake and Keats. Rapt with love of nature, the Romantics sought excitement, emotions, and the aesthetic motives over logic and science's preeminence (Russell, 1972). This exciting and revolutionary historical time also gave birth to one of the most highly regarded thinkers of the period known as modern—Immanuel Kant (1724-1804). According to philosopher/historian Bertrand Russell (1972), "Kant's most important book is the *Critique of Pure Reason* (1959). The purpose of this work is to prove that, although none of our knowledge can transcend experience, it is nevertheless in part *a priori* and not inferred inductively from experience" (p. 706). As Kant's (1959) work has evolved over the past three centuries, his early notions of the ways in which we understand experience may be as essential as they have ever been with regard to our personal identification with our earth. Kant's philosophy placed a value on the human connection with a real world, and as with Copernicus, he claimed man's ability both empirically and *a priori* (valid without observation or known intuitively) to know or understand the science that defined our earth (Russell, 1972).

Through the modern period up to today, and as we have grown into an ever more industrialized and urban society, our need to connect with our environment and its biodiversity may be more important now than it has ever been. Alienated from the environment and one another, many urban and suburban youth's only outlet for adventure and excitement is found in joining a gang or getting high (Goodman, 2002). Youth, especially adolescents, require sensation-seeking stimulation and adventure to correspond with the tremendous physical and emotional dynamics they experience. Adolescence, more than any other time, is characterized by a focus on others and narcissistic self-examination (imaginary audience). The goal, for most teenagers, is to connect with peers and to gain acceptance. Outdoor educational philosophy recognizes the importance of building connections to one another and to the environment through the use of active and experiential learning processes. The connection with peers and the environment can resolve the conflict of adolescent alienation and demonstrate the soulful inner peace that nature can provide. By applying the techniques of adventure-based experience, students are completely engaged in the learning process through mind, body and spirit, and the experiences become powerful metaphors of the possible. It is the rare individual who climbs a mountain or rappels down a cliff face and misses the prize of adrenalin and pride in his or her accomplishment.

The philosophy of outdoor education is an essential component of its practice. Sometimes referred to as pedagogy, the philosophical foundations of outdoor education work to inform the practice or praxis (critical application of pedagogy)—experiential learning. The principal questions concerning outdoor education philosophy pertain to the epistemological basis for using the outdoor classroom: Why outdoor education? How can outdoor education improve student achievement? What student outcomes are provided in the outdoor classroom? Answers to these questions form the foundation and philosophical underpinnings of outdoor education.

"The world is exceedingly complex, and it is damn confusing." This quote from Willie Unsoeld in Outward Bound's first movie/documentary addresses one of the major reasons why outdoor education is so important today. Historically, as in the time from primitive culture through the period of modern industrialization's transformation of experience with automobiles, televisions, and the like, people were much more closely connected to a physical and experientially based existence. Working with our hands, walking to work or school, and growing our own food, we were much more physically engaged and, therefore, we were more closely connected with our environment. In postmodern Western society, we may enjoy the convenience of fast food, drive-through markets, and loads of labor-saving devices; however, the benefits also carry risks. Problems of the labor-less existence include physical manifestations like obesity, lethargy, and a host of psychological problems including depression, attention deficit disorder, and alienation. What are we connecting to now?

CONNECTING INDIVIDUALS AND THE ENVIRONMENT

Postmodern philosophical foundations of outdoor education seek to address two essential problems of our world: (a) failed connections between individuals representing diverse cultural identifications, and (b) the enormous environmental or ecological problems associated with all of the earth's citizens (air, water, recycling, and energy). The need to create better connections with our fellow humans and the challenges we face within our environment provide enormous motivation for healthy outdoor experience and the application of outdoor educational philosophy within and around the schoolhouse itself. In sum, the crucial aspect of outdoor education's philosophy is to build better and healthier connections between individuals and the land that sustains them. In addition to believing that our earth's citizens and the place they inhabit are sacred, a fundamental philosophical notion is that real learning is more likely to occur in an atmosphere that is characterized by adventure (Lentz, Smith, Sentkowski, & Seidman, 1976).

Outdoor education provides multiple invitations to break down disability, color, class, and gender barriers. By bringing diverse individuals together to accomplish a task, the praxis of outdoor education can teach understanding, tolerance, and respect. The key to the accomplishment of this lesson is to re-invent and to make relevant the meaning of cooperation. According to Lentz et al. (1976), "Cooperation emerges as a group of people work toward a common goal which they can't accomplish individually. It emerges as a group of people begins to recognize, value, and make sense of differing talents included among the members of the group. It occurs when the group accepts and supports the efforts of the individuals within it" (p. 7). As educators continue their work to create well-prepared citizens for a democratic society, more teaching methods need to integrate building trust, understanding, and compassion for one another. The reduction of prejudice, racism, sexism, and other forms of alienation of underrepresented individuals is critical to the creation of citizens capable of sustaining healthy communities.

In recent years, hundreds of books have been published on the theme of multiculturalism and diversity (Goodman & Carey, 2004; Jacobson, 2003, McLaren, 1997, Nieto, 1996; Steinberg & Kincheloe, 1997). This outcry from individuals eager to promote tolerance and understanding is truly democratic and speaks to the continuing need to work to break down barriers that divide us. Using cooperation to enhance interdependence, outdoor education philosophy fosters practices that work to smash stereotypes and build real and meaningful relationships. By using real problems and challenges such as getting your group up a mountain or across a swamp, students and teachers alike must forge a relationship that transcends cliquey divisions. In adventure programming, everyone must reach the goal, not just a select and elite few.

Although many gains have been made in the effort to improve our environment, much work remains. From the development of a sense of ownership in the process of environmental protection to the creation of active participation in the real work of making the ecology safe and the earth sustainable, we have a real need to educate our future citizens about their responsibility to the earth. Outdoor education philosophy maintains that the most effective way to connect students to the relevance of an environmental problem is through direct contact or emersion. For example, to understand why recycling is important, outdoor education goes to the landfill. At the landfill, we visually and nasally attach meaning to the consequence of each act of tossing something into a "garbage" can. Questions turn into thoughts and possibly actions. Maybe this can, bottle, or paper might be reused, reinvented, or recycled?

ECOPEDAGOGY

David Jardine, a Canadian educator-philosopher, has developed a new term to describe the philosophical basis for the teaching of environmental education, an aspect of outdoor education. His neologism, *ecopedagogy*, is broadly encompassing of all space and related educational implications. Because we are ultimately the stewards of our earth, Jardine (2000) asked some important questions concerning our care of this sacred space.

> Ecopedagogical reflection thus involves drawing together our concern, as educators, for the presence of new life in our midst (D. Smith, 1988) (and for bringing forth this new life into the world, our world-educare) and "our most pleasing responsibility," caring for the earth. Such reflection simply asks: In what ways do questions of pedagogy interweave with questions of the continued existence of an earth in the embrace of which pedagogy is possible? (p. 21)

Outdoor education experientially connects all senses to open pathways to learning. By making learning more of an adventure than a test preparation or boring machination, students more readily connect to the material. Lentz et al. (1976) described experiential learning's appeal as "Adventure is important to us because it provides the emotional setting within which it becomes possible for the students to feel and know that they have been involved in something that personally mattered. It has been our experience that the student who has passed through an adventure has felt the adrenalin flowing and discovered that his senses were unusually alert" (p. 6).

The Appalachian Mountain Club (AMC) has also supported the concept of adventure learning. In their teacher's guide, *A Mountain Classroom* (AMC, 1973), the AMC contributes

> Learning in the natural environment is not only exciting for students but for teachers as well. The experience of learning together in this environment while engaging in the same physical and academic tasks can provide teachers with new awareness and insights about themselves and their role. It can also help teachers transfer the experiential curriculum to the classroom. (p. 3)

Adventure and excitement are cornerstones of outdoor education philosophy, and they make the learning come alive by connecting mind, body, and spirit.

A former student, Danielle, describes this connection artfully:

> At the Rockhouse Pond Rock Climbing Trip although I didn't go down, I learned that I have the will to make my own decisions and can stand behind them. I know that at first I really wasn't too happy with the situation but in the end after trying it I had a positive feeling about myself and the project because I knew that I had made the right decision for myself. I still felt a feeling of accomplishment because I had tried.

The power of self-efficacy, being in control of one's self, is critical in the creation of self-esteem and the development of personal strength. When we taught rappelling to seventh and eighth graders, we would be clear that we wanted everyone to "rope up" and try the experience. However, we emphasized that for some of our students, going down the cliff was just a cheap thrill. For others, maybe even those who couldn't make it that day, it may have required more courage to put on the rappel harness and come up to the edge because their fear of heights was so severe. In the kid's language, there were "no chickens" at Rockhouse Pond (not the place name of an actual climbing area. This private land was closed to the public). And for each of the students, what happened that day at Rockhouse really mattered to them!

Coming back to school and thinking about their experience is in line with one of the major contributions of John Dewey (1944); learning is the process of thinking about experience. In Dewey's words, "No experience having a meaning is possible without some element of thought" (p. 145). To connect the fieldwork (experience) with academic achievement, students would write reflection papers on their return to school. Like Danielle's observations and insights, the students' writing was inspired and deeply personal. Critical thinking, writing skills, and personal growth were enhanced through the writing process.

In our work at the Oyster River Middle School, we were lucky to be able to rub shoulders with two of the greats in the emerging discipline of the writing process, Don Murray and Don Graves. Frequently, these men would come to the middle school to provide in-service or to showcase their work to foreign visitors. One of our teachers, Linda Rief, took great interest in the work of these professors, and she successfully integrated their writing pedagogy within her eighth-grade language arts classroom. She also used adventure philosophy to enhance motivation and to overcome "writer's block." As she wrote in a *Learning Magazine* (Rief, 1984) piece, *Writing and Rappelling*:

> Sitting at the top of a sheer cliff, awaiting my turn to rappel down, building up my courage, I listened intently to Greg's words as he gently coaxed each student over the edge: "You can do it, just lean back, get a good grip. Nice control. I know you're afraid. Walk it back, feet apart, shoulders back—you've got it! Super job! Keep going. Lean back. What a pro!" "As I listened to Greg and watched each student overcome fear and disappear over the edge, the thought struck me that what Greg was accomplishing with these students was exactly what I wanted to achieve in my writing class." (p. 73)

Linda Rief saw the value of integrating the outdoor experience with the classroom to make learning relevant and exciting. The writing came to life in poems (songs), essays, and writing-art creations that celebrated the learning for each individual and personalized their achievements. Project Adventure's writers (Lentz et al., 1976) expressed the concept by stating the following:

> education should give students an opportunity to bring together and to integrate the physical, emotional, social, intellectual, and even the aesthetic aspects of their personality. We feel that if the intellectual aspect of the personality is emphasized to the neglect of the others that the person will suffer not only emotionally and socially, but also intellectually. (p. 9)

Integrating adventure and academic achievement is the best way to motivate students. Challenging themselves, the students can be rewarded for efforts they make toward their goals rather than seeing learning as an end or product that stands alone and isolated from personal meaning. Outdoor education philosophy values individual effort and replaces competitive exercises like times and distances with personal growth and satisfaction (Rohnke, 1981). The competitive spirit will always be present. In fact, it is probably a part of all of our DNA, but it does not need to be a focus in outdoor education. Cooperation and the holistic integration of mind, body, and spirit is the focus in this experiential pedagogy.

POSTMODERN CONTRIBUTIONS

Although the historical and philosophical foundations of outdoor education date back to modernist thinkers, there has been a significant and recent contribution to outdoor education philosophy by the postmodernists.

Postmodern refers to the time after (post) the modern period. Although these distinctions are not clearly black and white or good and bad, there are elements of modernist thinking that are anachronistic. Descartes' "I think, therefore I exist" represented the separation of mind over matter (Kincheloe & Steinberg, 1997). Modernist thinking was characterized by a desire to use science to describe the world and to comprehend causality. Reason and science build commerce, bureaucracy, and industrialization.

Postmodernists challenge the hierarchical thinking of linearity and separation that has supported misapplications of science to maintain social order (Giroux, 1991; Kincheloe & Steinberg, 1997; Willinsky, 1998). Postmodernists support multiculturalism, feminism, and other methodologies of inclusion. Postmodernism encourages new conceptualizations of human possibility, and it works to encourage individual and collective emancipation of all of us: African Americans, Native Americans, women, gay/lesbian/transgendered, and others living within subordinated positions (Goodman & Carey, 2004). The fit of postmodernism's pedagogical position with outdoor educational philosophy is in the restructuring of traditional relations of gender and class to create a cohesiveness between males and females characterized by equal relations. This is exemplified by the football quarterback high in the air on a ropes course postman's walk being belayed by an obese, nonathletic female with whom he would not normally make eye contact with in the school corridor. This new symbiosis includes someone who would have formerly been excluded being placed in a position of extreme trust. In this way, students get a concrete and vivid example of critical multiculturalism's postmodernist critique: We are all important members and contributors to this society, not just the privileged and the elite. Gender equity can be given immediate relevance and status when you are on the end of the rope that needs the other's attention and support.

KURT HAHN AND THE ICONS
OF EARLY DEVELOPMENT

Outdoor education philosophy owes much to the contributions of Kurt Hahn, Willie Unsoeld, Josh Miner, Bob Bates, James Schoel, and the thousands of men and women who have been involved with the evolution and development of Outward Bound and National Outdoor Leadership School (NOLS). Although we share some of their stories in depth at the end of this book in Chapter 10, their collective impact on the philosophy of outdoor education merits description here. Most of what we apply in outdoor education practices emanates from the lessons taught at Outward Bound and at NOLS.

Outward Bound and the myriad schools that have spun from it, owe their origins to British educator Kurt Hahn, (Smith et al., 1992). In the early 1940s, Hahn made some important observations. During this period, American Merchant Marine ships were convoying tremendous amounts of food and supplies to England in support of our allies fighting in the Battle of Britain. The Nazis, in turn, were trying to sink as many of these ships as possible to interrupt Allied supply lines. What Hahn observed was that of the ships that were torpedoed in the freezing North Atlantic Ocean, the older mariners were more likely to survive in the freezing water than their younger and supposedly stronger counterparts. From his observations and interviews, Hahn concluded that the older men had a characteristic that the younger men lacked: "the will to survive" (Rohrs, 1970). Hahn concluded that because the older men had families and other compelling reasons to stay alive, they resisted the waters cold effect longer than their younger counterparts.

From these observations, Hahn went on to develop a training school, now Outward Bound, and to instill this motto, "To serve to strive, and not to yield." From his early work at Gordonstone, an English boarding school, the concept spread to the United States through Josh Miner, director of admissions at the prestigious Phillips Andover Academy. At Andover, several staff members were acquainted with climbing and the American Alpine Club's forthcoming Everest expedition. Everest, as yet unclimbed by an American, was planned for the fall (post-monsoon) of 1963. One of the members of that famous team, Willie Unsoeld, was recruited from Nepal where he was working as the Director of the Peace Corps. After his breathtaking and successful summit via the West Ridge with Tom Hornbein, Willie Unsoeld returned victoriously (and toelessly) to America to become Outward Bound's first school director.

Philosopher/climber Willie Unsoeld left an impression that lives on to this day. Inventor of Zenism's like "internal navel contemplation" and one of the principal creators of the standard Outward Bound course, Unsoeld's legacy provided the framework for outdoor education for the next fifty years as he used the outdoors to create transformations in those around him (Leamer, 1999). Going from Outward Bound to Evergreen State College in Olympia, Washington, Willie's home, he used his brilliance to challenge students to explore physical and intellectual boundaries. A hero of many real and metaphorical first ascents, Willie's life was lost in an avalanche on his home peak, Mt Rainer, while leading a group of his students off that familiar summit. A man of great humor, intellect, courage, and conviction, Unsoeld left an indelible mark on the world of outdoor education.

In the most recent history of outdoor education, indoor climbing walls and the attendant technical advances have helped spread the application of outdoor education and adventure programming. The appeal of these activities is obvious; however, the philosophical foundations may be obscured by the bright lights and high C.T. factors (C.T. is a Jed Williamson expression for Cheap Thrills). Rappelling without closer examination of its metaphorical connection was just another carnival ride or cheap thrill. Like the cyclist's bright colors and flashing chrome bikes, the climber's accoutrement can be loaded with commercialism and all of the status of high-tech and fashion gear. Outdoor education philosophy eschews the collection of equipment in favor of looking, as Muir did, for the intrinsic rewards of active participation in a meaningful activity "to impel young people into value-forming experiences" (Smith et al., 1992, p. 9).

As we engage this new millennium, outdoor education philosophy is informed and receives benefit from the contribution of much of the educational and social critique of the past 25 years. Because all teaching and learning occurs within a social and political context, we believe that the current time requires that educators take an active role and position in support of true democracy. True democracy is characterized by equal opportunity. Nowhere is this opportunity more critical than among those who have historically been underrepresented and marginalized by individuals and groups that support hegemonic domination and suppression of difference. Typically, the excluded have been the poor, Black, Hispanic, gay/lesbian/transgendered, disabled, and religious minority. Outdoor education philosophy is well served by continuing to pay attention to the needs of educational equity and the role of social justice in all aspects of our teaching (McLaren, 2000). The pedagogy of love, a pedagogy first espoused by Paulo Freire (1970) and now known as critical pedagogy, is a perfect fit for today's outdoor educator. Building lessons that include all of the students and engage them in a meaningful process counteracts exclusionary practices and creates connections reflective of our educational ideals and emancipatory education (Leonardo, 2004). How we bring this philosophy to life as outdoor educational disciplinary knowledge is the objective of this book.

REFERENCES

Blanchard, S. (1985). *Walking up and down in the world: Memories of a mountain rambler.* San Francisco, CA: Sierra Club Books.

Dewey, J. (1944). *Democracy and education.* Toronto, Ontario: Collier-Macmillan.

Freire, P. (1970). *Pedagogy of the oppressed.* New York: Continuum.

Giroux, H. (1991). Introduction. Modernism, postmodernism, and feminism: Rethinking the boundaries of educational discourse. In *Postmodernism, feminism, and cultural politics: Redrawing educational boundaries.* Albany: State University of New York Press.

Goodman, G. (2002). *Reducing hate crimes and violence among American youth: Creating transformational agency through critical praxis.* New York: Peter Lang.

Goodman, G., & Carey, K. (2004). *Critical multicultural conversations.* Cresskill, NJ: Hampton Press.

Jacobson, T. (2003). *Confronting our discomfort.* Portsmouth, NH: Heinemann Press.

Jardine, D. (2000). *"Under the tough old stars" Ecopedagogical essays.* Brandon, VT: The Foundation for Educational Renewal.

Kant, I. (1959). *The critique of pure reason.* New York: E.P. Dutton.

Kincheloe, J., & Steinberg, S., (1997). *Changing multiculturalism.* Buckingham, England: Open University Press.

Leamer, L. (1999). *Ascent.* New York: William Morrow.

Lentz, B., Smith, M., Sentkowski, A., & Seidman, M. (1976). *Teaching through adventure.* Hamilton, MA: Project Adventure.

Leonardo, Z. (2004). Critical social theory and transformative knowledge: The functions of criticism in quality education. *Educational Researcher, 6,* 11-18.

McLaren, P. (1997). *Revolutionary multiculturalism: Pedagogies of dissent for the new millennium.* Boulder, CO: Westview.

McLaren, P. (2000). *Che Guevara, Paulo Freire, and the pedagogy of revolution.* Lanham, MD: Rowman & Littlefield.

Nieto, S. (1996). *Affirming diversity: The sociopolitical context of multicultural education.* New York: Longman.

Rief, L. (1984, September). Writing and rappelling. *Learning Magazine,* pp. 73-76.

Rohnke, K. (1981). *High profile.* Hamilton, MA: Adventure Press.

Rohrs, H. (1970). *Kurt Hahn: Biography.* London: Routledge Kegan Paul.

Russell, B. (1972). *A history of Western philosophy.* New York: Simon & Schuster.

Smith, D. (1988). Children and the Gods of war. *Journal of Educational Thought, 22A*(2).

Smith, T.E., Roland, C., Havens, M., & Hoyt, J. (1992). *The theory and practice of challenge education.* Dubuque, IA: Kendall/Hunt.

Steinberg, S., & Kincheloe, J. (1997). *Changing multiculturalism.* Buckingham, England: Open University Press.

Willinsky, J. (1998). *Learning to divide the world: Education at empire's end.* Minneapolis: University of Minnesota Press.

3

WOMEN AND OUTDOOR EDUCATION

Mary Breunig

*It was a beautiful fall day as I
bellyflopped onto the Grand
Traverse Ledge at the Gunks.
I looked up and was surprised to see
a woman, in her mid twenties, with
tears in her eyes. After securing my
own anchor, I turned my attention
to her. "Are you okay?" I asked.
"My boyfriend promised me that he
would not climb anything harder
than a 5.7 today and here we are
on Modern Times. I am so tired
of being a belay slave to my
boyfriend's 'tick list'" was her
exasperated response.*

When reading through the table of contents for this book, you may have been asking yourself, why a book chapter that is specifically related to the topic of women and outdoor recreation and education? Aren't all the chapters in this book relevant to both genders? These are queries that must be considered as an introduction to this chapter, alongside the introductory narrative to this chapter, which describes an experience that seems to represent a somewhat familiar "theme" and often recurring story in the field of outdoor education and recreation, the subordinated role of women in the sport. I have personally witnessed a scene similar to the opening example in many parts of the world; on the sea cliffs of the Freycinet Peninsula in Tasmania, the alpine crag of Rocky Mountain National Park, the sport climbs at Mt. Nemo in Southern Ontario, and the bolted cliffs of France. These experiences compel me to ask the question, "Where are all the women in the field of outdoor education and recreation, not only in the present-day context of outdoor adventure travel, but in the historical context of some of the early pioneering efforts within the field?"

INTRODUCTION

Patricia Stokowski (2000), a professor in the School of Natural Resources at the University of Vermont, noted her surprise at how issues of bias and gender never factored into her thinking and teaching as a professor of recreation and tourism—until one day. In October 1999, Stokowski purchased a copy of *National Geographic Traveler* magazine. That particular issue caught her attention because it profiled the "world's greatest destinations." Stokowski (2000) described how each place was introduced with a "vivid quote from an historical figure and then described by a notable writer" (p. 161). Although each image and accompany text captivated Stokowski, she was struck by the fact that there were almost no quotes or stories authored by women. "In fact, a quick count shows that of 51 articles, 48 (94%) are authored by men and only three by women. About 80 percent (46 out of 58) of the quotes from historic figures are also from famous men; eight others (14%) are attributed to women; I am uncertain about four others" (p. 161). Stokowski concluded that this particular issue of the *National Geographic Traveler* magazine seems to suggest that the "world's greatest destinations" are mostly male domains.

Stokowski's analysis of gender has helped me to consider the ways in which such subtle forms of bias and implicit assumptions about travel destinations and recreation and tourism are entrenched in our lives and in our work as recreational professionals. Perhaps this story helps to illustrate, at least in part, why there is a need for a chapter that specifically relates to women and outdoor education. Bialeschki (1992) encouraged all outdoor educators to ask, "Whose experiences are addressed and validated in the fields of outdoor education and recreation?" and "Who gets left out?"

As introduced in Chapter 2, there are certain groups and particular ways of knowing that have traditionally been privileged and have been predominant in the field of outdoor education. Historically, those groups and ways of knowing have either overtly or inadvertently been dominant, and they have, consequently, been given less credence to women's ways of knowing. As mentioned earlier in this book, a postmodern critique of outdoor education impels one to critically examine the individuals and groups who have historically been underrepresented and mar-

ginalized by those that support hegemonic domination and suppression of difference. The purpose of this chapter is to reinforce the fact that women have had a long and inspiring history within this field, but that because of the social and political climate in which we live, women's "voices" have not always been "heard," and have thus been less well-represented in discussions about the history of outdoor education. This chapter, therefore, focus as specifically on the role of women in the fields of sport, physical education, and outdoor recreation and education.

EARLY HISTORY OF WOMEN
IN THE OUTDOORS

Both *The Encyclopedia of Women's Travel and Exploration* (Netzley, 2001) and *By Snowshoe, Buckboard, and Steamer: Women of the Frontier* (Bridge, 1998) provide detailed accounts of women's early influence within the fields of outdoor travel, recreation, and education. These historical narratives cannot be comprehended in the same manner as present-day adventure narratives of outdoor travel are understood. Rather than representing the modern-day perspective of the trials and accomplishments of many present-day outdoor and adventure travel activities, these early stories represent feats of survival, the early pioneering efforts of women, and biographical accounts that describe these women as not only mountaineers and rugged outdoors-women, but as pirates, anthropologists, and governesses, among others

(Netzley, 2001). The successes and accomplishments of these pioneering women and
the challenging wilderness contexts that they
found themselves in have, in part, paved the
way for the women who have contributed to
our present-day understanding of the
accomplishments of women in the fields of
outdoor recreation and education. The next
section of this chapter takes a brief look at
women and sports and the field of physical
education before exploring the topic of
women in the fields of outdoor recreation
and education. It attempts to respond to the
central query posed in the introduction of
this chapter, "Where are all the women in the
fields of sports and physical education and
outdoor education and recreation?"

Women's Sport

Despite the many examples within the literature of sports and exercise that
seem to suggest that women had no active role to play (Hall, 2001; Smart,
2001), there is strong evidence that women have always been involved in
sports to some extent (Hargreaves, 1994). Unfortunately, many of these
male-orientated accounts make the task of even attempting to trace the participation of girls and women in sports and physical education quite difficult. This consequence may be because women's involvement in activities
and institutions were initially viewed as masculine (Duval, 2001) and were
defined around male norms.

Within Canada, Alexandrine Gibb has probably had as much to do with
the development of women's sports than any other individual in the country (Hall, 2001). Gibb distinguished herself as an athlete, a pioneering leader
and administrator of women's sports, manager of several international athletic teams and a pre-eminent woman sports journalist (Hall, 2001). Gibb's
own career as an athlete harkens back to the days when she could be seen
donned in the proper gymnasium costume of long black stockings, a knee-
length full-skirted tunic with a long-sleeved middy blouse top and loose-fit-
ting roped belt (Olafson, 1990). During that period, between 1902-1906,
sports and games were an important aspect of the daily life of a young
woman's private school educational experience and were comprised of such
activities as tennis, basketball, ice hockey, golf, and track. There are similar
accounts to this growth in the participation of women in sports within the
United States and Britain (Hall, 2001; Smart, 2001).

Prior to the onset of the war in 1914, women's sports in Canada and the United States had taken hold on both a recreational and a competitive basis (Hall, 2001). Most of this activity took place within private sports clubs and very little of the participation in the events was organized and/or controlled by women. The war brought about some major change in respect to this, however. Opportunities for more organizational responsibilities presented themselves while the men were away at war (Hall, 2001).

During the time of war, Gibb became less involved in her own athletics and focused her attention on the organization, administration, and promotion of women's sports, especially in Ontario. She helped organize the Ontario Ladies' Basketball Association and became a founding member of the Toronto Ladies Athletic Club, as well as its first president. Her philosophy was "girls sports run by girls." She later went on to write a women's sports column for the *Toronto Daily Star* and was manager of the highly successful women's track and field team at the Amsterdam Olympics, in addition to being elected president of the Women's Amateur Athletic Federation of Canada (Hall, 2001).

Through these efforts, Gibb promoted all varieties of women's sports, commented on issues of the day, and made clear her philosophy concerning, for example, opportunities for "working girls," gender equity, health concerns, and "mannish" women athletes. Alexandrine Gibb worked tirelessly and vigorously for the benefit of women's sports. Her pioneering efforts during the 1920s and 1930s won the respect and admiration of those who worked with her (Hall, 2001). Her commitment and vision contributed to the way that women were regarded within the arena of sports and within the field of physical education.

PHYSICAL EDUCATION

Perhaps one of the most noteworthy arenas within the discipline of outdoor recreation and education in general that has been significantly influenced by women is within the fields of outdoor and physical education in K–12 schools and colleges. Much of the development of this field can be attributed to some of the early pioneers in the field of women and sports, including Alexandrine Gibb.

Women's participation in physical education existed largely in isolation from men. Many of the early pioneers were actually expressly devoted to developing a unique tradition of women's physical exercise and education, rather than having it be defined around the hegemonic norms of a male tradition. Employing a scientific and therapeutic approach to physical activity, female pioneers had successfully created a profession that was premised on what has been referred to as Swedish gymnastics (Duval, 2001). Swedish Gymnastics, established and promoted by Per Henrik Ling, was different from callisthenics, which was previously seen as an acceptable form of activity for middle-class women. It was also clearly different from the competitive sports that characterized the cult athleticism so prevalent in the male public schools of the time (Mangan, 2000). Swedish gymnastics was inspired by dance, movement, and play.

Margaret Stansfeld, widely regarded as a radical English educator, was the founder of one of the foremost women's physical training colleges in England and was also a founding member of the Ling Association and the Swedish gymnastic tradition (Smart, 2001). In the early 1900s, she was both at the start and at the heart of a new profession, that of the female physical education teacher. Women's participation within this profession was not unusual at the time because it was not a role dominated by men, nor did it grow out of a male tradition. These women were trained to the highest standards as "games mistresses" who taught generations of middle-class schoolgirls (Smart, 2001). The intention of these early physical education initiatives was threefold: (a) to provide various physical activities for girls; (b) to challenge contemporary concerns about the problematic nature of vigorous exercise for women; and (c) to provide social opportunities to working-class girls and women, including both exercise and leisure pursuits (Smart, 2001). Stansfeld was particularly exceptional at promoting the academic and professional credentials of physical education and helped to establish a diploma of physical education program at the University of London in 1935 (Smart, 2001).

Duval (2001) suggested that much of this early history concerning women in the field of physical education has been submerged in the broader context of women's eruption into popular sports in the 1980s and 1990s, with such initiatives as Title IX in the United

States. Duval's main concern is that women's progress within this discipline was defined in reference to a more "male" conception of sports and fitness and in essence that sports and physical education during that era was concerned with establishing programs that emulated this male identification (Fletcher, 1984). This, either directly or indirectly, led to a devaluation of many of the unique aspects of women and sports during the earlier era of the early 1900s.

WOMEN AND OUTDOOR RECREATION
AND EDUCATION

Throughout history, there have been a number of women who have been influential in the fields of outdoor recreation and education such as Jane Addams (Dieser, Harkema, Kowalski, Osuji, & Poppen, 2004), Laura Mattoon (Raiola & O'Keefe, 1999), and Anne LaBastille (LaBastille, 1987), among others. These are women who have built on some of the early successes of those women who were pioneers in the fields of sports and physical education. It is interesting to note the breadth and depth of the influence of these women across the overlapping disciplines within the fields of outdoor recreation and education, including recreation and leisure, parks, outdoor and physical education in schools and colleges, the camping movement, tourism, and wilderness travel. "Who were these women and what were their contributions?" Each of these fields and the women who most influenced those fields are considered here.

JANE ADDAMS
AND OUTDOOR RECREATION

Jane Addams is best known for her work at the social settlement house of Hull House, located in a densely populated urban area of Chicago (Dieser et al., 2004). The idea of social settlements began in the 1880s in London in response to problems created by urbanization, industrialization, and immigration. Hull House in Chicago was one such settlement, comprised of Italian, Irish, German, Greek, Russian, and Polish Jewish immigrants. During the 1920s, African Americans and Mexicans began to put down roots in the neighborhood surrounding Hull House and became involved in the clubs and activities that it had to offer. Jane Addams and the Hull House residents provided kindergarten and day-care facilities for the children of working mothers, an employment bureau, an art gallery and library, citizenship classes and theater, art, and music classes, among other recreational opportunities (Dieser et al., 2004).

As a result of the success of her work at Hull House, particularly her efforts that focused on the field of recreation, Jane Addams was elected vice president of the Campfire Girls and became a member of the executive board of the National Playground Association (Brown, 2001). Jane Addams additionally contributed to the fields of outdoor recreation and education through her involvement in developing the first public playground in Chicago and the first public gymnasium in Chicago. During the course of her career, Addams worked with a number of other prominent women including Grace and Edith Abbott, Jelen Culver, and Alice Hamilton, as well as a number of men who are well known today as forefathers of the outdoor and experiential education fields, including John Dewey.

LAURA MATTOON
AND EARLY OUTDOOR EDUCATION

The early efforts of women who were devoted to the growth and development of women and sports and women in the field of physical education during both eras has helped lay the groundwork for the field of women and outdoor education in K–12 schools and colleges. K–12 schools began to adopt the wilderness trip model used by camps as early as the late 1800s. At the Gunnery School in Connecticut, the whole school went on a two-week, 40-mile journey at the end of the school year (Camp Kehonka, n.d.).

Although Laura Mattoon's career started at Camp Kehonka in 1902, some of her most influential work was as head of the science department at the Veltin School in New York City (Camp Kehonka, n.d.). As head of the science program at Veltin, Miss Mattoon was considered an exceptional teacher. She wished to show her students a kind of growth and adventure that only the outdoors could offer. She took students out camping. They slept in tents, built their own furniture, and swam and hiked in the pristine lakes and mountains of New Hampshire. She believed that this form of outdoor education would offer students training in the natural sciences in addition to engendering the "right" kind of values in students and serve as an aid in their character development. Laura Mattoon was one of many activists in the early 20th century concerned with the instruction and personal growth of young women.

There were similar programs at many of the folk and Quaker schools established in North America and Europe in the early 1900s. Within these traditions, it was believed that education should include not only those things that are practical but also those things that make students good citizens and participants in society (Heath, 1979). Outdoor education in both folk and Quaker schools was reflected in the curricular emphasis on physical activity, hands-on learning experiences that were both useful and practical, and wilderness trip experiences (Breunig, 2005). Within both of these traditions, women educators were common.

THE CAMPING MOVEMENT

During these same years, in the early 1900s, the girls' camping movement experienced tremendous success. Many of the women involved in this movement were those same people who brought the theory and practice of outdoor education into the K–12 schools and included Mrs. Luther Charles Farnsworth, headmistress of the Horace Mann School, Mary Schenck Woolman, founder of the Manhattan Training School for Girls, Florence Marshall, director and head of the Manhattan Trade School for Girls, as well as Mrs. Luther Gulick, co-founder of The Campfire Girls (Miranda & Yerkes, 1996). "The overriding belief they held in common was that a new American golden age depended upon the liberation of girls" (p. 64). The organized camping movement seemed to be one venue where this goal could be pursued.

As mentioned earlier, Laura Mattoon, alongside these other prominent women, took some of the educational aims and ideals found in the K–12 nature-based curriculum and applied them within the camping tradition. Miss Mattoon, and others, believed that camping was an important means for young girls to build character and develop some of the necessary skills to work toward the ideal of women's liberation. One problem was that although Laura Mattoon was regarded as a pioneer in everything pertaining to the progress of the summer camp (Sargent, 1924), neither she nor any of the other 200 women then directing camps, were eligible to join the Camp Directors Association of America (CDAA), founded in 1910 (Eells, 1986).

In Fall 1916, eight women met to plan what would soon be known as the National Association of Directors of Girls Camps (NADGS; Eells, 1986). The purpose of this association was to establish an approach to camping that was specific to the goal of challenging some of the antiquated boundaries that had been set for girls. These women believed that the only means to accomplishing this was to establish an environment and pedagogical approach that addressed the specific needs of girls. This approach would focus on "roughing it" in a primitive camp setting in addition to creating an environment where the aesthetic and spiritual links between girlhood and nature were created (Miranda & Yerkes, 1996). These eight women additionally believed that a women's-only association would only replicate the gender divide they hoped to reverse and thus believed that the NADGS would need to be an association that allowed for both female and male representation.

The form of educational progressivism that can be seen in the camping movement continued to grow and expand with the Girls Scouts, the YWCA, and the aforementioned settlement houses. As Teachers College in New York City drew increasing numbers of students seeking advanced degrees and support of this form of pedagogy, the NADGS received support from numerous prestigious faculty including John Dewey's disciple, William Kilpatrick and Kilpatrick's protégés, among them E. K. Fretweel and L. B. Sharp (Miranda & Yerkes, 1996). These men were to become important leaders in both the camping movement and the field of outdoor education. Although supported by Mattoon, this coalition did come at a price for women (Mattoon, 1925). The NADGC and the CDAA merged in 1924, with Laura Mattoon continuing to serve as secretary to the association.

These early initiatives in both outdoor education and the camping movement contributed significantly to a groundswell of interest in women-only outdoor pursuits programs in the later 1970s (Mitten, 1992). These early initiatives were also accompanied by an expansion of feminist-based theory and feminist pedagogy and their influence on the broader field of experiential education, which builds on the fields of outdoor recreation and education (Miranda & Yerkes, 1996). What is interesting to note is that some of these more recent efforts within the fields of outdoor and experiential education illustrate some of the same challenges that were faced by these early women pioneers from the time of the organized camping movement. Some of the queries are as prevalent today as they were during the early part of the 1900s: Whose experiences are addressed within the fields of outdoor recreation and education? Who is left out? and What "ways of knowing" (epistemologies) are valued?

WOMEN AND WILDERNESS TRAVEL
AND TOURISM

There are many chronicles of women's early adventures in the mountains, including *Scrambles Amongst the Alps* (Whymper, 1996) and the chronicles of Ruth Dyer Mendenhall's (1912–1989) early years of rock climbing. Many of the illustrations found in Whymper's book show drawings of men with a walking stick in hand scrambling up a route on Mt. Blanc, accompanied by a woman, in a hat and skirt, an outfit that would appear to be more suited for Sunday church, than for attempting a first ascent up a Swiss peak. It is difficult to imagine oneself without the conveniences of modern-day climbing and camping equipment and outdoor apparel attempting to engage in a similar feat. These stories serve as both entertainment to the "armchair traveler" and as a reminder of the ways in which women were an integral part of some of the early explorations and wilderness travel that took place in both North America and in Europe.

At the time that Ruth Dyer Mendenhall took up climbing and joined a rock climbing section of the Southern California Chapter of the Sierra Club, most of the pioneer rock climbers were men, but several outstanding women climbers had already retired from climbing or were overlapping with her (Goebel, 2004). This was in 1938. Climbing at that time did not appear to have a women's-only focus, as it does to some degree today. According to Mendenhall (Goebel, 2004), boys and girls enjoyed climbing together and most respected their own and each other's abilities and limitations. Many women during that era, including Mary Jane Edwards, Adrienne Applewhite (Jone), the first woman to climb the East Face of Mt. Whitney, and LaVere Daniels (Aulie), who appeared in a professional movie short, *Three on a Rope,* and was the first woman to climb Temple Crag (12,999) feet), were making their mark (Goebel, 2004).

Wildlife ecologist Anne LaBastille was another pioneer in the growing movement of women and wilderness. LaBastille encouraged women to pursue careers in wilderness-oriented fields, including: the field sciences, zoology, wilderness guiding, and speleology (cave exploration). LaBastille encouraged women to forge unique, self-reliant lifestyles in wilderness homesteads. These women, LaBastille herself among them, constituted a new and important category of role models for young women (LaBastille, 1987).

Anne LaBastille was both an Adirondack guide and a Commissioner of the Adirondack Park Agency of New York State for 17 years. While her books, the most well known being her trilogy entitled *Woodswoman I, II,* and *III* tend toward an underemphasis of women-only wilderness experiences, they do provide some foundation for other women and associations to pursue the idea of women-only wilderness travel and tourism. LaBastille does this in part by examining the complex web of social and psychosexual factors that have alienated women from wilderness in the past and shows how feminism and the rise of environmental consciousness have allowed the "wilderness within women" to emerge (LaBastille, 1987).

Today, we see evidence of some of the popularity and growth of women-only wilderness trip companies, including Wild Women Expeditions, Woman Tours, Woman FlyFishing, and Canyon Calling Tours for Women, among many others (http://dir.yahoo.com/Business_and_ Economy/Shopping_and_Services/Travel_and_Transportation/Tour_ Operators/Women_s_Tours/). There are many examples of women in the field of outdoor recreation and education with increasing numbers of women completing women's-only ascents of mountains (Nepal, South America, and throughout North America and Europe), women's first ascents of challenging rock climbing routes (including the well-heralded first free ascent of The Nose by Lynn Hill), women's-only ice climbing festivals (Chicks with Picks), female paddlers being applauded for gutsy first descents of whitewater rivers, and the widely heralded accomplishments of Ann Bancroft, the first woman in history to cross the ice to both the North and South Poles (www.yourexpedition.com).

These efforts and successes have come under some critical examination and scrutiny. For some people, men and women alike, there is an inherent problem when women are recognized for their accomplishments only when these are commensurate with or supersede the physical accomplishments of men (Warren & Rheingold, 1996). For others, there is growing concern about the potential for this emphasis on women-only activities to further exacerbate and further divide the gender gap, rather than work toward making it more equal. Many women believe that their "voices" and "experiences" need to be regarded as unique and gender-specific because of the fact that they have been left out of the outdoor recreation and wilderness travel "history books." For many, the goal of women-only programs and the need to highlight women's accomplishments within the field of outdoor adventure and wilderness travel is to consider the idea that what women bring to adventure experiences represent not only their distinct needs as women but a unique perspective on the field that would be beneficial if incorporated in all facets of outdoor and adventure education, regardless of gender, race, or culture (Warren & Rheingold, 1996).

CONCLUSION: FUTURE TRENDS

My discussion of women leads to the question, "What will outdoor recreation and education look like for girls and women and for all people in the new century?" Will some of the myths and realities of the previous century be dispelled? Will outdoor recreation and education continue to be considered around some of the previously dominant norms and will there be potential in the coming years for new norms and new standards to be formulated? Will the opening scenario become less a part of women's experiences within this century? These are queries that have yet to be answered.

As a professor in the Department of Recreation and Leisure at Brock University in St. Catharine's, Ontario, I teach a second-year undergraduate course on Outdoor leadership and one small part of the curriculum addresses issues of privilege, hegemony, and "voice." The students and I engage in a number of readings and experiential activities that allow us to explore gender, dominant epistemologies, and privilege in the fields of outdoor education and recreation. We further explore the value of acknowledging issues of dominance, privilege, various learning styles and intelligences and the ways in which we can use an understanding of these to work toward a more equitable and socially just world (or at least a more "just" classroom).

Over the course of the last 2 years, in particular, I have been struck by students' reaction to some of the issues that have been presented and discussed. Students have explained to me that they no longer see these issues (gender privilege, hegemonic dominance, and/or issues of justice) as particularly relevant to them. They often tell me that these issues are no longer prevalent. In essence, they consider themselves liberated and believe that education and society are just and equitable.

To assess the accuracy of their conclusions and to address this topic, I may ask students to read a book chapter (Martin, Cashel, Wagstaff, & Breunig, in press) or a journal article that uses "she" (the feminine voice throughout) instead of "he" (the male voice throughout). The self-described liberated students are invariably uncomfortable with this "different" use of "voice." I impel them to discuss what it is specifically that troubles them about these readings. They tell me that it is awkward and feels forced to read an article that uses "she" instead of "he." I ask them why? And they often respond that it is because it is different than what they are used to. I then encourage them to critically examine the ways in which this is one example of the ways in which hegemony and domination works and try to relate it back to why these issues may still be prevalent today, or, at the very least, are still necessary "talking points" for discussion.

I may ask students to explore some of the following questions that Warren and Rheingold (1996) have encouraged outdoor educators to examine, such as the following:

1. Is using high-tech equipment in wilderness trip programs and providing trip participants with a detailed list of "required" personal clothing, displaying an ignorance or insensitivity about class issues?

2. Do we schedule trips around certain religious holidays and not others?
3. Do you believe that you have had equal access to role models, including women and people of color in your own wilderness experiences and in your training and certification courses?
4. Are community service projects meeting the needs of the community or are they quick-fix trips into disadvantaged communities?
5. What do these experiences communicate about who gets "heard" and what gets valued within the field of outdoor leadership?

These questions and the use of case studies related to these specific queries provide students with an action-oriented approach to discussing some of the issues that are relevant to the topic of women's outdoor education, recreation, issues of hegemony, and dominant discourses within the fields of outdoor education and recreation. The educative value of exploring these issues in a nonjudgmental yet confrontational way holds great potential for a more equitable view of the fields of outdoor education and recreation, adding to both an historical understanding of the fields as well as to considering possibilities for the future.

REFERENCES

Bialeschki, M. D. (1992). We said, "Why not?"—a historical perspective on women's outdoor pursuits. *Journal of Physical Education, Recreation, and Dance, 63*(2), 52-55.

Breunig, M. (2005). Experiential education and its potential as a vehicle for social change. *Academic Exchange Extra, 4.*

Bridge, K.A. (1998). *By snowshoe, buckboard, and steamer: Women of the frontier.* Victoria, BC, Canada: Sono Nis Press.

Brown, V. B. (2001). Jane Addams. In R. L. Schultz & A. Hast (Eds.), *Women building Chicago 1790-1900: A biographical dictionary* (pp. 14-22). Bloomington: University of Indiana Press.

Camp Kehonka (n.d.) Retrieved October 1, 2005, from http://www.kehonka.com/laura_mattoon.htm

Dieser, R. B., Harkema, R. D., Kowalski, C., Osuji, I. P. & Poppen, L. L. (2004, September). Portrait of a pioneer. *P & R Magazine.*

Duval, L. (2001). In celebration—underestimated but estimable: Sheila Fletcher. *The International Journal of the History of Sport, 20*(1), 157-161.

Eells, E. (1986). *History of organized camping: The first hundred years.* Martinsville, IN: The American Camping Association.

Fletcher, S. (1984). *Women first: The female tradition in English physical education 1880-1980.* London: The Athlone Press.

Goebel, M. (2004, October 14). *Women on the rocks: The early years of the SMS & RCS*. Retrieved October 1, 2005, from http://angeles.sierraclub.org/skimt/text/basecamp.htm.

Hall, M. A. (2001). Alexandrine Gibb: In "no man's land of sport." *The International Journal of the History of Sport, 18*(1), 149-172.

Hargreaves, J. (1994). *Sporting females: Critical issues in the history and sociology of women's sports.* London & New York: Routledge.

Heath, D. (1979). *The peculiar mission of a Quaker school.* Pendle Hill, PA: Pendle Hill.

LaBastille, A. (1987). *Women and wilderness.* San Francisco, CA: Sierra Club Books.

Mangan, J. A. (2000). *Athleticism in the Victoria and Edwardian public school.* Portland, OR: Frank Cass.

Martin, B., Cashel, C., Wagstaff, M., & Breunig, M. (in press). *Outdoor leadership: Theory and practice.* Champaign, IL: Human Kinetics.

Mattoon, L. (1925). Secretary's report and resume of the work of the association. In *Camps and camping* (pp. 11-13). New York: Spaulding Athletic Library, American Sports.

Miranda, W., & Yerkes, R. (1996). The history of camping women in the professionalization of experiential education. In K. Warren (Ed.), *Women's voices in experiential education* (pp. 63-77). Dubuque, IA: Kendall/Hunt.

Mitten, D. (1992). Empowering girls and women in the outdoors. *Journal of Physical Education, Recreation, and Dance, 63*(2), 56-60.

Netzley, P. D. (2001). *The encyclopedia of women's travel and exploration.* New York: Oryx.

Olafson, P. (1990). *Sport, physical education and the ideal girl in selected Ontario denominational schools, 1870-1930.* Unpublished master's thesis, University of Windsor, Windsor, Ontario, Canada.

Sargent, P. (1924). *A guide to summer camps.* Boston: Wright & Potter.

Smart, R. (2001). At the heart of a new profession: Margaret Stansfeld, a radical English educationalist. *The International Journal of the History of Sport, 18*(1), 119-148.

Stokowski, P. A. (2000). Exploring gender. *Journal of Leisure Research, 32*(1), 161-165.

Warren, K., & Rheingold, A. (1996). Feminist pedagogy and experiential education: A critical look. In K. Warren (Ed.), *Women's voices in experiential education* (pp. 118-129). Dubuque, IA: Kendall/Hunt.

Whymper, E. (1996). *Scrambles among the Alps in the years 1860-69.* New York: Dover.

4

ALTERNATIVE AND CHARTER SCHOOL APPLICATIONS OF EXPERIMENTAL EDUCATION

Greg S. Goodman

The ignorant man is not the unlearned, but he who does not know himself, and the learned man is stupid when he relies on books, on knowledge and on authority to give him understanding. Understanding comes only through self-knowledge, which is awareness of one's total psychological process. Thus education, in the true sense, is the understanding of oneself, for it is within each one of us that the whole of existence is gathered.

—Krishnamurti (1953, p. 17)

Ever since Outward Bound and the National Outdoor Leadership School's (NOLS) beginnings in the late 1960s and early 1970s, individuals trained within these schools have branched out and sought sites to apply the skills and dispositions they acquired. One of the most popular applications of experiential learning has occurred within alternative educational and therapeutic communities. In this chapter, I attempt to articulate a pedagogy and praxis for use with those identified as needing affective, social, or other psychosocial education and/or therapy. Also included in this chapter are some stories that help to experientially connect the pedagogy of outdoor education with the daily praxis of the leadership.

At-risk youth require a psychosocial atmosphere that acknowledges these adolescent's essential and unique needs for safety, trust, and recovery following the many years of educational and other social failure that preceded their placement in an alternative program (Baker, Bridger, Terry, & Winsor, 1997). Because of these needs, the pedagogy for outdoor programming within alternative education must be well founded in psychological theory and supported with sound educational praxis (Goodman, 1999; Pianta & Walsh, 1996; Rogers, 1969). For purposes of enhancing the personal and relational needs of these students, the pedagogy for an outdoor program within the alternative education setting is distinguished from more traditional outdoor education philosophy in several important ways. The primary difference is the emphasis on psychological and psychosocial components such as individual and interpersonal growth. These psychological and psychosocial components are viewed as a precondition for the development of intellect and the enhancement of traditional goals of learning, such as reading, writing, or science education. In our descriptions of outdoor educational programs earlier in the text, outdoor education pedagogy and praxis was designed to primarily enhance student academic achievement and the secondary benefit was increased sensitivity and compassion for one another (i.e., psychological and psychosocial goals). In outdoor educational pedagogy and praxis for alternative education students, this paradigm is inverted to place the psychosocial before the academic. In fact, when the academic is even reached with disaffected youth, it will be cause for significant celebration for the teaching staff. Yet, no matter what the principal goals of one's specific program or school happen to be (recovery, re-education, or therapeutic), the needs of alterative education students match perfectly with outdoor education's experiential approach (Goodman, 1999).

As stated earlier, to understand how the experiential education philosophy is differentiated from the traditional, epistemological approach, it is instructive to examine their specific ideologies. Traditional pedagogy posits the school's mission as an academically driven, subject-centered process. This fact is apparent from the structure of the daily schedule to the reliance on formative and summative assessments; such as standardized testing to evaluate outcomes. Traditional schools sometimes support the emotional wellness of the students with psychological components; for example, a guidance counselor. However, the main goals of guidance are to further the academic success of students, not supplant academics with therapeutic or psychologically motivated interventions such as counseling (Goodman & Young, 2005).

Epistemological philosophy fails the needs of at-risk youth and reinforces their exclusion by woefully underacknowledging their psychological requirements. However, as an outdoor education teacher or instructor with these youth, you won't need a text to instruct you as to their proclivities. If you try to teach them without first establishing a positive connection, these former failures of our public schools will tell you straight up, "Funk you!"

One of my earliest learnings of the extreme difference between regular education and alternative education occurred while I was working as an outdoor education teacher at "The Alt." At the end of a magnificent climbing day at Rockhouse Pond, my instruction started. Up to this point, the day had been "perfect" (that should be the first clue that things are awry!), and the students were anxious to get back to the van and make the drive back to Hampton. Unaware of their true intention, I said, "Go on. I'll coil up the last rope and meet you shortly." Fairly humming with joy along the trail, my high from the success of the day's activity was quickly returned to earth's floor by the hanging scent of marijuana on the trail's corridor.

When I reached the van, I let my rage descend on the students and I pummeled them with questions until one of them admitted to the discipline breach. After the barrage of emotions, the van was silent for the 40-minute trip back to school. When we arrived back at school, I went to the appropriate disciplinarian and then promptly went outside to pace and reflect on the day's events. My frustration was palpable, and I could not let myself get into my truck to drive home. In my continuing rage and disappointment, I brought myself into the counselor's offices and sat down with friend/colleague Jamie Marston. I began by telling her of the day and my continuing issues with my new students in the alternative program. She knew these students well, and she had heard of the "head banging" that was going on between them and me over who was in charge at the Alt. As I spoke and she listened, all of my tangled up feelings began to unravel and I broke down in tears. I was so frustrated that these students would not listen to me or obey my rules. I felt as though I was a damn good teacher and that these students were wasting my time and theirs. I wished that I had never come to teach at that school and regretted my decision to leave the comfortable security of my old position as a middle school counselor. My situation was painfully disturbing and I didn't know what move to make. Hitting such a wall of rejection, I couldn't believe that I was fool enough to take that job at the alternative school! The students were rejecting me, and I felt like a failure!

The counselor was a great comfort to me. Knowing the students whom I was teaching, she said that their resistance was normal. She offered, "Perhaps part of the problem is that you are having trouble accepting your new students? Maybe the resistance you are getting is from the students' feelings that they are not acceptable to you?" After dismissing my first response of wanting to swear and reiterate that I was the teacher, I let Jamie's words penetrate. Maybe I was causing the resistance of the students to be exacerbated because of my rejection of them? This was now the time for my education—time to learn that the teacher of alternative education students needs to learn from the class before she or he can teach—period. My job was to accept them as they were and then, hopefully, they would accept me. I needed to stop trying to make them into something they weren't. The expectations that I had were unrealistic.

The adjustment that I made over the ensuing weeks and months improved my ability to win the students' trust and respect. I continued to learn about my students and to try to see the world through their eyes. Through understanding their point of view, I was able to meet the students in the middle between their ability to work and conform to rules and my ability to communicate a warmth and affection for them no matter what they felt about the given tasks. Why I thought the students would accept me unconditionally when I wouldn't do that for them stands out as one of the most naive notions of my career! The students and I both needed to come to the point of accepting each other through a natural process.

BRIDGING MULTIPLE WORLDS

Alternative education students have been fighting the molds of conformity for many years. They are much better at smashing a system than the adults are at maintaining these students within a tightly controlled classroom. Furthermore, it can be instructive to see this mismatch of the school's authoritarian or control pedagogy and the needs of at-risk youth through the lens of cultural reproduction theory (Bourdieu, 1977). Cultural reproduction theory states that groups or social classes tend to develop systems that reinforce the power and position that those groups hold. In the case of schools, success is marked by grades and advanced placement. These successes are the product of having the cultural capital (Bourdieu, 1977) to succeed within that system. Examples of cultural capital are homework, vocabulary, and personal experience. According to McLaren (1994), "Schools systematically devalue the cultural capital of students who occupy subordinate class positions" (p. 198).

I would suggest that a pervasive lack of hope of future success is also a part of the equation that sums as student failure. A student without the tools for success; for example, a strong and supportive family or habitus, is at a disadvantage because of his or her lack of resiliency (Goodman, 2002). In cultural reproduction theory, these students are already marked to repeat the failing from which they came. Again, according to McLaren (1994), "The end result is that the school's academic credentials remain indissolubly linked to an unjust system of trading in cultural capital which is eventually transformed into economic capital, as working-class students become less likely to get high-paying jobs" (p. 198). The net effect of a traditional, epistemological approach on disaffected youth is, simply, an ever-growing group of school dropouts.

The pedagogy for an outdoor program for at-risk youth must be fundamentally different than the epistemological foundation for regular education. Alternative schools need to work in a holistic fashion incorporating the best practices of mental health, education, and systems thinking (Pianta & Walsh, 1996) to build programs that address the needs of the youth they serve. This methodology is stated well by Altenbaugh, Engle, and Martin (1995) in their study of Pittsburgh's "school leavers." They state:

> Simplistic solutions, therefore, will only change the form of schooling, but not the substance and structure. Solutions must be comprehensive, acknowledging the complexities of the school leaving process. They must transcend the limits of the existing paradigm of public schooling, and seek creative and flexible approaches, overlooking nothing. All of this must begin with an atmosphere of caring and sensitivity. (p. 155)

It is paramount that the alternative school outdoor education pedagogy reflect a deep understanding of the needs of the student and their family as a system of human resources (Pianta & Walsh, 1996). For this reason, alternative education praxis is best structured so that it is primarily psychosocial in nature. This relates to the philosophical paradigms of existentialism and phenomenology. The focus is on the individual and his or her development as authentic self. To this end, all of the processes of the outdoor program need to reflect a positive valuing of the student and their culture. In daily instruction and programming, emphasis needs to remain on the dignity and respect of the student and his or her family.

The experiential process of the outdoor classroom helps to build a positive relationship bridge between the student, the family, and the school personnel. This connection is fundamental in demonstrating the school's desire to include in an educational experience those who have previously known exclusion (Comer, 1988). Inclusion begins with a psychological process to develop a self-esteem that allows growth and learning. Joy Zimmerman (1994), rephrasing the work of Bonnie Benard, said this well. "Essentially . . . all youngsters can thrive despite otherwise risky environments if in some area—home, school or the community—a child feels loved and supported; is the object of high expectations; and is given the opportunity to participate and contribute in meaningful ways to the world" (p. 3).

The foundation for alternative education students' successor is clearly rooted in their seeing themselves as lovable and capable individuals (Harris, 1969). It is from a foundation of acceptance of the individual and his or her culture that a successful relationship with school and society can be built.

ADD COMPASSION

For at-risk youth to achieve success of any kind, it is paramount that they have a close and personal relationship with their teacher, and the basis of this relationship is the teacher's compassion for the student. Compassion is defined as an empathy for the individual based on knowledge of the individual's history and a deep understanding of his or her experience. It is from this relationship or connection with the teacher that alternative education students then develop a personal reason to learn. This connection is very similar to the relationship that one develops with a mentor. In order to reach and teach these students, the teacher needs to recognize and remember that the influences that lead to the patterns of failure are deeply imbedded in the habitus of that student (MacLeod, 1995). Only compassionate acceptance will allow the teacher to overlook the resistance these students bring with them so that a connection can be forged.

Jay MacLeod eloquently described the role of habitus and social reproduction theory in his ethnography of disaffected youth in a Massachusetts housing project. MacLeod (1995) stated, "Put simply, the habitus is composed of the attitudes, beliefs, and experiences of those inhabiting one's social world. This conglomeration of deeply internalized values defines an individual's attitudes toward, for example, schooling" (p. 15). From this habitus, there tends to be a reproduction of values over time. Although not all poor and delinquent youth perpetuate habitus characteristics among themselves, the large majority continue the "traditions" set by older siblings, parents, and close friends. Breaking away from those values is the exception to the rules of social reproduction. In order to break the chains of habitus and to develop routines that foster success in school, a major paradigm shift needs to occur within the alternative education student. For teachers to gain the trust of at-risk youth, the students must first abandon their old connections and belief systems (habitus) before they will learn new ones.

Learning follows the development of safety and trust (Maslow, 1968). This is why the implementation of the "full value contract" is so essential (Schoel, Prouty, & Radcliff, 1988). One's locus of safety and trust is where the learning is taking place (Hart, 1983). The need for the development of trust is especially strong within the minority, at-risk learners. According to Ogbu (1995), "Because they do not trust the schools, many minority parents and adults in the community are skeptical that the schools can provide their children with good educations" (p. 98). The cultural capital or set of knowledge and experience that frames one's culture must be respected in order to build a bridge from one's culture to that of the school (MacLeod, 1995). The impact of disregarding the student's cultural capital (Bourdieu, 1977) is the subject of a recent research study by the California School Climate and Safety Survey (Bates, Chung, & Chase, 1996). This work revealed that approximately 40% of the students in the sample disclosed low levels of trust in their school. In the case of at-risk students, the failure to address their pain and alienation leaves the traditional school unable to reach these potential learners. Without compassionate teachers, these students will look for love outside the system in what is very often an antisocial affiliation such as a gang. Teaching at-risk or urban youth requires that outdoor education teachers develop respect and competency in the cultural identifications of their students (Andrade-Duncan, 2005).

MORE ON EXPERIENTIAL LEARNING
FOR STUDENTS AND TEACHERS

One of the learnings I have derived from teaching disaffected youth is that they are developmentally delayed as well as educationally deficient. The impact of years of substance abuse, truancy, and nonparticipation in learning has been to keep these students from achieving personal growth in all areas. Ironically, they appear mature; however, their social reasoning, decision making, and self-esteem are often more characteristic of preadolescents. To teach and reach these students, a student-centered curriculum works best. Using a team-teaching approach, the alternative school can focus on the needs of the individual first and the content of the curriculum second. As with the early adolescent, the challenge of teaching outdoor education in the alternative school is to change the self-esteem of the learners and to teach them by utilizing innovative and effective methods.

Many educators have found the process of "integrated learning" has much to contribute to middle school-age and alternative education students (Eggebrecht et al., 1996). According to Eggebrecht et al., "integration provides engaging experiences in which students encounter essential content in multiple and meaningful contexts in response to their own inquiry" (p. 5). Integrated learning uses the students' natural curiosity as the motivator for inquiry. As in Bruner's (1966) thematic teaching, students can participate in the learning of seminal skills through the process of exploring projects both grand and motivating. Outdoor education programs provide natural pathways for this application of knowledge.

Experiential learning also reinforces relevancy and enriches the learning process (Rogers, 1969). Experiential process, although everything we do is an experience, implies active learning. Learning by doing helps the kinesthetic learners as well as those who learn best through the auditory and visual modalities. This type of learning has been popularized by Outward Bound and Project Adventure (Gass, 1993; Rohnke, 1981). Many alternative schools in the United States and abroad use techniques based on this philosophy. This methodology is especially effective in the teaching of life skills (Moote & Wodnarski, 1997). Life skills, according to Brown and Mann (cited in Moote & Wodnarski, 1997) are those abilities that include self-efficacy, communication, and problem solving critical to the successful functioning or adaptive behavior of the individual.

Relevance continues to be a fundamental issue within an alternative setting. Students benefit from "reading" about specific content areas and relating their reading to their topic of interest. For example, students interested in whales can read about whales, write about whales, and research whales to achieve their desired knowledge. Additionally, all reading that is individualized and directed toward vocational or recreational interest has purpose and improves reading (Smith, 1978). High interest is achieved and reading is accomplished!

Paralleling reading strategies, math needs to be taught using the most highly motivating methods. Similar to reading, the successful math program needs to be individualized (Coxford & Hirsch, 1996). Coxford and Hirsch stated, "The individual work accommodates differences in ability, interest, and mathematical knowledge, and challenges students in heterogeneous classes" (p. 25). The salient point within all instruction is to motivate and inspire interest within the students.

A lot of the fun for alternative education teachers is in developing specific courses to address the psychological and social needs of these students. Courses in life decisions, health science, psychology, communication, outdoor education, community service, understanding cultural diversity, our environment, and conflict resolution can provide impetus for learning the reading, math, writing, and socialization skills these students must have to survive, or better still, to discover purpose and success! To call the classes by the same old names is to reinforce the resistance that an alternative education student loves to express.

In the period before I moved to California, I taught outdoor education in the Winnacunnet Alternative School (the Alt). The undisclosed motto of the Alt School was, "Funk that shit!" That motto was a true reflection of how my students felt about traditional education! Our challenge as educators was to devise curriculum that didn't evoke that expletive as a response. The students' challenge was to extinguish schoolwork that made them miserable and to reinforce us for providing lessons that were enjoyable for them to complete. I appreciate the fact that often the learning was two way. We both held opportunities for growth!

I joined the staff of the Alt in Fall 1985. The staff was comprised of a director, Ken Grossman; an academic teacher, Chris Spiller; an aide, Judy Hallisey; and an outdoor education teacher, me. Occasionally, our staff was supported by a part-time teacher or a counselor in times of large enrollment. Large for us was 55 students. The students chosen for the Alt were selected by counselors at the comprehensive high school, Winnacunnet High School. Winnacunnet was a school with an enrollment of approximately 1,000 students. Ninety-nine percent of the student body was Caucasian. The alternative education students were chosen from the cohort of students who had failed ninth grade. Many of these students were considered to be conduct disordered, and they were well known to the high school administrators. From that freshman cohort, we attempted to select 20 students whom we felt would be successful in our program. They would become our core group.

The core students would spend at least 1 year with us. They would take all of their academic classes with the alternative school staff. Outdoor education supplanted physical education. On Tuesdays and Thursdays, the core would split in half. One half would go on an outdoor education field trip and the other half would stay at the Alt. Their schedule was a block type. Several periods were combined together so that our schedule was not dependent upon the bell. We could have the students for as long as 8 hours at a time. In the case of our summer program, we had them for 3 weeks!

After successfully completing Grade 9, our students could return to the alternative school to take a two-credit class called Life Decisions. This class was designed as a follow-up to the more intensive alternative core and as a way to maintain contact with our students. The class also included an outdoor education component. Because Life Decisions was a seminar-styled class, the students were free to discuss topics of interest to them. This requirement left the class loosely structured. It could be repeated in both the junior and senior years. One of the goals of the alternative school was to reconnect its students with the high school and to have them graduate from there. To this end, the Life Decisions class acted as a link between the Alt and the comprehensive high school.

The habitat selected for our alternative school was very successful in its ability to connect students with their teachers. The alternative school's building was an old colonial period house. The house was vacant and located behind the campus of Winnacunnet High School, conveniently separated from the high school by a vocational building and a cemetery. For an alternative high school, the housing could not have been better. We had a kitchen to prepare meals and a home-like atmosphere. Most of all, we had large blocks of time to spend in the uniquely structured outdoor settings and within the alternative school itself. Those ingredients contributed greatly to the creation of a sense that the students were truly having an alternative school experience.

An especially effective component of the alternative school was the staffing. We almost always team taught. Therefore, our staffing allowed two adults on all trips and two adults to stay at school. This student–teacher ratio meant that there was always a person free to talk with an individual student, to answer the phone, to provide relief for a bathroom break, or to generally support the person teaching. Given the resistance that was often the companion to the alternative student's repertoire, the support of another adult was not a luxury, it was essential!

Our staff arrangement also recognized the importance of the influence of male and female staff persons working together. This balance was instrumental in developing feelings of familial support within the students. Often, we were in the roles of nurse, counselor, listener, or surrogate parent. Because our success with the students was accomplished by having their trust, having gender balance and respectful relationships among ourselves had a significantly positive carry-over with our students. Trust (Bates et al., 1996) was enhanced by having the time and the sensitivity to address our students' personal needs. Conversely, when we were not exhibiting our most positive and professional behavior, the students used that opportunity to reinforce negative attributes concerning the teacher, the work, or the school as a whole. Fortunately, discord among our staff was rare.

One of our earliest discoveries as teachers was that schoolwork was best accomplished at the moment. Readings that spanned a period of 20 to 40 minutes were more successful than lengthy articles or full books. The average attention span of our students coincided perfectly with that strategy. We also found homework to be essentially non-existent. Homework is an example of the type of cultural capital that our students lacked. Home life for alternative education students often lacks the protective features necessary for any of the requisite factors for work completion: quiet, space, or support. Therefore, assignments due the next day were a sure flop. The best practice was to have an activity that lasted about 20 minutes and then to move on to another. If the activity was a winner, great! If it was the inverse of winner, then no one had to suffer it for long.

Assignments that were tied to themes were more successful than work done in isolation or seemingly unrelated to any larger issue. When the student's "boredom button" was pushed, their internal alarms would rally them to full resistance! However, if entertainment could somehow be tied to the assignment, it was a guaranteed winner. The best example of what grabbed our students' attention had to do with a local blues man, T. J. Wheeler. T. J. would come to the alternative school on a regular basis. His lessons would fuse the topics of rock and the blues with stories about the old Blue's men of the south who worked their way across the country. The students were fascinated to learn how rockers from Elvis to today got their styles by emulating various obscure Blues men. T. J. would mesmerize the students by playing his guitar and demonstrating styles of play to show rock and blues interconnectedness. The music experience led naturally to further discussion of history and related language arts activities.

The film *Crossroads* is a good example of a language arts activity that was a natural follow-up to T. J.'s work with the students. After T. J. would come to the Alt, we would show the film *Crossroads* to reinforce the stories that T. J. shared and give additional credence to the role that the Blue's men played in the evolution of rock history. Whenever we could include a current film in the construction of a lesson or a unit, student interest was markedly increased.

The timely manner in which the work was introduced was also very closely related to the probability that it would get done or be met with a tsunami of resistance. We learned that if the students came to us with feelings unresolved from any earlier encounters or interactions, that those feelings would continue to hover about until they were resolved. It mattered not how enthralling our lesson was. If two of our students were angry at one another, those issues needed to be addressed before any teaching could take place!

Therefore, to facilitate any business or learning that needed to be attended, we would start our afternoon session with a whole-class meeting. The meeting would begin with a teacher or a student going to the blackboard and listing everyone's agenda for the day. Of course, the teachers would say, math, social studies, and the like. The students would interject break, movie, or whatever was on their minds. We would then divide up our time and vote on what went where in the day. Then we would all try to follow the schedule. This worked well in democratizing the experience and empowering the students in the process of their own education. This experience gave the students' voice and feelings of validity in the process of their learning!

One of my former students, Raylene Davis, sums up the importance of being able to deal with her feelings and the benefit that process provided. Raylene said,

> Like most of the kids that were there, I had a hard time coping with my feelings and the life that I had been living. [At the Alt,] I was given the freedom to feel any way I needed to at the moment. I was also given the freedom to have space to deal with it. Rather than be carted off for inappropriate behavior, I was shown a better way. I felt like I had the freedom to ask for what I needed. I learned how to express myself in my own unique way, how to have respect for others.

Raylene further concluded, "When you learn [to] trust the small group around you, you will find something of your own trust and self-worth." These learnings demonstrate how the process of listening to our students developed into the substantive social learning that made our program effective.

In addition to our teaching/counseling style, we found that the more divergent and engaging the topic of study, the more our students would get involved. When they had a successful day, it was very apparent in their faces. Conversely, when the students hated a lesson, we would have to teach through the gales of resistance. There is a lot of learning for a teacher in an alternative setting. Much creativity is required as well as a thick skin.

When I started at the alternative school, I was filled with excitement and idealism. I had wanted that outdoor education job since the school first opened in the 1970s. After I was hired, I was on cloud nine! However, after I met the students, I was shocked at the amount of resistance I encountered! The students basically said that they weren't ready to accept me as their new outdoor education teacher. They liked the old one, and they didn't want to follow me or any of the rules that I had established for them. The students informed me that the old teacher didn't make them do such and such. The old teacher was cool, and the old teacher understood them. In a nutshell, I didn't know what I was doing.

Alternative education students carry considerable frustration. They are angry to have failed in the traditional system, and they are unsure of their ability to succeed. The result is a confusion about where to place their blame; on themselves or on the system that did this to them. This phenomenon I call the "failed" student's dilemma. Letting go of the blame and anger is a hard process. To travel from anger and self-hate to acceptance and self-respect is the quest of all time. Since Plato's "Know thyself," teachers of the humanities have struggled to find the way to help students learn how to better themselves. In alternative education, it is the continual and quintessential question.

One of the best examples of a method to allow the venting of student anger came serendipitously on a gray, March day. Lying innocently beneath us on the Alt school's basement floor was a large number of antiquated, metal, folding chairs. These former student desks were of the bomb-proof, attached writing arm variety. Because they were school property and symbolically significant, the chairs took on one last utility for our students.

Matt appeared in the Life Decisions class with a load of rage on that March day. Failing to mitigate his anger with the usual counseling strategies, we discovered the chair's last utility. I suggested to Matt that he take one of the chairs from the basement, bring it out to the driveway in front of the school, and destroy it. This appealed to Matt. He took the chair outside and spent the better part of 30 minutes pounding the chair into the asphalt. Vented and sweaty, he came back into the class relieved. The process became known as "Doing a chair." The point of the process was that it gave recognition to the feeling of anger and it legitimized the process of venting one's anger against a tangible object and not hurting oneself in the process. So often, our students would be carrying anger only to have the release of that anger come back and hurt them further. A good example of that was when an angry boy would punch a wall or other hard object only to hurt himself more. Other examples of personal abuses abound; drug abuse, fights, body carving. Having an awareness of the true utility of intervention strategies that work for alternative education students is the difference between being able to survive as an observer to the wars they are waging or falling victim to the student's own undermining of their progress and education. At the Alt School, we were constantly experimenting with our methodologies to find pragmatic and psychologically correct techniques to help our students find successful solutions to their real life problems.

MODULATING THE EMOTIONAL TONE

The emotional tone of an alternative school is critical to the school's success. Developing feelings of support and trust between the students and the faculty is the single most significant component in the change process for the alternative education student (Schoel, Prouty, & Radcliff, 1988). Whereas these students were previously looking at education as an adversarial process because they were only experiencing the negative consequences of their inappropriate behavior, they now need to be convinced of the school's sincerity to be allies in their success.

The most important element in reversing the student's sense of failure is in demonstrating the school's understanding of the "failed" student's dilemma. Adolescents are notorious either/or thinkers. Their experience is most often expressed as black or white. Therefore, teenagers will usually be giving either one of two opinions. The response tends toward "It's the bomb!" or "This sucks!" Adults, too, can fall victim to the trap of reductive, either/or thinking. In the case of a "failed" student, often the reason for school failure is placed squarely on the shoulder of the student. Educators have become proficient at placing the responsibility for student failure outside the school. Examples of blaming the victim abound! "The parents don't support the teachers or demand the student complete homework." "The student doesn't attend frequently enough to earn credit to pass." "Despite modification, the student is not completing any of the work." These examples of reductive thinking resound in schools. Denial of the school's complicity protects the school from change.

The "failed" students' dilemma lies in overcoming the irony that they have been to blame for their school failure for the past 8 or 10 years. Why now would the new teachers treat them differently? Countering the blame of the schools, the students' responses to the either/or summation has been to conclude that school sucks. In order to overcome the naturally ingrained resistance on the part of the alternative education student, special understanding is required. These students need to let go of their ingrained assumption that they will be to blame if their school experience does not change for the better and that the school is a damned place for its historic condemnation of them. These realities require special expertise of psychological understanding and, often personal counseling finesse, to overcome the resistance that often accompanies these formerly failed students.

One of the solutions to reversing a self-esteem of school failure is built on demonstrated student successes. Success is first experienced through the development of a positive relationship with the teacher and then through a positive relationship with the work. There is the belief within the student that he or she is safe (Hart, 1983), and it is possible for him or her to achieve success.

Key to the development of trust at the Alt was the establishment of a few, simple rules. The first and foremost of the rules was the no put-downs rule. Put-downs include the entire range of racial, ethnic, gender, intellect, and other comments meant to place one student above another in a verbal joust. Put-downs are the leading cause of fights, disruption, and chaos in most groups and families. Often, the put-down is an expression of anger that is thinly disguised as a joke. Called "doing the dozens" within the African-American community, this experience is contrived to build a shield of defense against verbal abuse. In reality, the game is dangerous and leads to major social problems not the least of which are fights.

Establishing the no put-down rule takes constant vigilance; however, the reward in terms of school climate is huge! We all can work to remind ourselves that none of us are any better nor any less than anyone else (Kopp, 1989). Our lives are experienced within communities defined by varying amounts of diversity. In this context, our individuality requires nurturing and acceptance. We are all human, capable of mistakes, and, conversely, experiencing the rewards of our correctness!

The second rule of the alternative school was that everything that was spoken about at the alternative school stayed at the alternative school. (Except as required by laws regarding child abuse.) This rule reinforced the trust that we wanted to develop among the students. Often, on hikes or other trips, comments of a personal nature would slip out. We didn't want the students to feel that once a personal situation was revealed that the story would spread throughout the community. The confidentiality rule was hard to monitor, but the students generally respected it.

The significance of these two rules was within the emphasis on mutual respect and the protection of the individual. The value of these rules revealed itself in helping to establish a friendly tone within the Alt. Students certainly had their differences, but they were able to live within a culture based on mutual respect.

Balance of gender, race, ethnicity, and other human qualities is essential to the emotional tone of the school. An alternative school needs to reflect the positive values of the community that it serves and to be balanced accordingly. In this way, the staff can model the benefits of diversity and help the students see the value everyone possesses. This contributes considerably to the development of a positive atmosphere within the school. Although there are many factors that work together to shape the emotional tone of an alternative school, the fact that a person's psychological feelings are pre-eminent cannot be overstated. Staff and students alike are the essential players in the development of the school's tone, spirit, and atmosphere. Without buy-in to enhance the resiliency qualities partner to adolescent growth and development, learning is an uphill battle, and the development of trusting relationships will never occur. The net result will be both student and school failure. Just how those resiliency factors are enhanced is the focus of the remainder of this text.

Using outdoor educational methods within an alternative school requires that the teacher view the process of personal change and growth as being dynamic. Although this process encompasses the mistakes and learning of the past and aspires toward goals and benefits of a healthy future, alternative education exists in the here and now (Gaines, 1979)! The focus is immediate and very much present tense. The actions of the moment and the challenges they present provide numerous opportunities for learning and growth. Successful alternative schools incorporate modern psychological and resiliency theories to create an atmosphere that fosters the trust that allows positive development to occur. According to Bonnie Benard (1991), "Just as in the family area, the level of caring and support within the school is a powerful predictor of positive outcome for youth" (p. 10).

Alternative education philosophy and method allows each student opportunities to grow from self-defeat to self-fulfillment (Goodman, 2002). The word *alternative* implies that this process will be uniquely and deeply personal and developed individually (Bomotti, 1996). For the entire community, all individuals need to be successful and productive members. Alternative education recognizes and celebrates cultural pluralism and the need for meaningful inclusion of all. This means equal opportunity for each student with regard to ethnicity (Page, 1996), gender, and ability. Apple (1995) underlined the necessity for including a truly democratic process within the process of the alternative school by suggesting the following:

> If the development of clear alternative programs is essential, these alternatives need to be based on the democratic strength that actually exists in the United States. Without clear programs that seem to provide for at least partial solutions to local and national problems, "most people will accept the dominant view, which is inherently undemocratic and anti-egalitarian." Thus, these programs need to be sensible not only to hardcore activists but to working people with families and jobs. (pp. 158-159)

SPECIAL METHODOLOGIES
FOR ALTERNATIVE EDUCATION

How shall we approach oppositional and defiant students? By surprise, and in a way that they have not been solicited for learning before. When I began working at the alternative school, the principal of the high school, James Hawthorne, called me into his office and asked me how it was going at the alternative school. I told him that the students were a real challenge and that I had to think fast in coming up with new techniques to get their attention. James asked for an example and I hesitatingly offered this one. I told James that the students used the word "funk" all the time and that I needed to develop a "funk" lecture. James asked, "What's a funk lecture?" I replied that in response to the gross overuse of the word, I called my students together and said, "Hey, listen up! 'Funk' is my favorite word, but you guys are going to ruin it for me. Everyday I hear, 'Oh, funk. I've got to get my f**kin' lunch out of my f**kin' locker to go on a f**kin' trip in the f**kin' van . . . .'" I said, "Whoa, you are going to ruin this word for me. If you want to say the word 'funk' that is perfectly OK. But save it for something really good, like if a canoe fell on your foot or something!" The student response was to stare at me with their mouths agape. Then came the comment, "That's cool."

James thought that this story was one of the funniest things he had ever heard in his tenure as principal. For months after our meeting, I would be somewhere and be approached by someone recalling my "Funk" lecture. Showing that you can waltz to the edge of the envelope on occasion builds your credibility with the alternative education student. However, for your own professional security, you may want to check out some of the local linguistic norms first.

Swearing or obscenity is defined, psychologically, as displaced aggression. Displaced aggression is a term from Freudian psychology that defines the concept of displacement (Hunt, 1993). If, for example, students were angry at themselves for their current straits, that anger could more easily be released by swearing at some object or external person. As alternative education students are almost always carrying anger as a form of personal baggage, the attendant strings of obscenity are a natural vent.

The other aspect of obscenity that bears regard relates to the local norm. Coming from New England where the weather could foul the tongue of a saint, the "F'" word is often used merely as punctuation. Exclamation becomes "Oh, Funk!" Interrogatives degrade to, "What the Funk?" My biggest culture shock came after moving to the central valley of California, an area of predominantly White, middle-American values. Here the use of the "F" word is reserved for gutters and prisons. I made the mistake of using the word during an Individual Educational Plan meeting with some of my new colleagues. The resultant meeting with my supervisor was most instructive! I confess to still being linguistically challenged at times when there just doesn't seem to be a better word, but in deference to my survival needs, I try to be careful and pick my spots for that pleasant indiscretion.

Because language and image are so intertwined, at the Alt School I tried to strike deals with my students to keep the language appropriate to the situation. In the woods, and far removed from civilization, the linguistic standards were different than they were in the classroom or in the local grocery. The rationale was respect; respect for ourselves and the Alt as a whole.

True to the nature of adolescence, risk is one of the teenager's favorite companions. In the domain of risking, alternative education students pride themselves! Alternative education students are very desirous of adventure and challenge; fundamentals in a methodology first proposed by Kurt Hahn, refined by Willie Unsoeld, and utilized by Outward Bound. This methodology of outdoor and experiential learning well suits these here-to-fore resist-

ant learners. Rock climbing, canoeing, skiing, and other outdoor activities give opportunity for the satisfaction of the need to risk. The outdoor education component was essential in making our school alternative.

The outdoor/experiential approach also connects the students in a holistic way to their learning (Gass, 1993). Lab-like in structure, students are learning by doing (Leugers, 1997). The focus is on the process of the learning, and participation and cooperation are the only requirements. In the language of adventure-based counseling, this is referred to as a part of the "full value contract" (Schoel et al., 1988). No one is devalued in the learning process!

One of the unique characteristics of the outdoor education approach is the way in which it can feature multiple invitations to rejoin a learning experience. Using a variety of positive methodologies, we break new ground away from memories of past failures. Within a supportive small-group atmosphere, the alternative school teacher can foster a relationship that can achieve positive results. Between 1970 and 1989, I spent approximately 150 days teaching climbing and rappelling at a local ledge called Stone House. One of New Hampshire's most beautiful sites, Stone House afforded excellent climbing; solid rock, gorgeous views, and bomb proof belays. Over the years, I developed a lesson and routine at Stone House that had a 100% success rate for getting students to rappel (Reif, 1984). I accomplished this success by telling all of the students that for some of them, rappelling wasn't scary at all. For the unafraid, because they trusted me, the exercise was just another thrill like riding a roller coaster. However, for a few of the students, showing up at the top of that 200' cliff was the most courageous thing that they had ever done! Having redefined success, everyone was a hero and the term *chicken* was never evoked. This methodology maximized the use of social psychological theory by including everyone in the process of the day. "Doing" became the best demonstrator to overcome a self-esteem that supported nonparticipation. No one was devalued in the exercise.

Another successful tool to turn a "dropout" into a student is to let the student be the teacher. The peer instruction method has been proven to be very effective for both teacher and learners. Especially with peer-centered adolescents, the focus shifts from the adult to their own (ownership) of the learning process. One of the keys to success in this methodology is that we are not perceived as interfering with their learning! With all students, we are most successful when we remember to be the "guide on the side," not the "sage on the stage."

The strategy that I have found to be the most effective for the teacher's personal and professional survival in dealing with at-risk youth is humor. The alternative education students possess a great need to laugh and release frustration. The teachers, also, need to psychologically detach themselves from the immediate stress of their jobs to maintain their role as good-humored participants. To serve these purposes, the constructive use of irony, paradox, and humor in a variety of forms (remember, no put-downs!) can make the difference between a disaster and success. Humor can provide the release necessary to keep an absurdity in its place. Often the alternative education student is facing multiple paradoxes and, of these, the "stupid" teacher is one they constantly watch for. Having been put down many times by teachers, it is no wonder that the inverse of this hostility has found a home. By overstating our stupidity and showing our foibles, we allow the kids the opportunity to laugh at us in ways that enhance our relationship.

An example of the constructive use of humor relates to an old camp song. Often when we were in the woods, we would come across a beaver dam or lodge. To mark this event, I would call the students together, point out the lodge, and sing "The Beaver Song." The words are, "I'm a beaver, you're a beaver, we are beavers all; and when we get together we give the beaver call." For the finale of the song, you put your two index fingers in front of your mouth to simulate beaver's teeth and yell, "Hey!" This rendition's obvious silliness would always generate a flood of appropriate moans and laughs. Of course, the double entendre when I sang, "I'm a beaver" was not lost on many of our libidinous learners! The song became a part of the legend at the Alt (Goodman, 1999).

Although not a methodology, per se, understanding the power and effect of alcohol can enhance understanding of one of the other dilemmas that alternative education students face. An alternative education parent may verbalize that he or she want his or her child to be successful in the world; however, the parent's alcoholism is a glaring example of his or her inability to overcome personal obstacles and have a healthy resolution of his or her problems. This irony can be interpreted in many ways, but students often misunderstand their parents disease as a justifiable alienation from the world. The alcoholic parent blames the world for his or her own shortcomings. The boss fired him or her. The coach cut his or her son from the basketball team. In other words, the result of the alcoholic parent's effort or his or her child's effort is undermined by someone else. Blame is the defense of choice.

In any alternative school, more than a couple of the students will be coming from alcoholic and dysfunctional families. The rule in these families is chaos first! Don't count on anything! Dad could be home, or not. Mom could cook dinner, or be back in the hospital. This is a very insecure world! Because of their insecurity, any deviance from their school schedule hits these students right between the eyes. The message to them is that they are just like their parents; they are not trustworthy!

This "alcoholic" thinking of the parent is visited on the child. "The world is wrong!" This child comes to school looking for the teacher to be the "deceiver." "What time do we do math?" "What time do we get to go to the bathroom?" Endless questions. I used to think that these students were put in my classes just to delay the class from starting! It took me years to see that these children of alcoholics were so insecure that they needed to know what was going to happen minute to minute because in their personal lives, chaos was the clock. Life for them was totally unpredictable!

To be able to reach these students, tremendous understanding and patience is required (Baker, Bridger, Terry, & Winsor, 1997). Again, humor can be the fuel that keeps the engine of education going when the resistance is running at its highest. My favorite example of how the changing of the schedule can cause a predictable fury and how humor can be used to diffuse it has to do with one afternoon at the alternative school. The basic schedule for the alternative school was generally predictable. Although students and staff would negotiate the order of the day's activities, Mondays were an academic day. Tuesdays and Thursdays were trip days. Wednesdays were movie days, and Fridays were, well, TGIF!

One Wednesday, the academic teacher, Charles, usurped control of the daily calendar and declared that there would not be a movie that afternoon because he was behind in his teaching chronology. He dictated that there would be a math test in place of the movie. The students went wild! They declared, "You can't take away our movie!" "You're not fair!" The upshot of all of this is that they stormed out of the classroom and mulled around outside the building, smoking cigarettes and complaining. In a word, they went on strike! One girl even made a picket sign that said, "No Movie . . . No Test . . . Funk Math!"

After giving the students time to vent, my response was to get a camera and to go out and join the strikers. One of my favorite momentos from the alternative school is a picture of myself making the worst face I can make and holding the sign of protest. Shortly after I joined the strike it dissolved. It dissolved because adults got involved. The protest wasn't against anything anymore. For an oppositional and defiant teenager, nothing wrecks a party more than adult permission and consent. To move against something, that is the joy!

This example of the strike is a good one for understanding the two issues of schedule and oppositional and defiant behavior. Alternative education students are with us because they are not compliant. Realizing that, we need to not fuel their defiant nature by changing their schedule. A school works when it enlists the participation of its students. In an alternative setting, this requires finesse! Throwing a change in the schedule does no more than create angst.

Understanding the student's dilemma, alternative school educators can use humor to diffuse real and imagined catastrophes. Having the ability to see things differently has to be a key characteristic of an alternative school educator. This ability to work with conduct disorder is one of the premier skills of a successful alternative education teacher. As the students at the Alt would proudly disclaim, "What the Funk! I go to the Alternative School!" We, the staff, would sometimes echo, "What the Funk? We teach there!"

The ideal environment for alternative education invites discovery and doing. It inspires curiosity and participation as students are actively engaged in their education. Because of the unique needs of alternative education students, they require an environment that is not reminiscent of the one where they previously experienced failure. In my experience, I have found that atmospheres that are close to nature, or natural environments, provide the greatest opportunity for establishing a mental set conducive to learning. Moreover, the value of differing environments is strongly supported in educational research literature (Kellmayer, 1995). The modern educational system has created many examples of learning environments that diverge from the traditional classroom; such as science labs, shop classes, demonstration kitchens, gymnasiums, outdoor learning centers, and technology labs. As noted by Cairns and Cairns (1994), "The lessons are not restricted to the classroom . . . " (p. 259).

Because our desire is to achieve a more responsible and positively engaged citizen, these students need to see applications of their learning outside the classroom and in relationship to a real-world setting. The best subjects include those relevant to the lives of the students and their families. The biggest gripe of at-risk students is that the schoolwork and teachers in a traditional setting are not related to their lives. In MacLeod's (1995) ethnography, *Ain't No Makin' It*, the quotes of some of the "Hallway Hangers" sum up this sense of alienation well.

> Chris: I hate the f**king teachers. I don't like someone always telling me what to do. Especially the way they do it. They make you feel like shit. I couldn't take their shit. (p. 108)

Whatever the setting, be it outdoors or in a career lab, we recognize that the ideal environment for at-risk students is one that reflects their dynamic and physical nature. The appearance of the traditional classroom reinforces reminders of their experience of the past. Many of these students have attention deficit disorder, are anxiety disordered, learning disabled, and/or impaired in their mental process. Placing them in an environment that produces de'ja vu does not convince them that this is any "alternative." It looks like the same old structure in a different location or, as is the case in some districts, the location isn't all that different, either. The alternative education class is often on the same campus.

The first place alternative education should look for constructive change is in its environment. John Kellmayer's (1995) work on alternative schools places great emphasis on the value of setting for students. Kellmayer stated, "The richer the site, the more powerful the effect of the site on modifying the cognitive and affective performance of at risk students" (p. 93).

Of all possibilities, the outdoors offers one of the best choices for alternative education. "Climb the mountains and get their good tidings. Nature's peace will flow into you as sunshine flows into trees" (Teale, 1954, p. 311). My first work in an alternative high school was as an outdoor education teacher at the Winnacunnet High School in Hampton, New Hampshire. For 3 to 5 days a week, I would load up to 10 students and another adult into a 12 passenger van, and away we'd go. Being located on the campus of the comprehensive high school, administrators would often breathe a sigh of relief to see the students that I had with me leaving the campus for the day!

We would leave the confines of the high school campus and cruise off to mountains, seasides, rock faces, and rivers for a day of adventures and misadventures. Overall, the students loved these trips. The trips provided a challenge and a release from the ordinary. These adolescents loved risk taking, and the outdoor education program provided plenty of opportunity for adventure. Whether the challenge was climbing up an icy mountain or screwing up the process, there was something they could sink their soul into and get a response.

Above all, through the course of our experiences, we learned to respect and understand each other. There was not a single physical fight during my 4 years at the alternative school. Disagreements, arguments, and even a walk-out style strike, but no fights. I feel that the role that outdoor education played in providing an outlet for some of the frustration was a key ingredient in the process of keeping everyone going.

Not all alternative schools are as fortunate as those New Hampshire students in their proximity to natural habitats. However, the experience of getting out of the confines of a classroom is key to expanding the experience of the students. As Freinet used "learning walks" to inspire curiosity and develop literacy, the alternative school can incorporate outside experiences to build links with the community and enhance the inquisitiveness of its students.

In urban communities where fear is rampant, students and their families are even more alienated and fearful about the world around them. In his insightful ethnography of growing up as an African American in Portsmouth, Virginia, Nathan McCall (1994) wrote:

> Shortly after we moved in a neighbor warned my parents, "Be careful not to drive through Academy Park. Them is some mean crackers over there. They'll stone your car and shoot at you for driving through there."
>
> One night, when I was about ten years old, a little girl my age was shot to death while sitting near a picture window in her living room on Freedom Avenue. The killing brought home the fact that, nice neighborhood or not, we still weren't safe in Cavalier Manor. (pp. 9-10)

In communities where safety is a concern, looking for protective factors and working to maintain them is an important role for the alternative school teacher. Without a sense of safety and trust within the immediate environment, higher functions such as learning will not be accomplished. To this end, the entire community is key to the enhancement and betterment of itself. Within the contexts of our multifarious environments, we must seek affirmations for our student's future as well as our own. We cannot minimize the environment's value within the overall development of outdoor programs within alternative education settings.

REFERENCES

Altenbaugh, R. J., Engel, D. T., & Martin, D. T. (1995). *Caring for students: A critical study of urban school leavers.* Bishop, PA: The Falmer Press.

Andrade-Duncan, J. (2005). *Identifying, defining, and supporting culturally competent teaching in urban schools.* Paper presented at the annual AERA convention, Montreal.

Apple, M. W. (1995). *Education and power.* New York: Routledge.

Baker, J. A., Bridger, R., Terry., T., & Winsor, A. (1997). Schools as caring communities: A relational approach to school reform. *School Psychology Review, 26,* 586-602.

Bates, M., Chung, A., & Chase, M. (1996 Summer). Where has the trust gone? *CASP Today,* pp. 14-15.

Benard, B. (1991). *Fostering resiliency in kids: Protective factors in the family, school, and community.* Portland, OR: Northwest Regional Educational Laboratory.

Bomotti, S. (1996, October). Why do parents choose alternative schools? *Educational Leadership,* pp. 30-32.

Bourdieu, P. (1977). *Outline for a theory of practice.* Cambridge: Cambridge University Press.

Bruner, J. (1966). *Toward a theory of instruction.* New York: Norton.

Cairnes, R. B., & Cairnes, B. D. (1994). *Lifelines and risks: Pathways of youth in our time.* Cambridge, England: Cambridge University Press.

Comer, J.P. (1988). Effective schools: Why they rarely exist for at-risk elementary school and adolescent students. In *School success for students at risk: Analysis and recommendations of the council of chief state school officers.* Orlando, FL: Harcourt, Brace, Jovanovich.

Coxford, A. F., & Hirsch, C. R. (1996). A common core of math for all. *Educational Leadership, 53*(8), 22-25.

Eggebrecht, J., Dagenais, R., Dosch, D., Merczak, N., Park, M., Styer, S. & Workman, D. (1996). Reconnecting the sciences. *Educational Leadership, 53*(8), 4-8.

Gaines, J. (1979). *Fritz Perls: Here and now.* Tiburon, CA: Integrated Press.

Gass, M. (1993). *Adventure therapy: Therapeutic applications of adventure programming.* Dubuque, IA: Kendall Hunt.

Goodman, G. (1999). *Alternatives in education: Critical pedagogy for disaffected youth.* New York: Peter Lang.

Goodman, G. (2002). *Reducing hate crimes and violence among American youth: Creating transformational agency through critical praxis.* New York: Peter Lang.

Goodman, G.S., & Young, I.P. (2006). The value of extracurricular support in increased student achievement: An assessment of a pupil personnel model including school counselors and school psychologists concerning student achievement as measured by an academic performance index. *Educational Research Quarterly, 30*(1).

Harris, T. A. (1969). *I'm okay—you're okay.* New York: Harper & Row.

Hart, L. A. (1983). *Human brain and human learning.* Oak Creek, AZ: Books for Educators.

Hunt, M. (1993). *The story of psychology.* New York: Doubleday.

Kellmayer, J. (1995). *How to establish an alternative school.* Thousand Oaks, CA: Corwin Press.

Kopp, S. (1989). *Rock paper scissors.* Minneapolis, MN: CompCare Publishers.

Krishnamurti, J. (1953). *Education and the significance of life.* New York: Harper & Row.

Leugers, S. (1997, Summer). Experiential education: Learning by doing. *Paradigm,* pp. 14-15.

MacLoed, J. (1995). *Ain't no makin' it.* Boulder, CO: Westview Press.

Maslow, A. H. (1968). *Toward a psychology of being.* New York: Van Nostrand Reinhold.

McCall, N. (1994). *Makes me want to holler.* New York: Vintage Press.

McLaren, P. (1994). *Life in schools: An introduction to critical pedagogy in the foundations of education.* New York: Longman Publishing.

Moote, G. T., & Wodnarski, J. S. (1997). The acquisition of life skills through adventure-based activities and programs: A review of the literature. *Adolescence, 32*(125), 143-167.

Ogbu, J. U. (1995). Literacy and black Americans: Comparative perspectives. In V.L. Gadsden & D. A. Wagner (Eds.), *Literacy among African-American youth.* Cresskill, NJ: Hampton Press.

Page, C. (1996). *Showing my color: Impolite essays on race and identity.* New York: Harper Collins.

Pianta, R. C., & Walsh, D.J. (1996). *High risk children in schools.* New York: Routledge.

Reif, L. (1984, September). Writing and rappelling. *Learning Magazine,* pp. 73-76.

Rogers, C. (1969). *Freedom to learn.* Columbus, OH: Charles E. Merrill.

Rohnke, K. (1981). *High profile.* Hamilton, MA: Adventure Press.

Schoel, J., Prouty, D., & Radcliff, P. (1988). *Islands of healing: A guide to adventure based counseling.* Hamilton, MA: Project Adventure.

Smith, F. (1978). *Reading without nonsense.* New York: Teachers College.

Teale, E. W. (Ed.). (1954). *The wilderness world of John Muir.* Boston, MA: Houghton Mifflin.

Zimmerman, J. (1994, May). Resiliency versus risk: Helping students help themselves. *Far West Focus,* p. 3.

II

OUTDOOR EDUCATIONAL PRAXIS

5

BACKPACKING AND OVERNIGHT EXPERIENCES

James Jelmberg

A Light Among The Cedars

"I long to hear the mountain wind
whisper to the sea
pounding waves to silent shores
ancient song
awakening in me.

I long to see the mighty cedar
heart outstretched to heaven
protector guiding
standing firm
where others stood
to dare
to dream."

—Joseph Nadeau (1975)

A walk into the hills and mountains is a feast for the senses wherever the region may be. First, the visual treats have such an impact on students that the flora and fauna become images that they do not forget. Students inhale the fresh air, smell the damp earth, and rustle through the fallen leaves. They feel the euphoria that comes during a hiking experience.

Then there are the sounds. The birds beckon them into the woods with their territorial music. The sound of water is often heard in the hills and mountains. Water is the primeval force that shapes the landscape. The water arrives on the land with the rain and snow that, like Michelangelo's chisel, sculpts the earth and bedrock through freezing and cracking and erosion. Thousands of years ago this rain and snow, in the form of a glacial ice sheet

moved slowly southeastward through the northern states over the jagged peaks and through the deep V-shaped valleys revealing the rounded tops and U-shaped valley bottoms that exist today.

This mountain water has a multitude of other effects from providing musical sounds to the hiker to quenching the thirst for the countless numbers of animal and plant species that are found there.

The hills and mountains are majestic, motionless, and massive. These tall and venerable "massifs" are like wise and aging parents who have found their place in the world and despite occasional stormy weather, remain at home providing a source of stability for their children to return to for solace. Learning in the mountains can be a lifelong experience.

WHY A HIKE IN THE HILLS?

The obvious reason to take students into the forest is that the hills and mountains can provide an ideal outdoor classroom that will be both motivating and memorable. For a more detailed explanation, let's look at an example of an expedition where we took our middle school students to Zealand Notch in New Hampshire's White Mountains. The reasons that we chose this beautiful and mountainous area are many. Some of the most significant include the following:

1. Following a forest fire in the early 1900s, we found a forest succession that has been progressing toward a climax stage.
2. For a small fee we could use an Appalachian Mountain Club (AMC) cabin staffed by the AMC that provided bunk beds and a kitchen for student to use.
3. Dramatic evidence existed of the glacier in the forms of rounded valleys and peaks, glacial erratics, cirques, potholes, and scouring.
4. Other possibilities existed for the study of geology including views of the early metamorphic rock on the Presidential Range and firsthand observation of both plutonic rock in Zealand Falls and volcanic rock on an optional 4,000-foot climb to Mt Hale.

5. A variation in plants and animals were found in three different zones of elevation as well as unique arctic lichens in the falls, beaver ponds, a pond to bog succession, and other ecology studies.
6. We were able to study unique mountain weather including types of fronts and effects of wind in a mountainous area.
7. The location was a walking distance of 6 miles (with the option of 4 more miles).

THE OUTDOOR EDUCATION PROGRAM
AT THE OYSTER RIVER MIDDLE SCHOOL

Taken during the fall, this overnight backpacking trip into the mountains was the first of several expeditions that comprised a schoolwide outdoor education program at the Oyster River Middle School in Durham, New Hampshire. This program has historic roots dating back to 1974. Offered to all seventh graders, the outdoor program began as part of the science curriculum. The expeditions combined both academics and adventure and provided an opportunity for students, parents, and teachers to work together in the adventure-filled, outdoor classroom.

The philosophy of the program was to have separate groups of students go to diverse habitats during all of the seasons to experience different activities. In this way, students could return to school and share their different experiences with other classmates. In addition to the academic objectives were the adventure objectives of self-reliance, self-confidence, and values of conservation. The aim was to provide two general types of outdoor activities from which students could choose. For example, there were two-day overnight backpacking trips, a White Mountain backpacking trip in the fall and a New Hampshire seacoast backpacking trip in the spring. Another student option included a combination of two afternoons of forestry on skis in the local college woods and a full day of initiative exercises and technical rock climbing in the spring at a local site. These activities are described in full in the next four chapters.

All expeditions required moderate physical initiative, good academic standing, and appropriate conduct prior to the trips. Consistent with the program goal of improving student academic achievement, all students were required to gather data in the habitat, analyze it back in the classroom, and complete a report. Because these expectations were emphasized with students throughout the year, they generally rose to the occasion, and we don't recall any students who were excluded from the trips.

This particular expedition to Zealand Notch usually involved about twenty-five students and took 2 days and an overnight stay at an AMC cabin. The cabin provided bunk beds and a kitchen for use by the students who cooked in groups of five under the direction of their parent leader.

STUDENT PRIORITIZING PROCEDURE

In order to ensure that students would participate in different expeditions and return to share their experiences with each other, they had to be assigned to the different trips. To maximize student involvement, we wanted students to be active participants in this selection process. For example, students were asked to choose between day experiences and overnight expeditions. The overnight students were then randomly assigned to either the mountain or the seacoast expeditions. All day-trip students went on two forestry on skis trips and the initiative exercise and rock-climbing trip. This prioritizing procedure provided the students a choice of an experience that was different in habitat, season, and logistics so they could compare and contrast their experiences back in the classroom.

CURRICULUM ACTIVITIES
FOR THE HILLS AND MOUNTAINS

Geology

Young people are drawn to the mountains. They want to climb and explore them. The hills and mountains offer endless opportunities for curricular exploration in all subject areas. When students hike in the mountains, regardless of the region, they look at the rocks under their feet and inevitably ask the following question. How did these rocks get here? This and other questions are the teachable moments that we, as teachers, wait for. It is as if our students have asked us to teach them. The outdoor classroom offers many of these teachable moments (Hammerman & Hammerman, 1964; Hug & Wilson, 1965). Students might be surprised to learn that they might be walking on rocks that came out of a volcano or were formed at the bottom of an inland sea. The following learning activities in geology and ecology are just a few examples from a multitude of curriculum possibilities.

Every area across the country has its own unique geological history that has resulted from dramatic and interesting constructive and destructive forces. Here is one example of such a geological history. The White Mountains of New Hampshire are among the oldest mountains on earth dating back 400 million years. At that time weathering and erosion of an older mountain range to the east in the gulf of Maine resulted in the deposition of layers of sedimentary rock in southeastern New Hampshire in the form of sandstone, shale, and limestone. The inland sea, which covered the east coast from Maine to Georgia, receded leaving a geological surface that also resembled the sedimentary layers that are now seen throughout the midwestern states (Fowler, 1974).

Then something geologically dramatic began to take place. Immense geological forces of compression began to fold the layers of sedimentary rock slowly upward into a steep mountain range thousands of feet higher than the Appalachian range that remains today. One effective way to demonstrate this folding process to students is to take a stack of different colored dish towels and push the ends inward forming an upward fold in the middle. The colored layers will represent the sedimentary rock layers that have changed into metamorphic rock layers because of the pressure and heat from the compression. The upward fold represents the new mountain range.

The heat and pressure from this folding process caused the sedimentary sandstone, shale, and limestone to change into metamorphic rocks such as gneiss, schists, and minerals like garnet and mica. Some layers of metamorphic rock began to melt partially and form the older granites of this area (Laird, 2006). Metamorphic rocks are still prominent on New Hampshire's highest peak, Mount Washington, and in central New Hampshire, but have largely been eroded away, exposing the granite peaks and outcroppings that came in the form of volcanoes and plutonic (cooled underground) bedrock about 250 million years ago. Since then, the incessant erosion and glacial scouring from a mile-high ice sheet relentlessly reshaped this once jagged mountain range to the smoother contours that exist today.

Activities for Upper Elementary Grades 4 to 6

1. Collect and identify rocks and minerals.
2. Examine rock and mineral surfaces with a hand lens.
3. Make plaster of Paris molds of the mountains showing the pre-glacier jagged peaks and valleys and then the rounded peaks and valleys after the glacier.

Activities for Middle Grades 7 and 8

1. Look for bedrock formations that have deep scratches on them. Could these scratches have been caused by the glacier? In which direction do the scratches run? Hint: The glacier moved from northwest to southeast.
2. Find a gully and walk to where it begins. Look for evidence of erosion. Sketch what you see, and write what you observe (Hammerman & Hammerman, 1967).
3. Make a map of this area.

4. Observe folded rock layers. Have students hypothesize how these patterns may have been formed.
5. Use roofing tar to demonstrate the movement of a glacier. Pour tar slowly on top of another layer of tar, and observe the movement outward. Place an obstacle in the way of the moving tar, and see what happens to it (Hammerman & Hammerman, 1967).

Activities for High School Grades 9 to 12

1. Describe the continental glacier that receded from the northern states about 12,500 years ago.
2. Describe the process whereby the glacier picked up rocks and soil and moved them to different locations.
3. How do geologists know that the glacier moved from northwest to southeast?
4. Make observations to determine the differences between what appears to be a glacial valley and what is a river valley.
5. Identify a stream-eroded area and glacier-eroded area.
6. Study the movement of boulders and rocks in a stream. Have them hypothesize about the erosive force of river and streams.

Ecology

The hills and mountains provide homes for countless communities of plants and animals that vary according to the elevation. A hiker beginning a trek would usually begin at the lower elevation in a valley. Students in this lower zone would probably be moving through a hardwood or deciduous forest of trees such as birch, beech, and maple. They would also see shrubs and flowers that are specific to that particular region. In the White Mountains, for example, they would see Trillium and Bunchberry flowers (Fowler, 1974). The rocks that the students walk on would probably be covered with mosses and lichens, the beginning of the first layer of soil in a succession that would ultimately result in soil that is rich enough for more mature species of plants.

Small and large mammals such as rabbits, foxes, and deer abound in this deciduous forest habitat. Several species of birds such as woodpeckers and warblers also thrive here and can be heard busy at work establishing their territories.

As the students hike upward for several thousand feet on the trail, they can see the effects of the harsher weather that comes with higher elevation. They can see changes in plant and animal habitat that could reveal plant adaptations as well as different tree and animal species. They might see more evergreen trees such as spruce and fir as they enter a coniferous forest zone found on the sides of mountains upward from the valley bottom. The remaining hardwoods as well as some evergreens might be dwarfed reducing their exposure to the drying influence of the wind called desiccation. Because of this desiccation, the students may find these dwarfed trees between rocks and in other protected places, unable to survive in more exposed places. Students may hear different bird calls at this elevation from species like thrushes. Different animal tracks may also be found from larger animals like moose and even bear, a sign to stay together and not to leave the hiking trail.

These different elevation zones provide rich opportunities for the study of plant and animal adaptation to different habitats. Questions for teachers to raise on entering a different elevation habitat could include the following.

1. Have you noticed any differences in the plants as we hiked upward in elevation?
2. How have the plants changed as we entered this new zone?
3. What are the changes you have noticed with the plants?
4. What has caused the plants in this zone to change?
5. What are some specific adaptations that plants have made to this new zone?
6. Why are these adaptations necessary to the survival of these plants?
7. If there are different species of plants at this elevation, do you think there might be different species of animals also?
8. Why do you think there might be different species of animals at different elevations?
9. Have you found evidence of different animal species up here?
10. Why might there be different bird species here at this elevation?

Activities for Upper Elementary Grades 4 to 6

1. Have students look for evidence of animal activity such as footprints, feathers, boroughs, and scat (Hammerman & Hammerman, 1967).
2. Make plaster castes of animal tracks.
3. Sketch animal footprints and identify them using field guides.
4. Follow some animal tracks. See if you can reconstruct the direction of the animal and hypothesize where it might be going.
5. Look for evidence of animal homes, such as hollow trees, ground boroughs, and rock dens.
6. Look for evidence of food that animals might seem to be eating, such as empty nuts, root digging, and strips of bark.

7. Measure diameter and tree growth from one elevation zone to another.
8. Note plant adaptations as students hike upward to another zone.
9. Look for effects of wind on hardwood and evergreen trees.
10. Watch for flocks of birds and identify them.
11. Collect weeds for bouquets.
12. Collect seeds and hypothesize about how they travel.
13. Collect seeds and leaves and identify them.

Activities for Middle Grades 7 and 8

1. To show adaptations, set up five square-foot plots of soil in two elevation zones. Compare and contrast characteristics of the plants.
2. Compare protected and unprotected areas. Identify micro-climates by standing on top of rocks, beside rocks, and behind rocks taking temperature, humidity, and wind speed readings, and moisture observations.
3. Read about the succession from a pond to a bog. How does this relate to glacial activity?
4. Describe how soil develops during the succession from lichens to mosses, to flowers. How many years does this normally take?
5. If a forest fire destroyed all plant life, how many years would it take to establish soil that could support flowers?
6. Would this soil succession vary from elevation zone to elevation zone?
7. Watch caterpillars make cocoons. Put a cocoon in a box outdoors, and watch emerge in the spring.
8. What causes the autumn season?

Activities for High School Grades 9 to 12

1. Have students in the spring and early summer compare the dates at which the same plants flower in different elevation zones.
2. Compare the number of birds and the difference in species of birds in different elevation zones.
3. Compare the soil temperatures in sun exposed and shady areas. Are there differences in the organisms that might live in these areas?

4. Study the organisms in streams and rivers compared to lakes and bogs. State hypotheses that might account for the differences.
5. Describe some animal language and compare to human language.
6. Make a cross-section of a bog.
7. What kind of tracks do deer, rabbits, and foxes make?
8. What kinds of homes do these animals live in?
9. Why do birds and some insects travel such great distances at this time of year?
10. What is causing the weather to change?
11. How are plants changing?
12. Why are they changing?
13. How are animals preparing for winter?

Language Arts

So far the curriculum activities discussed in this chapter have been focused on science. The outdoor classroom offers limitless curriculum opportunities in all subjects. In a briefer format, the curriculum activities listed next are examples of how students can pursue language arts, social studies, mathematics, music, and art in the outdoors.

Activities for Upper Elementary Grades 4 to 6

1. Find a nature specimen in the woods or field, identify it using a field guide, and write a story about it.
2. Keep fieldnotes.
3. Label and identify specimens.

Activities for Middle Grades 7 and 8

1. Describe in a journal an outdoor experience and what it did for your self-confidence.
2. Use the library or the Internet to research an aspect of plants, animals, or geology that you have observed in the outdoor classroom.
3. Write poems, diaries, logs, student newspaper articles, stories, or songs related to an outdoor experience you have had.

Activities for High School Grades 9 to 12

1. Working in groups, write, rehearse, and present a dramatization about an experience you have had in the outdoor classroom.

2. Read outdoor adventure stories after lunch in the outdoor class-room.
3. Write stories and practice story telling related to an outdoor classroom experience you have had.
4. Read and report about the local history of an area after you have seen places and heard about events of historical interest.
5. Listen to bird songs and diagram the notes on a scale.

Social Studies

Activities for Upper Elementary Grades 4 to 6

1. Visit an abandoned farm.
2. Make craft items out of natural materials.
3. Make candles, brooms, quilts, traps, and slings.
4. Participate in a Native-American ceremony (Hug & Wilson, 1965).

Activities for Middle Grades 7 and 8

1. Visit local sites of historical interest.
2. Write a group report on a local historical event.
3. Re-enact a local historical event.
4. Demonstrate an understanding of democratic procedures in deciding which event to re-enact.
5. Make models of the historical site (Hug & Wilson, 1965).
6. Make maps to scale of the historical site.

Activities for High School Grades 9 to 12

1. Observe the physical geography of a historical site area, and analyze how early settlers adapted to it.
2. Create an understanding of the relationship between man and his environment.
3. Dramatize some of the conversations that may have taken place between the early settlers and Native Americans about trading and other mutual interests (Hug & Wilson, 1965).
4. Make a study of a small community or community organization nearby.
5. Demonstrate through group role-play how the democratic process in this community or community organization functions.
6. Demonstrate an understanding of some of the socioemotional needs of early settlers.

Mathematics

Activities for Upper Elementary Grades 4 to 6

1. Show the correct use of measuring instruments such as a compass, ruler, and tape measure.
2. Measure a board foot.
3. Measure the diameter of trees.
4. Measure the circumference of trees.
5. Determine the circumference of a tree by finding the diameter, and vice versa.
6. Determine the age of trees by counting growth rings.
7. Average the daily temperature readings over a week's time.

Activities for Middle Grades 7 and 8

1. Average barometer readings over a 2-week period.
2. How did the weather that week correspond to the barometer readings?
3. Discover the relationship between the circumference and the diameter of a tree.
4. Using the above discovery, discover the formula for determining the circumference when the diameter is known, and vice versa.
5. Determine the surface area of a site using scale drawings, scaled maps, and scale models.
6. Measure the distance hiked by pacing.
7. Estimate the distance hiked.
8. Estimate the height of a tree.

Activities for High School Grades 9 to 12

1. Determine the height of a hill using a clinometer.
2. Estimate the height of a hill or a building.
3. Determine the percent of slope of a hill (Hammerman & Hammerman, 1967).
4. Estimate the distance away of lightning using the relationship of the speed of sound (thunder) and the speed of light.
5. Estimate the width of a river.
6. Determine the speed of the current in a river.
7. Using triangulation, determine the distance across pond or lake.
8. Using the position of the sun, estimate the time of day.

Music and Art

Activities for Upper Elementary Grades 4 to 6

1. Observe and count color tones in distance.
2. Demonstrate an understanding of rhythm using sticks on rocks.
3. Use weeds, seeds, and grasses to create a nature picture.

Activities for Middle Grades 7 and 8

1. Draw maps of the camping area.
2. Draw maps of hikes showing compass bearings.
3. Produce artwork using a variety of natural materials.
4. Sketch or paint using natural pigments.
5. Find a natural deposit of clay, and work with it to produce a piece of artwork.
6. Get everyone in your group to sing a camping song for the fun of it.

Activities for High School Grades 9 to 12

1. Make a musical instrument using natural materials (Hug & Wilson, 1965).
2. Compose a piece of music from sounds in nature.
3. Demonstrate interests in art and music that will lead to a productive use of leisure time.
4. Lead a discussion of art and music as a part of everyday living.
5. Sketch or paint landscapes, mountains, hills, streams, rivers, ponds, or lakes.

ORIENTATION FOR PARENTS, STUDENTS, AND STAFF

Letter to Parents

Communication with parents is vital to the success of any outdoor education program. This communication needs to be early and thorough. First, parents need to know the answers to the "who, what, where, and when questions" of the trip. A well-prepared letter that addresses these questions will minimize the numerous headaches in the form of questions and complaints that would stem from a lack of information. Remember, at minimum, a passive partnership and cooperation on the part of the parents is important. At best you will need active participation from parents in the form of group leaders if needed. A good letter will often be the beginning of this cooperation and participation. The following is an actual letter to parents that explains who is going, what students are going to do, where they will be, and when they will be there.

Dear Middle School Parents:

Twenty-three seventh-grade students are planning an overnight science trip in the White Mountains to work on weather, geology, and ecology and astronomy activities. The teacher leaders from the school will be Mr. Jelmberg and Mr. Bonaccorsi, who will be assisted by other experienced group leaders.

The group will leave from the middle school on the morning of Monday, October 9, for the 3-hour drive to the Zealand Campground beyond Crawford Notch in the town of Twin Mountain. After lunch, students will carry their backpacks and sleeping bags into the Zealand Appalachian Mountain Club Hut, where they will locate their bunks, stow their gear, and prepare to work on afternoon science activities at Zealand Falls, Zealand Ridge, and Mt. Hale.

After preparing their hot evening meal, in cook groups of four, all will participate in a fireside sing-a-long, followed by an astronomy lesson.

After a hot breakfast Tuesday morning, we will make the 5-mile trek out of the Zealand Notch Area by way of Mt. Hale. The 3-hour ride home should bring us back to the middle school between 4 and 5 p.m.

Further information regarding necessary items for the students to bring is attached.

If you have any questions or concerns, please call me at the middle school at 868-2820. I will return your call.

Sincerely,

P.S. It has been the customary procedure for the past 3 years to send to parents of White Mountain backpacking students a list of parents' names and telephone numbers for the purpose of instituting a telephone chain as soon as we emerged from the woods in order to inform all parents of our exact time of arrival back at the middle school.

It seems more practical, however, to simply predict the arrival time as being about 5 pm on Tuesday and to ask that arrangements be made for their transportation home at that time.

Thank you for your cooperation.

Equipment List

Along with the letter to parents, leaders should include an equipment list of important items that students need to gather before the trip. These recommendations should be thorough and consider all possible weather conditions. The following is the list that we used.

Dear Students and Parents:

The following is a list of materials you will need for the science hiking trip:

1. Pencil or pen, small notebook, and most importantly, a curious mind
2. A good backpack or knapsack
3. Boots. This is the single most important item. Boots should be rubber lug, ankle-high, waterproof, and well broken in.
4. At least four pairs of socks, two pairs to be worn and two pairs to carry in the pack (many hikers use a lighter sock for an inner layer and heavy wool socks on the outside)
5. Hiking shorts
6. Long pants
7. Light shirt or blouse
8. Heavier shirt or blouse
9. Wool sweater
10. Windproof nylon parka (with hood)
11. Rain gear, such as a poncho
12. Underwear (carry extra with you just as you do socks, pants, and shirt)
13. Warm hat and gloves (carried year round)
14. Handkerchiefs or bandana
15. Toilet articles and towel
16. Flashlight
17. Canteen, small
18. Insect repellent with DEET
19. Sunblock, SPF-30
20. Plastic bags, small ones for wet boots, clothes, litter, etc., large ones to cover backpacks that are not waterproof.
21. Sleeping bag
22. Band-aids
23. Money for 2 coffee stops and telephone call for pick-up at the school, if necessary
24. Twine for tying on sleeping bags, etc.
25. Food for 2 days and 1 night (one breakfast, one hot dinner, two cold lunches)
26. Packs are to be brought in the day before the trip to be checked

Cell phones and a first aid kit should always be on hand for teachers on any outdoor classroom experience in case of emergency.

Permission Slip and Medical Release

The permission slip and medical release form should accompany the parent letter, and should always be pre-approved by the school district's legal officer. See Chapter 8 for alternative forms.

We give our child _____
(full name)

permission to participate in the hiking trip on October 2 and 3. We expect that the teacher-leaders will take reasonable precautions to insure the safety of our child and we absolve the school system from liability for any accident or illness that might occur in this trip. Should it be necessary to incur additional expenses and/or treatment during the trip, we give the trip leaders permission to use their judgment in such matters and will reimburse them for any expenses. We, as parents or guardians, have decided (with or without medical assistance) that any accident insurance we consider necessary will be our responsibility to locate and purchase.

Please indicate any medical problems or medicines that trip leaders should be aware of to insure your child's safety and comfort.

_____

_____

_____

Please list telephone numbers where you may be reached in case of emergency.

Day _____   Night _____

_____   _____
(Parents/Guardians Signature)   (Date)

Leader's Itinerary

Responsible leaders are the most necessary component for the success of an outdoor classroom expedition. These leaders become responsible for the small groups of students from the beginning to the end of the outing. They take attendance, monitor academic work in the field, and generally keep the group functioning as a team. Good group leaders can be recruited from dependable parents, community leaders, school board members, school administrators, fellow teachers, student teachers, teaching interns, university volunteers, and trusted older students.

First, each leader needs a trail map that shows distances and elevations. Each leader also needs to be oriented to the curriculum objectives and the who, what, where, and when questions of the trip. This orientation could be accomplished in the form of a leader's itinerary. The leader's itinerary is a chronological sequence of events with notes about what the leader might expect in terms of student questions and concerns. This enables the leader to anticipate and troubleshoot any problems that might arise, ranging from backpack and equipment difficulties to curriculum activities and sights not to be missed. Informed leaders are critical to get the groups from one point to another intact and functioning as a team. Once the groups have arrived at these points, the overall expedition leaders can address curriculum issues with the whole group, thus reinforcing the group leaders.

The following is an actual leader's itinerary we used for the White Mountain trip.

DAY 1

FIRST 30 MINUTES ON THE ZEALAND TRAIL

Students will have problems with adjusting packs. Helping them is optional. Cheerfully encourage self-reliance. The group can also work as a team to solve these kinds of problems.

Assigned groups with leaders will be allowed to go at their own pace. Students will never go in front of the first leader, who will stop after three quarters of a mile and regroup at the stream for lunch. The order of groups will be rotated periodically.

AFTER LUNCH

Groups with leaders proceed slowly and do science observations on wildlife activity with the species, activity, habitat, elevation, and temperature being recorded. Students also need to be observing plant life, noting the types of trees, their approximate age (young, mature, old), and the soil type, water, and elevation. Then notes on the weather should be taken with details on the types of clouds, temperature, wind speed and direction, and a weather prediction for the day. Finally, the geology should be observed with notes on the effects of the glacier, i.e., rounded peaks, U-shaped valleys, and glacial erratics (large isolated boulders).

Students should divide the labor with the thermometer, map, compass bearings, etc. Each should record his or her own observations, however.

ZEALAND FALLS HUT

Students will have a short time to locate a bunk and drop off packs before beginning the 1-hour trek (self-paced, not to pass the first leader in each group) up the Zealand Ridge Trail to Zeacliff.

There are lichens to observe on the way up the Zealand Falls. This is an alpine habitat.

ZEACLIFF

Views of the Presidential Range (metamorphic rock, once the bottom of an inland sea 400 million years ago). Whitewall Mountain is igneous rock, part of the White Mountain Magma series (200 million years ago) like Zeacliff, Mt. Zealand and Zealand Falls. This is plutonic rock with large quartz and mica crystals that cooled underground.

Evidence of glacier (receded approximately 11,000 years ago) in the form of rounded peaks, U-shaped valleys, scouring on the rocks, and a glacial cirque (precipitous, rounded out, ravine) on Mt. Kerrigan.

Plant adaptations to the desiccation (drying effect of the wind, as in the way laundry dries on a windy day).

1. Stunted growth
2. Waxy leaves of the mountain cranberry hold moisture as small pores produce little transpiration
3. Spruce and fur trees protect the leeward branches
4. Landslide on Whitewall Mountain, new plant succession beginning
5. Bog formation—glacial pond with no inlet or outlet—gradual succession of plants

DINNER

AFTER DINNER

Groups have discussion on following topics and elect spokesperson to report highlights on:

1. Scientific findings
2. Teamwork

Sing-Along
Astronomy observations outside the cabin
Sound hunt outside the cabin
Bed

DAY 2

FIRST 30 MINUTES ON THE ZEALAND TRAIL

MORNING

Make beds
Sweep bunk rooms
Breakfast prepared in groups
Cleanup
Prizes for best bunk

Two large groups: one to Beaver Pond Lecture; other to Solo at the Falls Activity. Students walk away from leader in "spokes on a wheel" fashion. Sit alone for 20 minutes, out of sight of everyone else. Return and share imagination, sights, sounds, and what it would be like to be lost and alone. What would you do?

Switch groups. Repeat.

LUNCH

Slower group returns via Zealand Trail
Faster group returns via Mt. Hale (volcanic Rock) in 3 hours

Narrative for the Drive

If there are important sights along the drive, the leader's itinerary might include a short narrative that would describe the location and features of these sights as well as suggestions about where the group will be stopping for gas and snacks. Following is an actual narrative that was given to group leaders for the White Mountain Expedition.

SIGHTS TO POINT OUT ON THE DRIVE UP

The first peak visible is Mt. Chocorua, which is a monadnock (standing alone). This mountain is composed of an igneous dike formation that was harder than the surrounding rock. The adjacent rock has long since eroded leaving Mt. Chocorua standing alone.

Carter Notch is an example of a V-shaped valley that became u-shaped by the glacial scouring. (The glacier receded about 11,000 years ago.)

Crawford Notch is another U-shaped valley with steep walls of metamorphic rock (once the bottom of an inland sea 400 million years ago). The steep walls feature loose jagged rock eroded with straight fissure lines formed along the original sedimentary layers.

The mountains have gentle slopes on the northwest sides and steep "plucked" slopes on the southeast sides, because the direction of the glacial flow was from northwest to southeast.

Reminder: Please fill gas tanks before the trip.
We will stop for coffee or a quick snack at Ellie's Coffee Shop in Conway.

SPECIAL CAUTIONS ASSOCIATED WITH OVERNIGHT EXPERIENCES

Spending the night away from home and school presents the teacher, student, and the parents with both challenges and opportunities unique to outdoor education. It is recommended that several well-planned day trips be successfully accomplished before attempting to take students overnight. When you then feel ready for an overnight trip, however, you will be better prepared to take advantage of the outdoor classrooms that are rich in curriculum possibilities and that lie some distance from the school.

Anticipating problems before they arise is always the best policy. Having clear consequences and procedures for emergencies is always the best policy. Not leaving yourself with sufficient supervision and oversight can create significant stress in emergencies. Sending students home is rare but may be necessary when students are not feeling well or when behavior problems become unacceptable. Medications should be on hand with written instructions from the school nurse about how they are to be administered.

EVALUATION FROM ADMINISTRATORS, PARENTS, STAFF

Every outdoor classroom expedition and program needs to be evaluated. In addition to the academic work evaluated back in the indoor classroom, objective opinions and observations are needed from people not directly related to the planning or formation of the expedition activities.

During these expeditions, our students from the Oyster River Middle School have been highly thought of by the adults who have observed them first hand including parent group leaders, school administrators, and the AMC hut masters. Following is a sampling of their observations.

After returning from an overnight student expedition to the White Mountains, I received a letter from Lincoln Cleveland, the hut master at the AMC, where 24 seventh-grade students, 3 teachers, and 2 parent leaders stayed.

Administration and Staff Responses

This group really added spice to a day that was starting to get slow. They were inquisitive about hut operations but not obnoxiously so. They were old enough and outgoing enough to help themselves instead of having to be told what to do time and time again. . . . Their behavior was excellent for a seventh-grade group. They were prepared and did clean up their mess as well as sweep out the hut in the morning.

There was not one complainer in the group and they seemed to be genuinely interested in the mountains. Their leader had oriented them well stressing education in terms of weather, ecology, and geology and encouraged strong group interactions and had briefed his group thoroughly on what their roles, duties and experiences would be. They were energetic and focused. The evening's activities included a whole series of skits performed by the group.

A parent said the following: "The group took any inconveniences, such as wet weather, extra academic work, less than great food, sore feet and other instances inherent in 'roughing it' in stride and demonstrated their maturity."

The principal wrote the following letter about a similar trip to Zealand Falls in the White Mountains.

Dear Jim:

We appreciate your leading the recent seventh-grade Outdoor Education Program. From all reports, the venture was a success and the major reason was the role you played.

We are pleased that the students responded so well. These are the times they will remember and the experiences that make this school the positive place it is.

Please convey to all the students who participated in this trip the pride we have in them and our compliments on how well they represented the middle school.

Finally your time, effort, willingness, and, of course, "boundless energy" contribute immeasurably to our kids' education.

Sincerely,

One parent who attended a trip to the mountains as a group leader wrote the following letter.

Dear Principal Rocci:

The Zealand Trip was such a success I felt a note to you was in order. Both Tom and Greg are to be commended for the excellent job of organizing and directing the trip. As a parental participant I observed, first-hand, how well the students worked together. Some individuals succeeded outdoors for the first time, in large part due to Tom's and Greg's sensitive and well thought out pre-trip preparation and on-site leadership.

Experiencing the colossal views, physical exertion and comradeship with their classmates, constitutes a most meaningful 2 days for which I feel fortunate to have been a part.

Please feel free to share this note with Tom and Greg.

Sincerely,

The recognition for this program went beyond the students, teachers, parents, and administrators who participated in these expeditions. The following represents the superintendent's and the school board's unanimous support for the schoolwide Outdoor Education Program.

Dear Jim:

At its meeting in May 16, the Oyster River District School Board acted to award a $300 bonus to you as a recognition of your outstanding performance. This decision is based in part on the recommendation of your colleagues, your principal or Board members and reflects the Board's unanimous support for this award.

The Oyster River School Board is pleased to have the opportunity to recognize the outstanding performance of staff members such as yourself, and conveys with the enclosed check its sincere appreciation for your most significant contributions to education in the Oyster River School District.

May I add my personal congratulations and thanks.

Sincerely,

Student Response

A student who attended the Zealand trip wrote the following article for the student newspaper:

Grade 7 Science

On Monday morning, 24 students from the seventh grade, 3 teachers, and 2 parents left on the first of four trips in the seventh-grade Outdoor Education Program. It was about a 10-mile hike from the Zealand Campground on Route 302 to a hut where we slept and two other hikes, one to Whitewall Mountain and the other to Zealand Mountain.

On the 3-hour drive up, we looked at the foliage and talked about the weather. On the hike up to our cabin, Mr. Jelmberg and Mr. Bonaccorsi had us stop often to tell us about the mountains and to answer any questions we had about where we were. At the hut, we unpacked and left for a short hike to Whitewall Mountain where we studied some plants. The next day we went up to Zeacliff, where we could see a lot of the white mountains and how glaciers had carved the valley below us. It was in my opinion, a very good trip.

ACADEMICS AND CONDUCT

In order for students to participate, they were required to have good standing with their teachers prior to the trip. Good standing means that students have had to demonstrate good effort both academically and in terms of conduct. These expectations were explained to students and reinforced continually throughout the school year. Students consistently made these efforts and very much wanted to participate in these expeditions. I cannot recall a single student over a 10-year period who was excluded for failing to meet this test.

REFERENCES

Fowler, B. (1974). *Zealand Falls*. Unpublished trail guide, Appalachian Mountain Club, Boston, MA.

Hammerman, D. R., & Hammerman, W. H. (1967). *Teaching in the outdoors*. Minneapolis, MN: Burgess.

Hug, J. W., & Wilson, P. J. (1965). *Curriculum enrichment outdoors*. Evanston, IL: Harper & Row.

Laird, J. (2006). *Expert interview*. University of New Hampshire, Durham.

Nadeau, J. P. (1975). *A light among the cedars*. Somersworth, NH: Lebanon Enterprises.

6

DAY TRIPS IN THE WOODLANDS AND FORESTS

James R. Jelmberg

The Road Not Taken
"Two roads diverged in a wood, and I-
I took the one less traveled by,
And that has made all the
difference."

—Robert Frost

The purpose of Chapters 5 through 8 are to provide a "how-to" approach to several outdoor classroom expeditions that are adaptable to the different regions of the country. Although the expedition in this chapter includes a forest succession curriculum that occurred in southeastern New Hampshire, forest succession happens in every forest and woodland in every state. By describing the curriculum and orientation activities for trips that actually took place successfully over a period of many years, these activities can be adjusted and replicated in other schools and outdoor classrooms throughout the country. With the additional curriculum activities section in each chapter, these expeditions are also adaptable to elementary and secondary schools.

THE OUTDOOR EDUCATION PROGRAM AT ORMS

This trip in the local woods during the winter season was the second of several expeditions that comprised the schoolwide outdoor education program for seventh graders at the Oyster River Middle School (ORMS) in Durham, New Hampshire. This expedition combined both academics and adventure and provided an opportunity for students, parents, and teachers to work together in an adventuresome, outdoor classroom.

As with the overnight backpacking trip into the White Mountains in the fall, the idea of the program was to have different groups of students go to different habitats, in different seasons, for different activities, so that students could return and share their experiences with other classmates. In addition to the academic objectives were the adventure objectives of self-reliance, self-confidence, and values of conservation. The aim was to provide both overnight and day trips from which students could choose. The day trips option offered a combination of two afternoons of forestry on skis in the local woods in the winter along with a full day of initiative exercises and technical rock climbing in the early spring at a local site.

All expeditions required moderate physical initiative, good academic standing, and good conduct prior to the trips. Students were also required to gather data in the habitat, analyze it back in the classroom, and complete a report.

CITIZENSHIP FOR DEMOCRACY

We feel that in order to foster democratic citizenship in our students, we needed, above all, to teach them to feel responsibility for each other. Students feeling and being responsible for each other speaks to our better selves as teachers and students and is a quintessential theme of this book. In order to do this, we needed to provide students with opportunities for making informed choices, building consensus and voting in diverse and equitable groups, and giving opinions for future expedition planning that would benefit future students.

There are several choices that students were encouraged to participate in. First, there was the choice of which expedition they wanted to go on. As in a democracy, choices are not always guaranteed. Students listed their choices in order of priority, and every attempt was made to honor those choices within the necessity that the numbers of students had to make sense for each trip.

Second was the choice of which classmate to choose as a partner for their expedition. Partners need to help each other and are usually friends or acquaintances of the same gender. In order to ensure the all-important objective of gender equity, the pairs of girls were combined with an equal number of pairs of boys. This gender equity truly comes into play as these groups of four to eight students hike together, help each other, and make decisions together in a democratic way. These groups also become pathways to multicultural experiences where underprivileged kids work hand in hand with more privileged kids.

Third are the choices that occur as matter of course as the expedition proceeds. Sometimes this choice is simply in the form of voting for which trail to take or activity to pursue. Often the choice becomes based on a consensus that transforms the groups into microcosms of multicultural and democratic action as they assume their responsibilities, such as helping each other get around on skis and preparing their group presentation on their chosen forestry site. Providing an exciting outdoor classroom environment for students to participate in can also bring about transformational friendships for kids who ordinarily would not choose to work together.

Asking students for their opinions in debriefing sessions was an all-important part of each expedition and was done without fail. After each trip, students were asked to share

their experiences with their classmates who had chosen the other options. Students were also asked for strengths and weaknesses of each expedition in an attempt to use student opinions as a way to improve future expeditions (see students' responses in Chapters 5–8). This was one way that students were made to feel that their voices were critical for future expedition planning.

DAY TRIPS

Day trips are easier to plan and implement than overnight trips. Because of this, we advise that teachers choose day trips as a beginning point before trying to plan an overnight expedition. Because the woods were within walking distance of the school, the forestry on skis class was especially easy to schedule. In fact, the woods were so close by that we scheduled two afternoon classes for each student group that selected this trip option.

The first afternoon was to orient the class to each of the important forestry sites after the students had read about them. The second afternoon trip was when each group presented the significant forest succession information and concepts to the whole class.

INNER SKIING

Cross-country skiing or snow shoeing in the woods in winter is an exceedingly beautiful experience. It is completely different from being in the woods during any other season. Because the leaves are gone, one can see greater distances giving the viewer a greater perspective of the forest as a whole. Unobstructed by leaves, students can stand and clearly see distinct groves of different kinds of evergreens. As these groves become some of the stations of study, it is easy to supervise students, because you can easily see where they are.

Our first impression in these winter woods is the silence of the snow-laden landscape that surrounds the sites. This silence is interrupted only by teachers and students speaking about the trees, and then by the sounds of student laughter as they step into their snowshoes or slip, slide, and schuss their skis through the snow from station to station.

It is a simple gift to teach your students how to use either snowshoes or cross-country skis. In order to encourage beginners to ski through the woods, we suggest only four simple techniques. First, show them the diagonal stride. This simply means that when one is sliding on the left ski, use the right pole, and when sliding on the right ski, use the left pole. There is not even a need to insist on this, because most beginners do this naturally after a few strides. Second, show students how to get up after a fall by removing one ski and stepping up. Third, pair non-skiers with experienced skiers or naturally athletic people so they can help each other. Fourth, stay on terrain that is fairly flat, sidestepping up the inclines and snowplowing down to slow down or stop.

Beyond these simple steps, the fewer instructions the better. Do not try to teach too much. Let the kids discover their own skiing skills by doing it rather than overthinking it. It is better that students relax and trust their bodies to balance themselves by beginning with a slow walk on skis. As long as they are able to make forward progress, they will "pick it up" as they go.

Early champions of this approach are Tim Galway and Bob Kriegal (1977), who wrote the landmark book for this intuitive approach to ski instruction entitled *Inner Skiing*. Paying homage to Guru Maharaj Ji, Galway and Kriegal advocated relaxed concentration, trusting one's own body, and quieting the conscious mind as pathways to skiing competence that allow us to think of the ski terrain in front of us as "a great canvas and that your skis are brushes" (p. 133). Another valuable piece of advice is the Zen guidance of focusing on your naval as you ski. The fact that this works with students is related to the naval being our natural center of gravity, the "point of perfect balance" (p. 134). As a ski instructor for 16 years at the Waterville Valley Ski School in New Hampshire, I heartily endorse these inner skiing concepts to encourage people to learn to ski, whether it is downhill or cross-country. The wonderful sport of skiing has brought me all over the Alps, but my all time favorite has always been New Hampshire's Tuckerman's Ravine. It never occurred to me to not return to Tuckerman's each spring (Hertz, 2006).

CURRICULUM ACTIVITIES FOR THE FORESTRY ON SKIS CLASS: FOREST SUCCESSION

College Woods in Durham, New Hampshire, has been undisturbed by human timber cutting activity since 1961. All changes that have taken place, therefore, are natural ones, making these woods an ideal habitat to observe forest succession and ecology. The eastern entrance to these woods is also the beginning of a forest ecology trail that has many sites that have been observed and described in a trail guide written by faculty members and their students from the University of New Hampshire Forestry Department under the supervision of Richard Weyrick. This guide, entitled the *Forest Ecology Loop*, provided the forest succession concepts for the Forestry on Skis class for a 10–year period starting in 1974. This trail guide has been recently revised under the supervision of James Barrett (2005) and is the foundation for the curriculum activities that follow. This revision is titled *The Paul Bunyan Woodlands Trail*.

I tried to write this curriculum in a way that would be understandable to middle school students. To achieve this, I prepared a question–answer dialogue with my students on selected parts of the trail. I also chose to focus on the relationship between just two evergreen tree species. Once this competitive relationship was clear to the students, I could add other tree species to the dialogue.

The following is a dramatic struggle of survival between the majestic Eastern White Pines and the younger Eastern Hemlock trees. It is a story of trees and hurricane winds, sun and shade, water and soil. The following is a typical outdoor classroom conversation that is representative of the teacher-led discussions with ORMS seventh graders that occurred in these woods over a 10-year period. It is our attempt to bring the reader into the forest with us, where one can eavesdrop on the class and listen to the thoughts of our students as they constructed their ideas on how a forest succeeds or progresses from an open field to a climax forest that will maintain itself with the same species of trees, generation after generation.

The starting point for this trail is at the path entrance to the right along the road leading to the Ritzman Animal Nutrition Laboratory, beyond the baseball field. Each station is indicated by a numbered tree-shaped marker posted on a tree. Tree-shaped markers with arrows indicating the direction to be followed are posted at certain intersections. The stations described are labeled by numbers corresponding to the number in the description.

Site 1: White Pine Grove

Teacher: Here we are just inside the eastern entrance of the woods at the first of several sites that make up this woodlands trail. It is a grove of very large white pine trees, which can be identified by the sets of a certain number of needles on the twigs. How many needles are there in each set?

Students: I count five.

Teacher: Yes, five. This set of five needles means this is a white pine tree. This particular species of tree is called the Eastern White

Pine tree. It can live for more than two hundred years, if they get plenty of sun. When you take a close look at these trees, what is it about them that tells you that they need a lot of sun?

Students: The lower branches are all dead.

Teacher: Yes. The lower branches are not getting any sun, and they have died. And even though they can live a long time, Eastern White Pine trees are not necessarily present in really old forests. That is because the young white pine trees cannot grow in the shade of the adult trees. So, when these pines die, there will be no young pines to take their place.

Are there any young trees here that do seem to be able to grow in the shade of these pines?

Students: Yes. They are right here.

Teacher: Look at the needles. How would you describe them?

Students: They grow opposite one another.

Teacher: Yes, they grow on opposite sides of the twig in a symmetrical pattern. So, these young trees are a different species called the Eastern Hemlock tree. And since these hemlocks are the only plants growing under these white pines, they are unusual. The fact that they can grow in the shade is an important factor for the hemlock that we will talk about and think about in some of the other sites on this trail.

Suddenly, like fleet-footed forest ferrets, the students following the trip leader scamper and slide to the next site along the trail.

Stay to the left at the trail intersections. The next station is on the right side of the trail about a half minute walk from the intersection.

Site 2: Hemlock Grove

Teacher: Using what you learned from the last site, can you tell what kind of trees these are?

Students: Hemlocks.

Teacher: How can you tell these are hemlocks?

Students: The needles have an opposite pattern.

Teacher: The needles have an opposing pattern. The needles are often the key to identifying evergreen trees. Notice how dense these hemlock thickets are. So how are these young hemlocks able to grow here?

Students: Hemlocks can grow in the shade.

Teacher: Very good. The young hemlocks seem to be thriving in this shade. So, what trees do you think will probably be growing here 20 to 30 years from now barring a hurricane?

Students: Hemlocks.

Teacher: Yes, hemlocks. What about hundreds of years from now?

Students: Hemlocks.

Teacher: Very good. Any questions?

Teacher: This competition for future dominance is slow, silent, and stoic in the steady and stationary search for sun and shade. It brings to mind Henry Wadsworth Longfellow's poem, *Evangeline*. Here are the first few lines.

> This is the forest primeval. The murmuring pines and the Hemlocks,
> Bearded with moss, and in garments green, indistinct in The twilight,
> Stand like Druids of eld, with voices sad and prophetic. . . .

How many have heard that poem? [A few hands go up.]

Stay to the left at the trail intersections (note the large Natural Area sign at the first intersection). The next marker is on the right-hand side—about a half minute walk from the second intersection.

Site 3: Field Growing Back To Forest

Teacher: About 40 years ago this area was used to store lumber. Since then it has been allowed to grow back to a forest. When you start with an area like this that was cleared to be a field, the forest grows back in stages. First you see weeds and bushes like raspberries, blackberries, and sumac. Then the first trees begin to appear including birch, aspens, cherry trees, and junipers. Why would these species grow in a field like this? What would there be plenty of in an open field?

Students: Sunlight.

Teacher: Yes. There is a lot of full sunlight in an open field because there aren't any tall trees to provide shade. The tall trees come later. They are already growing here as young white pine and young oak trees. When they become taller, they will begin to produce more shade. What will happen to the earlier species then?

Students: The younger trees from the earlier species won't be able to grow in the shade.

Teacher: Very good. So when the earlier birch, aspens, cherries, and junipers die, there will be no younger offspring to take their place. Therefore, the earlier species will eventually disappear from this forest area. What kinds of trees will eventually dominate the forest here?

Students: Hemlocks.

Teacher: Why?

Students: Because hemlocks will be able to grow in the shade of the taller trees.

Teacher: Very good.

Soon the students become less verbal as they think about which trees will survive and listen to the sounds of their skis on snow in an otherwise silent world.

Retrace the path back to the large Natural Area sign.

Site 4: Post-Hurricane Growth

Teacher: This area was hit hard by two hurricanes in 1938 and 1956. What two kinds of evergreen trees do you see here?

Students: White pine trees and hemlocks.

Teacher: Yes, white pines and hemlocks. Which species will eventually win the struggle for survival and why?

Students: The hemlocks will grow in the shade of the white pines, but the young pines will not grow in the shade of the hemlocks.

Teacher: What other species are growing at this site?

Students: Hardwood trees.

Teacher: Yes. There are hardwoods like beech and sugar maple. Like the hemlock, the young seedlings of these two species are also able to grow well in shade. Now that you know that, what kinds of trees will eventually survive and dominate the forest here?

Students: Hemlocks, beech, and sugar maple trees.

Teacher: Excellent. So unless there are more hurricane winds here or some other disturbance, these three species that you just mentioned will be able to dominate this forest for hundreds of years. That is called a climax forest, because it is the last stage in forest growth.

Teacher: Do you have any questions?

Continue left down the trail into the Natural Area. The next marker is on the left.

Site 5: Forest Streams

Teacher: Summer streams from silent springs score the landscape and slake the thirst of the stationary and somnambulant forest. What poetic technique is that?

Students: Alliteration.

Teacher: Very good. Is this stream important to the trees in this forest?

Students: Yes. The trees need water to grow.

Teacher: Yes. And lots of trees like these need lots of water. In fact, this stream is full of water in the spring and fall, but is not so full during the summer. Why do you think that is?

Students: Because the trees are growing in the summer and need water when they are growing.

Teacher: Questions?

Continue along the road. At the small path designated by a marker with a directional arrow, turn left and cross the stream. The next station is located on the left side of the trail.

Site 6: Grove of Old Hemlocks

Teacher: What kinds of trees do you see here?

Students: Hemlocks and white pines.

Teacher: So, once again we have the struggle for survival between our old rivals. What about the younger trees? What kind are they?

Students: The young trees are hemlocks. They can grow in the shade, so they will eventually win the struggle for survival.

Teacher: Does everyone agree with that?

Students: Yes.

Teacher: You are really catching on to how these forests grow. Any questions?

Continue down the trail. The next marker is on the right.

Site 7: Uprooted Trees

Teacher: Just up the trail here you will see a large tree tipped over. What do you think tipped it over like this?

Students: Wind. Hurricane winds.

Teacher: Yes. This tree was tipped over by the hurricane that we talked about earlier. Notice how shallow the root systems are on the large white pine trees. Do you think the soil here is deep or shallow?

Students: Shallow.

Teacher: Why do you think the soil is shallow?

Students: The roots don't seem to reach down very deep.

Continue along the trail. The next marker is on the left.

Site 8: Grove of Old Hemlocks and Beech Trees

Teacher: I know that you can recognize these hemlock trees, but can you identify the hardwood trees here?

Students: Beech trees?

Teacher: Yes, there are beech trees. Remember, young beech trees, like hemlocks, are able to grow in the shade of taller trees. The beeches and the hemlocks here are over 70 years old, which means they were young trees growing here at the time of the 1938 hurricane. The hurricane winds damaged the older trees which allowed the younger beech and hemlocks to grow faster. This is a situation where the hurricane actually helped the growth of the beeches and hemlocks. They have really taken over here, so can you make a prediction about what trees will dominate here in the future and why?

Students: The beeches and hemlocks will dominate because their young seedlings will be able to grow in the shade.

Turn to the right, cross the same stream and take a path to the right which takes you back to the woods road. At the road turn to the right again and walk to a point just past a triangular road intersection. Bear to the right, following the woods road. The next station is a few yards along a small path to the right.

Site 9: Paul Bunyan Tree

Teacher: What do you notice about this tree besides the fact that it fell down?

Students: It's huge.

Teacher: Yes. In fact, this was the largest tree in these woods. At about your height, this tree has a diameter of over four feet. It was over 135 feet tall and was more than 200 years old. So, this was a young seedling shortly after the revolutionary war, when our country was just getting started. The amount of lumber that could be cut from this tree could side a small house. Any questions?

Students: Enough lumber for a small house?

Teacher: Yes. There would be enough to put siding on a small house, and there might be enough left to do the roof.

Return to the road.

Summary of Forest Succession

Teacher: So far we have talked mostly about young hemlocks being able to grow in the shade of taller trees. There are other kinds of trees that can also grow in shade. Can you remember what they are?

Students: Beech and sugar maple?

Teacher: Very good. So you now can predict the future of this forest. What kinds of trees will dominate here in the future and why?

Students: Hemlocks, beeches, and sugar maples will dominate because their young can grow in their shade and other trees can't.

Teacher: Excellent job out here today in the outdoor classroom, everyone.

Teacher: The next time we ski here, it will be your group's responsibility to present to the class the forestry succession concepts that

we learned here today. We can read the trail guide and spend some class time preparing for this. Another assignment from this experience in the forest will be for you to choose a group project that represents something significant you learned from this experience. It could be related to any subject or subjects such as math, science, language arts, social studies, art, or music. For example, there were several references to poetry mentioned here today. So writing a poem or a song would be one way to do this project. You could also do a report on how many Paul Bunyan trees it would take to build your own house, or even your dream house. That would take some research. You might want to interview a house builder for that. Those are just two of many ideas you could pursue.

ADDITIONAL CURRICULUM ACTIVITIES: ECOLOGY

So far, the curriculum activities discussed in this chapter have been focused on forest succession. The following additional activities are in the area of animal and plant ecology in general. We would also like to point out that the outdoor classroom offers limitless curriculum opportunities in all subjects.

Activities for Upper Elementary Grades 4 to 6

1. Food Webs
   Copy this chart into your notebook and complete it: Name of Food Web Member
   The Job That It Does
   a. Producer
   b. Plant-eater or herbivore or primary consumer
   c. Meat-eater or carnivore or secondary consumer
   d. Variety eater or omnivore
   e. Scavenger or decomposer

Participate in a teacher-led discussion on "Food Webs." Make a poster using pictures of a food web of animals found in your state.

The different food groups of a community include: food makers, plant eaters, flesh eaters, variety eaters, and decomposers. In any community, some members of all of these groups are almost sure to be present.

2. Activity

Materials needed: trowel, collecting can, wide-mouth jars, hand lens, guide books. Go on a field trip to an area where you can study a meadow and an adjoining forested tract.

   a. In both the meadow and the forest, find examples of the six food groups. Keep a record of what you see. Go as far as you can, find out how each type obtains its food.

   b. Be sure to observe examples of algae, mosses, ferns, fungi, and seed plants. Do the same in the case of mammals, birds, reptiles, amphibians, insects, and any other animal types that may be present.

   c. If you find a log or stump that is well decayed, pull it apart. Note what organisms may be present. You may find various insects and worms in the decaying wood. You will see the cobweb-like parts of fungi. Millions of bacteria are also present, but they are too small to see.

   d. Dig up about 1 quart of soil from the forest floor. Take it back to the laboratory. Spread the soil out on a sheet of paper. See what kinds of plants and animals you can find in this soil sample.

3. Your Interpretations

After making the necessary observations, respond to the following items:

   a. Food makers seen included

   b. Plant eaters seen included

   c. Variety eaters seen included

   d. Decomposers seen included

Activities for Middle Grades 7 and 8

1. The following are all populations. In each case, tell if it would be easy or difficult to arrive at the actual number in the population.

   a. The number of students in your middle school today

   b. The number of people in your state

    c. The number of fish in an aquarium
    d. The number of grass plants in your front yard
    e. The number of maple trees in your yard
    f. The number of deer in your count
    g. The number of fish in a lake

2. Propose a way to count each of the hard to count populations listed above. Check your methods with your teacher. What possibilities for mistakes are there in each of your methods?

3. Find out how the United States census is taken every 10 years. How accurate is it?

4. Attend a teacher lecture and discussion on populations and censuses.

5. How would you count the number of mice in a field? Add a known number of marked mice to the field. Then trap and find out how often you trap a marked mouse. If 1 in every 10 you trapped was marked and there were 10 marked mice in the field, the population would be about 100 mice.

6. Populations that are not changing in size are said to be in balance. Members of human populations and animal populations both die. What are some causes of human deaths? What are some causes of wild animal deaths?

7. It is Spring of 2006. There is an island with a population of 10 sparrows—5 males and 5 females.
Lets pretend:
    a. Each year each pair of sparrows produces 10 offspring, always 5 males and 5 females.
    b. Each year all the parent birds die before the next spring.
    c. Each year all offspring live through to the next breeding season.
    d. During our time of study, no other sparrows arrive on the island and none leave. Figure out the size of the sparrow population in Spring 2007, 2008, and 2009. Put your figures on a graph.

8. A meadow has a population of 1,000 rabbits in March. In April there are 400 young born and 10 rabbits move from a neighboring meadow that a farmer has just plowed. From May to October, 160 rabbits are trapped or shot by hunters and 100 are eaten by foxes and hawks. During the winter, 19 die from the extreme weather and 100 are eaten by foxes. When the next summer comes, what is the rabbit population in the meadow?

9. Think: Imagine an island with deer living on it. Each spring many fawns are born. Will the population keep increasing every year? What things could limit the number of deer on the island?
10. Participate in a lecture discussion on "limiting factors, carrying capacity, and environmental resistance."
11. Think: List as many examples as possible of man's attempts to raise or lower environmental resistance of different organisms.
12. Do research on the Lemming, a small Arctic rodent.
13. Name four things that could limit the size of a herd of deer in the woods.
14. Use the phrase "carrying capacity" in a sentence.
15. List three attempts of man to raise or lower the environmental resistance of certain organisms.
16. How does having a territory help an organism?
17. What happens to animals that don't get territories?
18. How does a territory reduce competition among the same species?
19. Make a list of animals that have territories.
20. Many animals live together in societies—like ants, termites and bees.
    a. How does this social life benefit the animals?
    b. In what ways are these insect societies like human societies?
    c. The number of fish in an aquarium
21. Some animals move or live together in packs, herds, flocks, and schools. Some even choose a leader, like a pack of wolves.
    a. How do these animals cooperate?
    b. What benefits do they get from cooperation?
    c. What jobs does the leader do when he/she is present?
22. What methods are used for protection or escape other than cooperation?
23. Name three things animals of the same species may compete for?
24. List three ways a robin with a territory is better off than a robin without one.

Activities for High School Grades 9 to 12

1. Define the term population and give two examples.
2. Explain at least two methods of counting a population. Explain the strengths and weaknesses of each method.

3. Write an essay to demonstrate that you are able to predict the effects of births, deaths, and dispersal on a given population.

4. Name three factors that determine the carrying capacity of a given area for a given species.

5. Define the territory and explain three advantages an organism with a territory has over an organism that does not have a territory.

6. Give three examples of cooperation among members of a species. For one species, explain:

   a. How the animals cooperate?

   b. What benefits they get from cooperation?

   c. What jobs does the leader do, if present?

7. Explain plant and animal dispersal as a result of competition.

8. Given a set of organisms, arrange them in a natural food web and give each member the appropriate label:

   a. Producer

   b. Primary consumer (plant-eater, herbivore)

   c. Secondary consumer (meat-eater, carnivore)

   d. Decomposer or scavenger

9. Explain the effects of the removal of one member of the food web on all the other members of the web.

10. Write an essay or present a model or diagram showing that all living things are dependent on each other.

ORIENTATION FOR PARENTS, STUDENTS, AND STAFF

Letter to Parents

Because the forestry on skis class was a day trip close to the school, the orientation for parents, students, and staff was easier and required less communication and less equipment than overnight expeditions. Communication with parents, however, is still vital to the success of both day and overnight trips in any outdoor education program. This communication still needs to be early and thorough.

Parents need to know the answers to who, what, where, and when questions of the trip. As with an overnight trip, a well-prepared letter that addresses these questions will minimize the numerous headaches in the form of questions and complaints that would stem from a lack of information. The following is an actual letter-to-parents artifact that explains who is going, what students are going to do, where they will be, when they will be there, and will answer the questions that parents might have.

Dear Middle School Parents:

Twenty-five seventh-grade students are planning an afternoon science trip to College Woods to work on forest succession and ecology activities. The teacher leaders from the school will be Mr. Jelmberg and Mr. Bonaccorsi.

The group will eat their bag lunches in my classroom and leave from the middle school at 11:30 A.M. on the morning of Monday, December 9, for the walk to the Outdoor Sports and Camping store on Pettee Brook Street to rent X-country skis for a price of $5. The class will then proceed to College Woods to begin forest ecology activities at the eastern entrance near the railroad bridge. Students will return by the end of the school day in time for the buses.

Further information regarding necessary items for the students to bring is attached.

If you have any questions or concerns, please call me at the middle school at 868-2820. I will return your call.

Sincerely,

Jim Jelmberg
Teacher, seventh-grade science

Equipment List

Along with the letter to parents should be an equipment list of important items that students need to gather before the trip. These recommendations should be thorough and should "err on the side of caution."

The following is the list that we used.

Dear Students and Parents:

The following is a list of materials you will need for the forestry on skis class trip:

1. Pencil or pen, small notebook, and most importantly, a curious mind.
2. A good backpack.
3. X-country skis, boots, and poles. You may bring your own, or rent from the camping store on Pettee Brook where we will stop on the way to College Woods.
4. At least two pairs of socks, one pair to be worn and one pair to carry in the pack (many X-country skiers use a lighter sock for an inner layer and a heavy sock on the outside).
5. Light shirt or blouse.
6. Heavier shirt or blouse.
7. Wool sweater.
8. Windproof nylon parka (with hood).
9. Warm hat and gloves.
10. Canteen or water bottle.
11. A bag lunch.
12. Sun block, SPF 30.
13. Plastic bags, small ones for wet boots, clothes, litter, etc., large ones to cover backs that are not waterproof.
14. Band-aids.
15. Money for ski rental ($5) and telephone call for pick-up at the school, if necessary.
16. Twine for tying items on the backpack.

Permission Slip and Medical Release

The permission slip and medical release form should accompany the parent letter. This is the one that we have used year after year. Whatever permission slip and medical release form you choose should always be checked by the legal officer for your school district. (See Chapter 8 for alternative forms.)

We give our child _____

(full name)

permission to participate in the hiking trip on October 2 and 3. We expect that the teacher-leaders will take reasonable precautions to ensure the safety of our child and we absolve the school system from liability for any accident or illness that might occur on this trip. Should it be necessary to incur additional expenses and/or treatment during the trip, we give the trip leaders permission to use their judgment in such matters and will reimburse them for any expenses. We, as parents or guardians, have decided (with or without medical assistance) that any accident insurance we consider necessary will be our responsibility to locate and purchase

Please indicate any medical problems or medicines that trip leaders should be aware of to Insure your child's safety and comfort.

_____

_____

_____

Please list telephone numbers where you may be reached in case of emergency.

Day _____   Night _____

_____   _____
        Parents/Guardians Signature   Date

Please return as soon as possible so that trip planning may begin. Thank you.

Leaders Itinerary

Responsible leaders are necessary for the success of an outdoor classroom expedition. These leaders become responsible for the small groups of students from the beginning to the end of the outing. They take attendance, monitor academic work in the field, and generally keep the group function-

ing as a team. Good group leaders for a day trip like the Forestry on Skis class could be fellow teachers and staff who may be familiar with the students. It is necessary to have at least one other leader who can ski or walk in the snow at the end of the class to make sure that students keep up with the group. Group discipline needs to be maintained and the group needs to stay together. This other leader should either know the area or have a map. Only one teacher needs to know about forest succession and ecology in detail. Cell phones and a first aid kit should always be on hand on any outdoor classroom experience in case of emergency.

PROGRAM EVALUATION RESPONSES FROM ORMS STUDENTS AND TEACHING INTERNS

A formal evaluation was done on the ORMS Outdoor Education Program where quantitative and qualitative information was gathered from many different sources including administrators, teachers, experts, parents, students, and teaching interns. This completed evaluation was submitted to and approved by the principal, superintendent, school board, and professor in program evaluation at the University of New Hampshire. In addition to the academic work evaluated in the indoor classroom, objective opinions and observations were obtained from people not directly related to the planning or formation of the expedition activities. The following are responses to the overall program, first by a random sample of seventh graders representing a class of 150 students, and second by a seminar class of teaching interns at Brandeis University in Waltham, Massachusetts, following a presentation of the goals and curriculum of the ORMS Outdoor Education Program. Other parts of the program evaluation can be found in Chapters 5, 7 and 8.

Responses From ORMS Students

The following are the responses to a student questionnaire that was distributed to a random sample of seventh-grade students representing a class of 150 students for the purpose of evaluating how the curriculum activities matched the goals of the Outdoor Education Program.

The following Likert scale was used:

Strongly agree: SA   Agree: A   Strongly disagree: SD
        Disagree: D   Can't tell: CT

Goal I. The Outdoor Education Program presents growth experiences in academics, self-confidence, and teamwork.

	SA	A	CT	D	SD
A. Students are likely to learn academic concepts in these outdoor classrooms.	78%	22%			
B. Students are likely to gain self confidence from completing these initiatives, i.e., rappelling or hiking the N.H. seacoast.	89%	21%			
C. Students are likely to work together with new groups of friends in mixed boy–girl groups to complete the hiking, cooking, and academic activities.	78%	22%			

Goal II. Gains in overall self-confidence are likely to lead to gains in academic achievement and vice versa.

	SA	A	CT	D	SD
A. Students are more likely to try an academic challenge after participating in the program.	11%	56%	22%	11%	
B. Students are more likely to have success in the academic challenges because of the increase in general confidence.	78%	11%	11%		
C. Gains in academic success are likely to lead to increased self-confidence.	100%				

Goal III. The Outdoor Education Program experience is likely to cause students to want to preserve the forests and natural areas.

	SA	A	CT	D	SD
A. Students are likely to view conservation of the forests and natural areas as important.	67%	33%			
B. Students are likely to voice this view.	11%	78%	11%		
C. Students are likely to refrain from littering in the forests and natural areas.	56%	44%			
D. Students are likely to refrain from littering in other places.	33%	44%	22%		
E. Students are likely to verbally object to someone of the same age littering.	44%	33%	22%		

Responses From Teaching Interns

The following narrative responses are from all of the participants in a seminar for education interns at Brandeis University in Massachusetts following a presentation on the ORMS Outdoor Education Program.

Intern 1: I thought the presentation was very good. The slides and pictures were informative. I think the philosophy of allowing the kids to work together (I noticed you stressed this point) is fantastic. This program is obviously well planned. The comments from different educators and parents were very positive. There is psychology involved. If the kids are quiet in class, they may be more verbal outside the classroom. This is also a perfect time to get to know the kids. I really enjoyed the presentation. I hope I can accomplish something like this at my school. I may be in contact for some help.

Intern 2: The presentation of outdoor education goals was very informative. I initially thought that my previous experience had given me all the answers. I was pleased to learn otherwise. Development of program activities, administrative support, parent–teacher involvement and specifics of financing and discipline were presented in an informal, concise, and interesting fashion.

My previous experience was not over extended periods (overnight trips) and tended to focus on immediate natural history and ecology goals. Your work seemed to stress individual development and fulfillment. Important values and skills were expressed. Judging from the amount of participation (adult and student). It appears that the program is an overwhelming success.

The visual material was helpful for understanding and appreciation of actual experience.

Intern 3: A very good exhibition, even though I am not into the outdoors. Very interesting programs. I think many kids will love it.

Perhaps, this kind of exhibition can be shown to students themselves, especially those who are not initially willing to go on such trips. Personally, I would give it a try just from observing the excitement of those who did it.

This has given me ideas about making more use of the outdoor environment, even though I would keep projects close to school grounds and within the community. Lots of luck, Jim.

Intern 4: Your presentation was very well prepared and organized. I had no idea any such program was available for middle school-aged children. Your audiovisual materials were great and nothing else could have made it more appealing. I can't think of any way to improve your presentation. It was very enjoyable.

Intern 5:   I was impressed with your curriculum. I found it to be enlightening and informative, and I thought you were well organized in your presentation and in your program.

I enjoy learning creative methods in any aspect of teaching, and your outdoor science program is informative, interesting, and an excellent way to teach children not only science but some methods of social behavior. Keep up the good work.

Intern 6:   Jim, I really enjoyed your presentation last Tuesday. The slides gave a very good idea of what your outdoor science program is really like. They say more than words. You can see cooperation among students, whether it be in climbing a mountain or cooking a meal. The only suggestion I can think of is maybe allowing a few of the students who participated in the program to comment, either via tape or by accompanying you on short distance trips to other schools, or maybe just student commentaries. A very worthwhile program and an excellent presentation. Thanks.

REFERENCES

Barrett, J. (2005). *The Paul Bunyun woodlands trail* (An unpublished forestry guide). Durham: University of New Hampshire.

Frost, R. (1939). *The road not taken.* In G. Leggett (Ed.), *12 Poets* (pp. 254-255). New York: Holt, Rinehart and Winston.

Galway, T., & Kriegal, R. (1977). *Inner skiing.* New York: Random House.

Hertz, S. (2006, Winter). Tuckerman! *University of New Hampshire Magazine,* pp. 34-38.

Longfellow, H. W.. (1847). *Evangeline, A Tale of Acadie.* Mount Vernon, New York: The Peter Pauper Press.

Weyrick, R. (1973). *Forest Ecology Loop.* An unpublished forestry guide. Durham: University of New Hampshire.

7

ROCK CLIMBING AND INITIATIVE EXPERIENCES

Greg S. Goodman

As we pushed upward on the scary, hollow-ringing of rock, the rope allowed our trespass: without it, there would have been no such tip-toeing in the sky. As the climb got hard, and the hours of concentration devolved into trance, we became the most privileged of explorers, for there is no terrain so exquisite and unknowable as vertical rock.

—*Roberts (1986, p. 237)*

One of the most memorable and vivid experiences one can have will be found either dangling off the end of a rope or trying to find a nubbin of granite for a finger hold on the face of a large cliff. But no matter the size or location of the face or pseudo-face, the elements of adventure and challenge are ubiquitous in the climber's world.

Since Outward Bound and the National Outdoor Leadership School (NOLS) began using rock climbing as a critical course component, the adaptive programs and other spin-offs like Project Adventure have incorporated climbing and high ropes activities in their curriculum. Because of the adrenaline pumping nature of high ropes and cliff ascents, words like "boring" and attendant resistant comments like "We did this" drop from the student lexicon. As instructors, we always felt that teaching climbing was the favorite lesson. We're sure the fear and related safety relevance issues contributed to the student's peaked attention. The danger for us was to fanaticize that we were Gaston Rubaffet or to succumb to some ego-trip gratification of teacher turned "rock jock."

For climbers, irony is part of the peak experience. Overcoming fear by placing oneself in the middle of a challenging climb brings forth acts of courage that one would not typically access in a normal day in the classroom (unless, of course, you teach in Grades 7– 9). Facing danger requires considerable knowledge of safe practice. Surviving in difficult situations gives a greater appreciation of life itself. In the climber's world, interesting juxtapositions of courage and fear, knowledge and the unknown, leading and following, delicacy and brutality, grace and profanity can all intermingle in the day's experience. All in all, this is a really interesting sport. Reading stories about the climbers, in our armchairs we discover diverse personalities ranging from engineer/mechanics to madmen.

Although not all, most of the best mountain writing is done by outdoorsmen/women—climbers themselves. People like Jon Krakauer, Gene Rose, John Roskelly, Greg Childs, and David Roberts have fabulous stories to tell. These great authors of mountain literature follow in the traditions set by historic icons and notables John Muir, William O. Douglas, and Sir Edmund Hillary. All of these writers proclaim the beauty of the places and the agony of the ventures as individual and nature collide and intersect in duels of weather, wit, and courage. For our students, the moral and physical equivalent of Willie Unsoeld's first ascent of Everest may be a day on a rock face with you, their 10th-grade science teacher!

Much of my favorite mountain writing has been done by my students. After taking them to the rock for a day, they return to school and write about their experiences. Very often the writing contains passion, growth, and enthusiasm. The students' reflections are self-rewarding with the prize of experience: personally relevant learning. Rock climbing is filled with learning opportunities and the students' reflective writing demonstrates their growth. At the end of this section, we have included examples for your enjoyment.

ORIENTATION FOR PARENTS, STUDENTS, AND STAFF

The main concern in all outdoor activities is safety. In climbing, it is no different. Ironically, however, the need to emphasize safety's relevance is not as critical because all of the participants get the danger concept when they see the objective. It is clear to all but the most oblivious: cliffs are dangerous places. Our job is to guarantee that this is a safe activity.

The first step in being sure that the activity will be safe is in the provision of a comprehensive orientation. Having everyone understand the purpose of the day and how we will make it safe is critical to having a successful day on the rock. Our goal is to be in harmony with nature and in sync with all of the members of our group from the leaders to the participants. Promoting respect for the environment and each other are the critical or crux issues to successfully meeting the safety requirement.

Respecting the environment carries all of the same rules for any outdoor activity concerning littering, toilet or personal needs, and wildlife or plant life considerations. These guidelines were presented in Chapter 1. However, of special consideration is the nature of cliff experience. Respecting this environment means not succumbing to the urge to throw things off the face (genetically wired in seventh-grade boys), not running or dashing about, and not being careless about helmets, water bottles, or other items that could accidentally be knocked over and rolled off the edge. These caveats are just a few examples of the myriad creative responses possible with large groups of young folks unaccustomed to the unseen dangers of a new environment. Adventure on—ignorance off.

As examples of two situations where I experienced a negative outcome, I offer these. Nature's bathroom requires a bit of special training for the uninitiated. Because of its basic and fundamental status as a part of the experience for an outdoor person, it is easy to overlook the possible trepidation it can evoke in the shy or inhibited student. In the middle of a beautiful, fall, foliage-filled New Hampshire day, I was enjoying my position as cliff manager for a collection of middle school students when a seventh-grade girl emerged from the woods in a state of hysteria. After composing herself to be able to relate the story, it was revealed that she was excused by one of our adult supervisors to enter the woods to use "nature's bathroom." Because she was seeking privacy and was unfamiliar with the terrain, she wandered off and became lost in the wooded area behind the rock face. Not having a sense of comfort in the woods, she panicked at the thought of being permanently lost. A hyperventilating adolescent was the result of failing to predict disaster off and away from the "action" in front of us. The real lesson for me was compounded by the debriefing conference with the parents and my principal after the girl's parents heard the tale of horror their daughter presented. The trauma was real, and we failed to see its possibility.

The second story also involves on off belay episode. Our climbing spot was a wonderful, open 150-foot face of solid granite with few objective dangers. Most of the vegetation was cleaned off the face and there were no loose chunks of material to rain on the unsuspecting below. However, the route we chose for our rappels and climbs, The Roost, had a tricky exit, and we would use a hand line or an actual hand to "spot" students on completion of their descent as they rounded the cliff edge on a narrow ledge.

One winter day, we were finishing up coiling ropes and readying to descend to aid the last of the students around the precarious corner at the climb's end when screams erupted from below. Apparently, one of our students was perched on the edge of the corner and slipped off the snow-covered ledge to fall 30 feet into the snow below. When she hit the bottom to the fall, her head jerked back, and she connected with the granite wall behind her. The result was a mild concussion; however, it was an inexcusable and avoidable accident. This accident could have been prevented with proper supervision at the base of the rappel and enough helmets for all of the students to be wearing at all times. (Because we were short of helmets, we would share them on rappel and upon completion of each descent haul them up to the top of the rock face with the descenders, karribiners, and slings. Any family's lawyers could have easily understood our equipment paucity issues and complied with a huge lawsuit!) The result of the head trauma was nonconsequential; however, the learning for us as instructors was profound. We always roped the end of the climb after that incident.

Because of these experiences and through other debriefing processes, when we would bring a large group such as an entire class to the cliff, we would split the class in two, and this would give us two smaller groups of approximately 15 individuals. Then these smaller groups would be staffed with a ratio of at-least one adult to every five students. With alternative education or other at risk students, we would bring one small group of 8 to 10 students and stay together for the whole day. The grouping depends entirely on your participant's needs and the possibilities within the environment you select for climbing. The overarching point is that there must be sufficient supervision to cover all aspects of the requirements of the particular group.

The dangers of climbing are generally exacerbated by careless maneuvers off belay rather than the result of a fall or slip while climbing or rappelling. Preventing injury is accomplished with good management and discipline. As the belayers are engaged in interaction with the individual sharing the rope, the students waiting to climb or rappel need supervision. Given the age of the students a ratio of five to eight students per adult is usually best practice. By having adequate adult supervision and setting a proper tone of respect, much in the way of potential problems is eliminated. Because almost all of the instructor's attention is absorbed by the facilitation of best climbing practices on the rock face, it is critical that other adults manage the needs of the students anxiously awaiting their turn or other students bored or inpatient with a long period of inactivity.

A final safety/supervision consideration concerns the age and caliber of the participants. After coiling the ropes at the end of a particularly rewarding day on the rocks with my alternative education students, I received heavy wafts of marijuana smoke along the pond's return trail. This would not have occurred if I had kept the group together and maintained my connection with them. Giving students too much liberty often generates undesirable results. I now realize that student's desire to break away from the supervision is often inspired by a desire to engage in activities that would not occur under the eye of a responsible adult. The supervision needs of each group and individual must be commensurate with the requirements that are present.

Permission Slip and Medical Release

The permission slip and medical release form should always be pre-approved by the school district's legal officer. Cell phones and a first aid kit should always be on hand on any outdoor classroom experience in case of emergency.

Equipment

Climbing is a very technical and scientific endeavor. As a result, the equipment of choice and the lexicon to describe it vary according to innovations and changes in best practices. When we began climbing, the use of brake bars attached to nonlocking karabiners was just giving way to the use of figure eight descenders. The choice for rappelling is always the most bomb-proof or infallible tool available. The safety key is in comprehending and preventing the potential failure of the "infallible."

Helmets are the essential safety item and their relevance as a risk management tool is more determined by the possibility of loose rock falling on the participant than the possibility of banging one's head into the face while on rappel. Whatever the possible injury, the same protection applies to items launched from above. Be it accidental, like a rolling water bottle, or intentional, like an item thrown for thrilling effect, the helmet can be essential protection.

Footwear can run the gamut from Royal Robbins finest friction soles to fairly dilapidated tennis shoes. The only caveat for footwear is no flip-flops or leather-soled city shoes. Anything with a decent grip will suffice. Comfort and compatibility with the environmental requirements seems to be the best bet.

As all climbers know, the ropes used in climbing are standardized and recommended for dynamic belays. This means that the ropes stretch when stressed. This stretch allows the climber some resiliency when they are belayed. For rappels, we used a non-dynamic, kernmantle 7/16-inch rope. These ropes were less expensive than the costly climbing ropes, and they were more than adequately safe for our participants. Your program's choice of ropes is best dictated by following recommended safety standards. Your school district's insurance agent will sleep better knowing you followed the best practice route here.

Technique

In almost all of the climbing and rappelling we have taught, we have chosen to employ top roped technique. This means that the belayer was atop the climber or that this was simulated by placing "protection" on top of the climber. By having a well-secured belayer atop the climber or rappeller, as much security and safety as could be afforded was in place. In hundreds of days of teaching with this technique, not one student or adult received an injury greater than a mild concussion. This is not to say that we were so skilled that no one could have been more seriously injured. Looking back, I believe that we were damn lucky! Following the irony rule, because of climbing's tremendous danger the implementation of best safety practices may mitigate the possibility of serious injury. And in the event of a serious or deadly accident, one could muster a personal and or legal defense knowing that best risk management procedures were in effect.

Objectives for Learning

One of the favorite aspects of the day on the cliff was giving the opening lecture and outlining the day's experience. The greeting would set the tone for the entire day. The goals of the brief lecture were to center our student's attention on our safety and protection of the environment we were sharing with its natural residents: the birds, bugs, and other animals of the habitat. Building respect for each other within the environment was always one of the essential curriculum ingredients.

As important as the space that sustains us are the individuals participating in the activities. To build respect for everyone, we emphasized the elemental feelings of trust, fear, and empathy. As Jed Williamson used to say, rappelling had a high "C.T." (cheap thrill) factor. For some of our participants, it was a cheap thrill akin to an amusement ride or an experience like bungy-jumping. But for many others, this was something that was the moral and physical equivalent of climbing Mt. Everest. And for some, completion of the rappel was not going to happen that day.

We asked that all participants would simply try the activity. That meant putting on the harness, clipping into the belay and rappel system, and taking a few steps back on the ledge top. Our instruction to the entire group included this tidbit: for some, just clipping in to the system would take more courage than completion of the activity would require for our eager beavers. What one was feeling at the top was their own experience, and with the respect for each individual's difference, we were not going to have any "chickens" on the trip today. For this particular activity, the concept of a "chicken" did not exist. For most everyone, cheers and yelps of applause would accompany the participant's arrival off rappel: either on top or at the bottom.

The "full-value contract" was a concept developed by the Project Adventure staff to articulate the backbone of bonding and trust development (Schoel, Prouty, & Radcliff, 1989). Essentially, three commitments formed this contract:

> Agreement to work together as a group and to work toward individual and group goals;
>
> Agreement to adhere to certain safety and group behavioral guidelines;
>
> Agreement to give and receive feedback, both positive and negative, and to work toward changing behavior when it is appropriate. (Schoel, Prouty, & Radcliff, 1989, p. 95)

The full value contract clearly defines a way for a group to become safe in both physical and emotional domains.

Curriculum and Activities

A favorite paraphrasing of a Dewey quote that I liked to share with my students summarized that we are all experience rich yet we spend little time thinking about those experiences. Learning, according to Dewey (1944), is the process of thinking about experience. Because we were in school (in the outdoor classroom), we needed to invest time and energy in the thinking process to enhance the meaning and value of our experience. To follow up our day on the rock, we would hand out homework to be completed the next day. Examples of these assignments are included to demonstrate possible follow-up activities. We felt these assignments provided valuable assessments of our program's effectiveness. As you read the student writing responses, you will see how these student expressions were invaluable to the program, the parents, and the participants.

Example From a Middle School Climbing Day

The rock climber's homework would be to complete one of the following assignments:

1. Explain the physical forces including friction and gravity that applied to the activity you experienced today at Rock House Cliff.
2. Explain what you have learned about yourself today. Include the effect of the initiative exercises and the rappelling experience.
3. Using either a prose or poetry format, describe your feelings about what you experienced today. Include images of the environment, your feelings, and the interactions with your peers. Blend facts of the day with your creative writing energies.

Examples From Student Journals and Interviews

Some of the best rewards of a day on the cliff were the arrival of student writing. Reading their reflections brought back the day and allowed special satisfactions. Here is some of what we received:

> At the Round Pond [fictitious name] rock climbing trip, although I didn't go down, I learned that I have the will to make my own decisions and can stand behind them. I know that at first, I really wasn't too happy with the situation, but in the end after trying it, I had a positive feeling about myself and the project because I knew that I had made the right decision for myself.
> I still felt a feeling of accomplishment because I had tried.
> The area was beautiful. I really enjoyed the activities before the descend (sic). They were fun and educational. I thought Nancy and Matt were really good. They helped us to understand and appreciate the woods. Another thing we learned was to trust each other. With the blindfolds, we learned to trust each other because we didn't have sight. With the trust fall we learned to trust each other because if we didn't, we'd get hurt. (Student essay)

> I felt very proud of myself when I got down to the bottom of the cliff. I was very scared going down the cliff.
> The trip taught me to listen, think about what I'm listening to, to observe and preserve your environment, and the most important thing is

self-confidence and faith. I needed self-confidence just to look over the edge of the cliff and also walk down. I needed faith to go down also because the safety people had my life in their hands. When I say in their hands, I mean their hands.

I really enjoyed the day and it was very self-rewarding just to think of what I accomplished today is like winning a prize at a fair. (Student essay)

> Rappelling is really neat.
> When you stand by the edge on a Swiss seat.
> The rope can lift 500 pounds
> Enough to lift a car off the ground.
> No one will call you chicken if you don't go,
> Because it's not for play or show.
> It's more to gain self-esteem,
> And the good thing is you do it as a team.
> As you go down the view is really nice,
> And you wish you could go down at least twice.
> Rockhouse Pond is really peaceful,
> And no one could ever call it dull
> With all the wild life around,
> It takes you away from the things in town.
>
> Many people do not go but that's OK,
> Because even though you're scared,
> You're never ever dared.
> Instead people just say, what the hey,
> (That's why Oyster River kids are the best.)

(Student poem)

Example From a High School Climbing Day

High school curriculum integrates outdoor experiences and writing skills to provide clarity and depth of meaning. The challenge for students at this level of learning is to improve critical thinking skills and communicate those thoughts in clear expression. Although the classic five-paragraph essay is often touted as the classic example, we believe that giving students multiple opportunities for personal expression is most effective in maintaining momentum for the important tasks of reflection and synthesis.

Rock Climbing Reflections

As we emphasized throughout this class, learning is a process. Teachers and students can continue to experience learning from the rock climbing day by reflecting on what they have done. The students' reflections or thoughts can

be communicated to the teacher and the
class in several forms.

1. Write a classic form, five-paragraph
   essay. For this assignment, reflect
   on one significant aspect of the day.
   Choose some part of the day that
   stands out as being particularly
   meaningful to you. This could
   include observations of yourself,
   your peers, or any other aspect of
   the day you choose to make significant. State in the introductory
   paragraph an overview of your
   observation, and proceed in the
   next three paragraphs to clarify the
   learning that took place for you.
   Conclude with an overall summation of the experience's meaning to you.
2. Reflect on the experience of the day and identify a feeling that
   you encountered. Create a poem, song, or other written expression of the feeling and how it unfolded or occurred to you.
   Think of your feeling as a sacred object and give it as much
   respect as you can muster.
3. Write a children's story based on the experience you had at
   Rockhouse Pond. Think about the story as having a conflict and
   give the resolution or failure to reach resolution a life. What was
   the challenge needing resolution? What magic occurred to bring
   resolution to this crisis

Example of Student Writing and Reflection

My Feelings at Rock House Pond
Before I went rappelling, I was very scared. I didn't want to go at all. I
think I was scared because I'm afraid of heights, and the cliff we were to
rappel on was high!
My group had the initiative exercises first. I'm glad we did that first
because it calmed my nerves. I had time to do fun things before I did something scary.
The exercises to me were a great of fun. You had a chance to explore the
woods and enjoy yourself. The exercises taught me how to use my other
senses when I had lost one of them. Also, when we all were blindfolded and
we walked through the woods holding onto the rope, we had to learn to
trust the person that was leading us through the woods.

The exercises taught me to like the woods and to keep the woods like it was when I found it because the woods was a home of many animals.

When we went to the rappelling part, I wasn't as scared, but I was still scared.

In the end, I didn't go down the cliff. I didn't care if everyone else went down but me, and I didn't care if they saw how scared I was. I still had a fun time watching all the other kids go down. But I think I was scared at the end when I was told that I had to try! I found out though that trying meant only putting the gear on and not going over the edge. So I did that with no worry.

In all and all, I had a great day at Rock House!

Recognitions

An example of a favorite post-experience writing came in the form of a special connection made by a teacher-participant on one of the best Rock House days. Linda Rief, a seventh-grade language arts teacher from the Oyster River Middle School, had been a student of Don Murray and Don Graves in the now-famous University of New Hampshire Writer's Program. Nationally renowned for contributing the writing process pedagogy and praxis that has revolutionized the teaching of writing, Graves and Murray had a large effect on the middle school staff, and Linda was one of the recent converts to this work. After spending a day with her class at Rock House, Linda published "Writing and Rappelling" in the September issue of *Learning Magazine*. She contributed:

Last spring I volunteered to accompany the sixth graders in our middle school on a rappelling adventure led by counselor and outdoor educator Greg Goodman. The thought of descending on a rope over the edge of a sheer cliff terrified me, but I was determined to conquer my fear. With Greg's guidance and support, I did rappel down the cliff, and so did every student but one. The experience taught me not only about rappelling but also about reading.

Sitting at the top of a sheer cliff, awaiting my turn to rappel down, building up my courage, I listened intently to Greg's words as he gently coaxed each student over the edge: "you can do it, just lean back, get a good grip. Nice control. I know you're afraid. Walk it back, feet apart, shoulders back— you've got it! Super job! Keep going. Lean back. What a pro!"

As I listened to Greg and watched each student overcome fear and disappear over the edge, the thought struck me that what Greg was accomplishing with these students was exactly what I wanted to achieve in my writing class. The way I had been teaching writing was anything but an adventure for my students. I was the teacher who circled misspelled words, inserted proper punctuation, and added or deleted whole sentences or thoughts. Often I wrote more than my students. I loved what they wrote, and why not? The writing was mostly mine!

The way Greg taught rappelling was entirely different from my own teaching approach. With gentle words and knowledgeable guidance, Greg built a supportive environment around each rappelling student. Interweaving positive, confidence-building comments ("You can do it. I have confidence in you") with simple, clear instructions ("shoulders back, feet apart, lean back"), Greg supported risk taking. Nothing he said threatened the children. The students trusted him and themselves.

Greg's rate of success in teaching rappelling was high. Every child in the group but one dropped over the edge. I couldn't claim such success with my writing class. My students hated writing, and I was exhausted from the effort of teaching them. I saw the solution clearly as I listened to Greg. I needed to create a supportive environment in which each child could experiment with writing. (Rief, 1984, p. 73)

A day at Rockhouse Pond was always rewarding, but to have student and other writing affirm the values and the learning that occurred made the experience transformative for me as a teacher. Teaching climbing and rappelling can also be problematic. The risks associated with climbing are great, and the possibility of error always looms large in the minds of instructors. On the edge of a cliff, there is no riskier endeavor a teacher could undertake; risk is what we choose to embrace.

REFERENCES

Dewey, J. (1944). *Democracy and education.* Toronto, Ontario: Collier-Macmillan.

Rief, L. (1984, September). Writing and rappelling. *Learning Magazine*, pp. 73-76.

Roberts, D. (1986). *Moments of doubt.* Seattle, WA: The Mountaineers.

Schoel, J., Prouty, D., & Radcliff, P. (1989). *Islands of healing: A guide to adventure based counseling.* Hamilton, MA: Project Adventure.

8

BACKPACKING ALONG OCEANS, STREAMS, AND PONDS

James R. Jelmberg

Sea-Fever

"I must go down to the seas again,
to the lonely sea and the sky,
And all I ask is a tall ship and a star
to steer her by.
And the wheel's kick and the wind's
song and the white sail's
Shaking.
And a grey mist on the sea's face and
a grey dawn breaking."

—John Masefield

A spectacular way to get students involved in the outdoor classroom is to first locate a body of water. Depending on the region of the country in which you live, this body of water could be a stream, river, pond, lake, or an ocean. The sights and sounds of streams, ponds, and oceans provide a natural attraction to students of all grade levels. They are symphonies of sound, motion, and changing color. Youngsters are irresistibly drawn to these bodies of water, whether it is the call of crying gulls, the freshwater sounds of rushing streams, or the bird songs of the ponds and lakes. It is an all encompassing world where students see the waves and the water, feel the wind and the sand, and smell the salty sea. As John Masefield beckons in his poem "Sea-Fever," students will be called to return to these bodies of water, and their learning in these habitats can provide lifelong experiences of pleasure.

The material presented within this chapter stems from more than thirty years of interdisciplinary learning developed by the teachers at the Oyster River Middle School (ORMS) in Durham, New Hampshire. Most of the curriculum activities that these students accomplished along the seacoast are adaptable to a hiking trip along streams, rivers, ponds, or lakes. These environments can provide an ideal outdoor classroom habitat that students will remember for years to come.

THE OUTDOOR EDUCATION PROGRAM AT THE OYSTER RIVER MIDDLE SCHOOL

The overnight backpacking trip along the New Hampshire seacoast was the last of several expeditions that comprised the schoolwide outdoor education program at the ORMS, a program that began in 1974 and continues today. Originally part of the science program, the curriculum evolved to become interdisciplinary. The program's expeditions provided an opportunity for all students, parents, and teachers to work together in an outdoor classroom that involved adventure in an integrated way.

The process of working together is most observable among the students in their diverse and gender-equitable hiking groups. Because of their all-important goal of being responsible for each other, these multicultural groups have additional challenges to accomplish on this overnight expedition. Having to help each other fix backpacks, cook food, and pitch tents as well as completing group academic challenges provides opportunities that necessitate more democratic consensus building and decision making. Students develop their minds, bodies, and spirits through accomplishing challenges in an atmosphere of support. The student hiking groups provide that support. Working together and achieving consensus adds a transformational dimension to the exciting, adventuresome outdoor classroom goals of teaching the whole child by providing equal opportunities for diverse students to make group decisions and bond together.

One of the principle goals of the program was to have different groups of students go to different habitats representing varied seasons, to perform unique and stimulating activities. The students would then return and share their enthusiasm and experiences with their classmates. Student sharing took many forms. What the students who chose the seacoast expedition shared with their classmates back in the classroom after their trip is described here by a reporter in a *Transcript* news article about a typical seacoast trip.

48 ORMS Students Complete Science Trip Along Seacoast

DURHAM—Forty-eight Oyster River Middle School students recently completed a two-day, overnight backpacking, science trip along the New Hampshire seacoast as their component of the seventh grade Outdoor Education Program.

"The success of the Outdoor Education Program has been the result of a team effort all year long with all students participating and all special and team teachers, as well as administrators, helping with the organization," said Jim Jelmberg, originator of the program.

The students began work in Seabrook, and a day of activities and lectures on weather and geology saw students eight miles northward in Rye. After pitching tents and cooking the meals they had planned, students grouped around the campfire to recount the science observations of the day and to select the most self-reliant in each group. Skits were performed by each group, and students finished the evening with a campfire sing along.

Reflecting back on the trip, Jayne Goding, trip transportation coordinator, said, "It was important for me as a teacher to be able to get to know another dimension of the students outside the confines of the classroom."

Following more science activities the second day, the group arrived, tired but happy, at Odiorne Point. After an evaluation and debriefing of the trip came the long awaited "ride" home.

"These trips are successful in many ways, not the least of which are the science and self confidence aspect," said science teacher Tom Bonaccorsi.

All expeditions required moderate physical initiative, good academic standing, and good conduct prior to the trips. Because these expectations were emphasized with students throughout the year, students generally rose to the occasion, and very few if any were excluded from the trips. Additionally, all students were required to gather data in the habitat, analyze it back in the classroom, and complete a report.

The curriculum topics on the seacoast expedition originally included geology, ecology, meteorology, geometry, and compass orienteering if time allowed. Later, as other teachers became involved in the hike, their interests enriched the curriculum in all subject areas. In addition to the academic objectives were the adventure objectives of self-reliance, self-confidence, and values of conservation.

This hike ventured northward from the Massachusetts state line in Seabrook to Odiorne Point in Rye. The time of year was usually near the second week in May. The exact time was determined by the tide, and was noted on the permission slip sent home prior to the trip.

This particular expedition usually involved about 50 students and took 2 days and an overnight stay, where students pitched tents on the back fairway of a local golf course. Students cooked in groups of five under the direction of their parent-leader.

ENVIRONMENTAL CLEANUP

When students find themselves in adventuresome, outdoor environments, they are motivated to learn about natural areas that have been conserved by earlier generations. They also learn to respect these environments using environmentally friendly modes of transportation such as hiking, skiing, snow-shoeing, and rock climbing as opposed to gasoline propelled mini-bikes and four-wheelers, and by packing out all litter that they brought in, leaving no trace behind.

Students were always expected to pick up any litter that was dropped along the way. They were more than willing to do this, in part because they were inspired by the pristine environment they found themselves in. Occasionally, there was an unusual opportunity for them to go above and beyond the everyday desire to leave the environment the way they found it. One day while hiking on the beach, a Coast Guard officer hailed us, and asked to speak with the students. There had been an oil spill from one of the many oil tankers that come in and out of Portsmouth Harbor. The officer asked the students for help in locating evidence of oil on the beaches or rocks as we hiked along. Our hikers were excited about their new responsibility and began to enthusiastically look for oil residue. A few places were found, and we reported them when we finished the trek. I'm sure these students still remember that day when they were asked by a Coast Guard officer to help him out with an oil spill. I'm also sure that because of that experience, they will be much more vigilant and pro-active about protecting their environment.

CURRICULUM ACTIVITIES FOR WATER-BASED EXPEDITIONS

The rocky shorelines of the streams, rivers, ponds, lakes, and oceans provide rich habitats for study in all curriculum areas and at all grade levels. From almost the first moment our students walked onto the beach to begin their hike, they were asked to open their working manual. This manual became a journal that documented a journey of inquiry that was characterized by the questions that occupied their minds. As our students were guided by this manual, the following questions give the reader a look into what they were thinking at that time.

THE NEW HAMPSHIRE SEACOAST: A STUDENT WORKING MANUAL

THE MASSACHUSETTS BORDER TO HAMPTON HARBOR INLET

Oceanography: Notice where the tide is when you begin your hike. As you proceed along the beach, notice whether it is coming in or going out. Will the tide be right for digging clams this morning? Notice the time it takes for the tide to come back to where it is now.

Geography: As you look approximately 30 miles southward, you will see a point of land reaching eastward into the Atlantic. What point of land do you think this is and why is it called such? Now look offshore to the northeast and sight a group of large islands miles out to sea. What islands are these and how far away do you think they are?

Navigation: Take a compass bearing to see what course you would steer if you were to navigate by boat to these islands. What direction is the wind coming from? How many miles per hour do you think it is blowing? What people use this information while they work? What effect is the wind having around you?

Geology: Where did all this sand come from and how was it deposited to form beaches like this? How were these sand dunes formed?

Harbor Navigation: After you have walked approximately a mile you will notice buoys in the water. What is their purpose? Is there a pattern to how they are placed? Why are some red and some black?

Geology: At the northern end of this beach you will notice some rock formations. Can you name some of these kinds of rocks? Name some minerals that you can see contained in these rocks? How are the striations (different colored streaks) formed in these rocks? How have these rocks come to be some jagged and some smooth?

THE HAMPTON HARBOR CLAM FLATS

Oceanography: What natural advantages here in Hampton Harbor have provided a favorable place for clams to live? How do clams travel?

Zoology: How do they dig into the sand? What do they eat? How do they reproduce? Are there males and females? How do they make their shells? What kinds of fish come in here? Why? What things happen in the westward marsh that makes it an important place for birds and fish and other animals?

HAMPTON HARBOR INLET TO BOAR'S HEAD

A tunnel carries hot water from a nuclear plant built here to generate electricity. What are your feelings about a nuclear plant being built near the clam flats and the salt marsh? If the hot water or the tunnels coming from the nuclear plant would be harmful to the salt marsh or the clams, would you want such a plant built here?

As you stand here on the other side of the harbor inlet, you have covered approximately a mile and a half of the roughly eight mile trip to our first day's destination, the Friary in Rye. Since the walk from here to Rocky Bend (the first cluster of rocks) is approximately one mile, time your walk and see what your walking speed will be in miles per hour. Then on the basis of this walking speed, estimate the number of hours it will take to finish the remainder of the trip.

CONFIDENCE COURSE ACROSS THE ROCKS
AT BOAR' S HEAD

Coordination Exercise. Caution: Walk slowly, look where you are going, and be careful. Good Luck!

Now that you are around Boar's Head, how do you feel? How did you feel when you were slipping and tripping among the rocks? How many miles do you have to go now? When do you think you will arrive at the Friary? What is the compass bearing to the Isles of Shoals now?

BOAR'S HEAD TO PLAICE COVE

Geography: When you reach Plaice Cove, you will have gone from the town of Hampton to another town. List in order, from south to north, the names of all the New Hampshire towns along the seacoast.

Biology: Notice the tidal pool here in Plaice Cove. If we had the time, what things might we look for in this tidal pool? What natural advantages does the pool provide here for microscopic life? Do you think the temperature here is the same as in the ocean? Why or why not? What are the actual temperatures of the pool and the ocean? Do you think there is more or less salt in the pool? Why? What effect might the amount of salt have on the animal life? What animals and plants do you see in the pool? How are they able to hold on to the rocks?

LITTLE BOAR'S HEAD TO THE FRIARY

Oceanography: Where is the tide now compared to where it was this morning when you began the hike? How many hours does it take the tide to go from low to high? How many hours will it be from low to high to low again? What causes this constant rise and fall of the tides? How? Where is the wind coming from now as compared to this morning? Conclude from this the compass pattern by which the winds changed direction today? Do you think that this wind pattern is related to the weather? How has the weather changed from this morning? What causes the waves? How high are they compared to this morning? How fast is the wind blowing compared to this morning?

Geography: What is the compass direction to the Shoals now? Sketch a map of the land that you have walked today. Label the sections of your walk using the Massachusetts State Line to the Hampton Harbor Inlet, and the other parts of your walk. Use a scale of one inch equals 1 mile, and include Cape Ann, the Isles of Shoals, and the town you have passed through. Label N, S, E, W and the direction of the Gulf Stream.

THE FRIARY TO RYE HARBOR STATE PARK

Second Day

Oceanography: What is the Gulf Stream and in which direction does it flow? What great current affects these northern New England waters? Where is the tide now that you are about to begin hiking? How long will it take to ebb and flow to return to where it is now?

Weather: Observe the weather and fill in the following: 1) air temperature; 2) water temperature; 3) wind speed; and 4) types of clouds. On the basis of this information, make a weather forecast for today. During the day, observe the above conditions and see how accurate your prediction is.

RYE HARBOR STATE PARK TO THE STATE BEACH

Sensory Awakening: For the entire stretch of this next beach, remove your shoes and walk alone in single file, without any talking whatsoever. Use your five senses to experience all

the stimulation affecting what you hear on this beach. Describe your feelings about: 1) what you hear; 2) what you smell; 3) what you feel; 4) what you taste; and 5) what you see.

WALLACE SANDS BEACH

Sensory Awakening: Here at Wallace Sands you will blindfold a partner and lead him half way across the beach; leading him into sensory experiences such as touching things of different texture and temperature of the beach. Your partner will do this with you on the next half of the walk, doing similar things with you. Describe how it feels to have to trust someone completely like this.

Navigation Mathematics: Take a compass bearing on the Isles of Shoals and compare it to the bearing taken at the Massachusetts Line. How many degrees on the compass have you covered thus far? Draw a circle with the Isles as the center and show the circumference segment. How long would the actual radius of this circle be?

CURRICULUM ADAPTATION TO DIFFERENT GRADE LEVELS

The curriculum manual was originally developed and used with eighth graders. We have explained how the curriculum activities in this book are adaptable to other schools and other grade levels. The following is an example of how the above eighth grade curriculum manual was adapted to the sixth grade by John Parsons and his teacher colleagues on the ORMS Phoenix Team, John MacArthur, Linda Becker, Katie Firczuk, and Sue

Williams. The adapted curriculum continues to evolve, and the Phoenix Team members now anticipate sharing more of the curriculum development responsibility with their students.

PHOENIX Seacoast Backpack Worksheets

You can do this work by yourself or in small groups. All work is required of everyone. Students who complete work appropriately will be eligible to participate in campfire and other fun activities. Any students who do not complete their work will spend campfire time finishing the work with a teacher.

All answers go into your journals as directed by Mrs. Becker. Label all answers with the corresponding question number (and letter, if present). Do not number your answers in advance. In many cases, answers do NOT have to be in complete sentences. There are quite a few exceptions, however. You will be notified when sentences are required.

DAY 1

1. As we walk onto the beach, look south. Which state are you seeing? Notice the Salisbury water tower. Don't write anything, though.
2. Look north. Which state is it?
3. Record the time as we start walking.
4. In which general (compass) direction is Hampton Harbor?
5. At what time this morning was high tide at Hampton Harbor?
6. At what time will be high tide this evening?
7. How long an interval is there between high tides?
8. Take a compass bearing (magnetic) on the White Island Light (Isles of Shoals) and record it.
9. As we walk north, notice the sand piles on the west side of the beach. What are these piles called?
10. Why is the sand piled up here? Answer in a complete sentence.
11. What is the most common plant you see growing in these sandpiles?

Now put your worksheets away and just walk for awhile.

HAMPTON RIVER AREA

12. What is a river mouth?
12A. Take a compass bearing on the White Island Light and record it.
13. When we arrive at the mouth of the Hampton River, WALK carefully on the rocks. What types of rocks are most of these?
14. Find some stripes of a black rock running through the other rocks. What type of rock is the black rock?
15. What is one of the names for this stripe structure?

16.   What causes this striping to occur? Answer in a complete sentence.

Notice, but don't write down, the orientation (direction) of the break-waters here.

17.   See the cabinet attached to the navigation tower atop the rocks. Who put it there?

18.   What the cabinet is being used for. Answer in a complete sentence.

19.   We are about halfway to the bridge, stop and find visual evidence that the tide is going out. Your tide chart doesn't count, silly. Using a complete sentence, write a brief explanation.

20.   While you're standing here, notice the difference in sound the cars make as they cross the middle portion of the bridge. Write a complete sentence with your guess as to what causes this difference.

21.   Not far south of here is a large rock called Bound Rock that we will not go to look at. It marks the boundary between Hampton and Seabrook. Many years ago, it used to be in the middle of the river, but the river has shifted course over the years. Why is it unlikely that the river will shift course much in the future? Explain in complete sentences.

22A. Go under the bridge and just beyond it, and look at the large structures located on the salt marsh across the estuary. What are the two domes?

22B. Why are they different colors? Use a complete sentence to explain.

22C. What are cooling tunnels used for? Use a complete sentence. Go back under the bridge to climb up to cross the sidewalk on the east side. If you see harbor seals in the river, point them out to an adult. Bonus points!

23.   What is the official name of this bridge?

24.   Look at the large boats in the harbor. What (specifically) are they for? Walk through the State Park and out onto the beach again. Continue north toward the "Sea Shell," but don't go up into the soft sand until told to do so. We'll use the bathrooms here again. We'll walk the sidewalk (stay to the right) for a short distance to the NH Marine Memorial.

25.   What does USN mean?

26.   What does AF mean?

27.   What does USA mean on this monument?

28.   What does USMM mean?

29.   What is the former name of Pease International Trade Port?

30.   After whom was it named?

31.   Take a compass bearing on the White Island Light, and record it. Notice, but don't write about, the tower on Boar's Head. Walk the beach, then sidewalk, to the north side of Rocky Bend. As you

walk, notice the location of the
Hampton Beach water tower.
Don't record.

32. What is a "boar"?

33. What is a "headland"?

34. Where were Vikings from?

35. In the legend about Thorvald
    Ericson, why did the surviving
    Vikings not give Thorvald a tra-
    ditional Viking funeral? Explain
    in complete sentences. From
    here, we'll walk a bit more on the
    sidewalk, and then it's back on
    the beach.

36. Which beach are we on now?

From the base of Winnacunnet Road to the far end of this beach is exactly 1 mile. You are going to walk briskly for this distance and time yourself to see how fast it takes you to walk a mile. The far end of this beach
is defined as the last seawall opening and steps.

ALONG THE WAY

37. Record your start time.

38. Record your end time.

39. How long did your mile take?

Rest stop at Comfort Station

40. The shotgun shells floated in from the ocean. Why were they in the
    water? Use a complete sentence.

41. What do the steel doors cover?

42. What is the purpose of the breakwaters at the mouth of the
    Hampton River? Use a complete sentence.

43. Look at the "breakwaters" all along this beach? Why are they per-
    pendicular to the ocean (while the ones at the river mouth are not)?
    Use a complete sentence.

44. Take a compass bearing on the White Island Light.

45. On the northernmost stretch of seawall (the uncurved part), there
    is a sealed up opening. What was the opening used for?

46. What structure used to sit behind the seawall?

47. The cove on the north side of the rocks is called Plaice Cove. What
    is a "plaice?"

48. Look south-southeast. See the peninsula that sticks way out. What
    is it called?

TIDE POOL EXPLORATION

Language Arts and Science at the same time! It doesn't get any better than this, folks!

First, see page entitled Language Arts Activities.

Second, you will work in groups to look for various plants and animals that appear on the blue sheets in your folders. You will record the names shortly in your journals. Be sure to put specimens back precisely. Please put all rocks back in their original locations. You should be able to find at least the following:

- plants—knotted wrack, sea lettuce, rockweed, Irish Moss, kelp (probably all three kinds shown)
- animals—barnacles, various snail species, probably various crabs, blue mussels, possibly green sea urchins, sea stars, amphipods

48A. Is the tide pool temperature about the same as the ocean temperature?

48B. Why or why not? Use a complete sentence.

48C. Some upper level (splash zone) tide pools do not get flooded regularly at high tide.

They tend to have a higher salt content (they are more salty). Explain, using complete sentences, why this happens.

If you see loons in Plaice Cove, show them to an adult. Bonus points!

48D. What do you notice about the orientation of the rocks just north of our lunch spot? Explain in a complete sentence.

As we travel north beyond Plaice Cove, we'll see a small area of peat on the beach.

60. The mansions across the street are all part of whose estate?

49. What is it composed of?

50. There is a lot more of this buried under the sand along this coastline. Why is it located right near the shoreline and under the water? Use a complete sentence.

51. What have the Irish (in Ireland) traditionally used this material for?

51A. When there is a high tide on the New Hampshire coast, what sort of tide is there on the exactly opposite side of the earth?

52. What do we call the little brown, shingled buildings at the north end of North Hampton Beach?

53. Explain, in a complete sentence, what they were used for.

54. What is the name of the small headland just beyond these buildings?

55. Which famous poet used to spend summers at his house near this headland?

56. Take a compass bearing on the White Island Light and record it.

57. According to some local people, what sank in the waters off this headland in September of 1942?

58. What do they believe caused the alleged sinking? Explain using a complete sentence. Notice the location of the water towers at Salisbury and Hampton Beach.

59. Find the benchmark in the rock. What does it say on it?

About 400 meters north, stand near the bench just before the last lone cedar tree. Look south and notice the Boar's Head tower. Look up the coast a similar distance. On a compass heading of 43 degrees, just left of the flashing Whaleback Light, see another tower similar to the Boar's Head tower.

60. The mansions across the street are all part of whose estate?

61. Which political office did the patriarch of the family hold?

62. Why did the family tear down the largest of the mansions in the early 1960s?

MATH

63. The white house in the middle of the estate is about 70 feet long. Use that information to figure approximately how many square feet are in the entire lawn area. If you have a more efficient way of doing it, check with an adult, then go ahead.

64. An acre is roughly 41,000 square feet. How many acres does the lawn cover?

65. All along the coast there are lots of small buoys in the water, and here you are up high enough to see them well. What are they?

From this spot, you will walk the sidewalk above the rocky beach for about 10 or 15 more minutes, until you arrive at the Rye town line. Just past the line, we'll turn inland for our last few hundred meters to Abenaqui.

DAY 2

Today you will have fewer questions to answer. As you walk, notice whichever types of BIRDS you see (from those listed in your packet and any others we mention) at any time between here and Odiorne. Record them at Question 88.

66. Record the time we start walking.

67. Take a compass bearing on the White Island Light, and record it.

68. What time was high tide this morning?

69. What time will it be this evening?

70. How much time is there between high tides today?

71. How does the interval compare to yesterday's?

72. Which beach are we walking on from here to Straw's Point?

ISLES OF SHOALS LORE

73. See the Language Arts sheet.

74. There are two historical features of the area at the north end of this beach. Which one was human-made?

75. Why did the ocean drown the sunken forest here? Use a complete sentence.

PLEASE WALK CAREFULLY ALONG THIS STRETCH AROUND STRAW'S POINT!

76. Look at the huge wooden structure. What is the official geometric name for this specific shape of polyhedron?

76A. Write, in a complete sentence, your guess about what this thing is and why it is here.

77. Why is there a great deal of sand on top of the marsh behind the beach? Use a complete sentence.

78. Look west across the marsh. What is the name for the group of short posts sticking out of the marsh?

79. Using a complete sentence, explain what they were used for.

80. How did people keep horses' hooves from breaking through the surface of the marsh? Use a complete sentence.

81. Think of a situation in which humans wear similar footwear to avoid sinking too deep into a different material. Use a complete sentence.

81A. The straight-line ditches in the marsh are not natural formations. Why are they there? Explain using a complete sentence.

81B. What is the value of a salt marsh to the coastal environment? Use complete sentences.

Photo Opportunity

AS WE RETURN TO A SHORT STRETCH OF ROCKS, BE CAREFUL. IF WE WALK THE PRIVATE ROAD INSTEAD, PLEASE BE QUIET.

82. Saunder's Restaurant is right next to the spot where ORMS sixth-grade students pulled an Alaskan King crab out of the tidal creek. You should remember the slide of this you saw in science in January. Which phylum of animals does a crab belong to?

83.   Describe, using a complete sentence, the characteristics that place the crab into the phylum you named.

From here, we'll walk along the road, single file, to Rye Harbor State Park.

84.   Take a compass bearing on White Island Light, and record it.

You can put worksheets away until we reach the south side of Concord Point. Here we'll walk the stony Foss Beach or the top of the "seawall" or both walks. Walk on the rocks south of Concord Point.

85.   Here are several of the "stripes" in the rocks as you saw in various places yesterday. Which rock is the dark "stripe" material made of?

86.   What is the stripe called?

86A.   What causes ocean tides?

86B.   What causes waves?

86C.   What does the word "fetch" mean? Use a complete sentence.

WALK CAREFULLY ON THE ROCKS FROM HERE AROUND THE POINT

87.   On the north side of the point there is a stream coming in. List three types of seaweed you find here.

88.   Record your bird sightings here.

FROM HERE WE'LL WALK BRISKLY ALONG WALLIS SANDS TO THE STATE PARK "BREAKWATER" AT THE NORTH END. STAY WELL AWAY FROM THE DRY SAND.

89.   From the breakwater, take a compass bearing on White Island Light, and record it.

90.   At Seal Rocks, notice the angle or orientation of the rock layers. What is an upward fold of rock called?

91.   What is a downward fold of rock called?

92.   What caused the folding? Explain using a complete sentence.

If you see seals, show them to an adult. Bonus points!

93.   When we get to the next stony beach, you'll find rocks that range from about hand size to about brick size. What kind of beach is this called?

94.   Where did the rocks come from? Explain in a complete sentence.

95.   Why are some beaches made of sand? Explain in a complete sentence.

96.   Late yesterday you looked north and saw a tower (like the Boar's Head tower) in this area. Near here you can see it close up. What are (were) these towers for? Use a complete sentence.

IF THE TIDE IS LOW ENOUGH, WE
MIGHT SEE THE SUNKEN FOREST AT
STONY POND. DO NOT REMOVE
ANY TREE PIECES, INCLUDING
ROOTS.

97. On the shore at the south end of Odiorne
    Point, take your final compass bearing on
    White Island Light, and record it.

98. Look up your very first compass bearing.
    How many degrees have we covered since
    the Massachusetts state line?

**PHOENIX Seacoast Backpack Resource
Pages**

Your required worksheets cover a large amount of information representing many different topics. There are four ways for you to find or develop answers.

1.   Information that has been presented in class at any time during the school year is material we expect you to know. It is generally NOT included here (except geology).

2.   Lots of written information IS included in this packet (some of it in outline form) and in the packet you received recently — containing descriptions and drawings. Read it carefully before the trip, so you'll have an idea of where to go to find specific items when you get to them on the walk.

3.   Mr. Mac, Mrs. Becker, and Mr. P (and possibly other adults) will be discussing various topics with you as we go. Listen carefully.

4.   You must PARTICIPATE in direct observation of the world around you. This is perhaps the most important of your sources. We want you to develop your ability to notice, analyze, and interpret what exists and occurs in your world.

ALL the information you will need is in one or more of the sources above. We have not attempted to include all of the information in all of the sources, so it is likely that NONE of it is in all four. That means, of course, that you'll have to read, listen, look, and think.

An example of Tides for Hampton Harbor: June 2-3

Thursday, 6/2: Low 2:42 a.m. Sunrise 5:07 a.m. Moon Phase:
    Waning crescent

High 8:36 a.m. Sunset 8:16 p.m. (new moon on June 6)

Low 3:01 p.m.

High 9:04 p.m.

Friday, 6/3: Low 3:42 a.m. Sunrise 5:06 a.m. Moon Phase:
    Waning crescent

High 9:36 a.m. Sunset 8:17 p.m.

Low 3:54 p.m.

High 9:55 p.m.

GEOLOGY

Most of this should sound very familiar to you. The southern areas of our walk will present about 2 miles of sand dunes on the upper reaches of the beach. These piles of sand have been formed by wind blowing off the water, which tends to be the strongest wind direction here, although not always the most frequent. Various plants can be found growing in sand dunes, but the most common is beach grass, whose roots help to hold the dunes in place, much as the roots of trees and other plants help to hold soil on hillsides in forests.

The sand itself is the product of weathering. The ocean waves crash down on the shore, sometimes quite violently, and have gradually broken solid rock down into large rock pieces, then smaller chunks called cobbles (as in old cobblestone streets in cities), and finally into pebbles and sand. When rocks and sand are moved around by waves and wind, they act like sandpaper, wearing away rock and eventually eroding it into these tiny pieces we call sand. If you come back to a rocky shoreline several million years from now, you will most likely find a sandy beach. On our 2-day excursion, we will be walking on rocky shores and cobble beaches, as well as on the sandy areas that people most often picture when they think of beaches.

The rock along the New Hampshire coast is of several types. Most of what you will see will be:

1. Granite, which is fairly easy to recognize with its three minerals—mica, quartz, and feldspar. Granite is an igneous rock, meaning that it is cooled and hardened magma. It is hard, but not as hard as metamorphic rocks described in 2 below.
2. Gneiss, schist, and quartzite, which are very hard rocks made from softer rocks and sometimes thick, ancient layers of mud that have been buried, then squeezed (by the tectonic forces described later here) into harder rock. These rocks are from the general type called metamorphic rock, which can be recognized by the layers and folds and swirls it usually contains. These rocks have been exposed by erosion wearing away the upper layers, leaving what we see today.
3. Basalt, which is another igneous rock. Most of the basalt we see occurs in long, usually narrow channels or stripes in the surrounding metamorphic rock. These channels are called dikes, because they look somewhat like a dike holding back water along a riverbank. They are also called intrusions (as in the root word "intrude"), because the hot, liquid rock was forced up into cracks in the metamorphic rock above it. It then cooled and hardened into the black basalt we see.

The crust of the earth is made up of about two dozen huge plates that slowly move in various directions, sometimes as much as 1 to 2 inches per year. These plates are actually floating on a thick layer of hot, liquid rock called magma. As hotter areas of magma rise up through cooler layers (still very hot), currents are created. These currents actually push the crustal plates around above them. As the plates move along the surface of the earth, they sometimes collide with each other. Several things can happen as results of these slow, but awesomely forceful collisions. Only one result, however, is very relevant to our study here: If two plates of similar size and strength hit each other head on, they will both buckle upward, so the rising land becomes mountains—like the White Mountains. This takes millions of years to happen, sometimes hundreds of millions of years.

Here at the coast, although we don't see mountains, we do see other evidence of the pressure that squeezes plates together. Much of the rock here is metamorphic rock—very hard rocks that used to be softer rocks or even layers of mud that were jammed together very hard for a long time—millions of years. Some of the rocks show "banding" in which certain minerals get packed together into rough layers. Some areas show waves of these bands going up and down in actual folds in the rocks. Imagine how strong the pressure must be to compress and fold rock!

The downward folds in the rock are called synclines, and the upward folds are called anticlines. Some anticlines and synclines are only a few inches in size; others can be many miles in length. If there are large anticlines, and the tops are gradually worn away by erosion, you will be left with deposits of rock that are bent upward toward the sky, but with sheared-off tops. There are many anticlines visible along the New Hampshire seacoast, and the Isles of Shoals have a lot also.

The long, narrow, human-made piles of cube-shaped rocks that are seen in several locations along the coast are usually called breakwaters, or jetties. They often jut out from the shore at river mouths and harbors to provide more protection for the boats at anchor in the harbor. Sometimes they are constructed along the shoreline to try to prevent erosion of the sand and the inconvenient shifting of river channels. In other locations, they are actually called "sand-retention structures" and are built at right angles to the shoreline to try to prevent down-coast movement of the sand on the beach. Without them, the beach would gradually be scoured free of much if its sand by south-flowing currents, and the tourists would not come to soak up the sun and spend money here.

This might sound unimportant, but the Hampton Beach economy depends almost totally on the tourist industry. Many people would not have jobs without the sand on these beaches!

As part of efforts to monitor tidal flow in and out of the Hampton-Seabrook estuary, the UNH Department of Ocean Engineering has placed sensors in nine locations, including on the old navigation tower at the Hampton River mouth. You'll see wires running from the cabinet down into the river. Mr. P might explain more information about this effort during the stop at the river mouth.

Another chapter in geological history that has had a substantial effect on this coastline is that of the continental glaciers in the last 20,000 years. At the height of the last ice age, this area was covered with ice between 1 and 2 miles thick. As the earth warmed up over the next 10,000 sand years, the ice gradually melted. As the ice melted, the water all ran into the world's oceans, so sea level rose approximately 220 feet and flooded the coastlines. In fact, the ocean went as far inland as the current location of Route 125 in Lee and Barrington. Durham, Madbury, and much of Lee were under water. Stratham Hill was an offshore island.

However, another shift took place, too, but more slowly. When thick glacial ice covers a huge portion of a continent, it weighs so much that it actually depresses the surface of the land a long way, because the crust is pushed down into the magma it is floating on. When the ice melts, and the weight is gone, the land eventually rises back up to a normal floating level. This is called glacial rebound. When this occurred, the ocean flowed back out some distance.

Since then, the water and land levels have varied back and forth a bit, but the world's oceans have continued to rise slowly for about the past 4,000 years. During some of the earlier periods of slightly lower sea levels, forests and salt marshes have grown and thrived in shoreline locations that are now underwater or on the water's edge, because at later times of higher water, the ocean has advanced and flooded and killed the vegetation. Thus, we can find tree stumps in a few spots, and there are several deposits of peat that are found along beaches, especially when storms temporarily wash away a shallow layer of sand on top.

ASTRONOMY AND TIDES

The earth has ocean tides because of the gravitational attraction between the moon and our planet. All objects actually exert a gravitational pull upon each other, but the attraction is not noticeable if the objects are small. However, the moon and earth are extremely large. The gravitational attraction between them holds the moon in orbit around the earth. Since about 70% of the earth is covered by oceans, we see the effect of gravitation in our high and low tides. The moon actually pulls the water a few feet toward the moon as it passes overhead. When the moon is as high in the sky as it gets, there is a high tide directly beneath it. What do you think is happening on the exactly opposite side of the earth at that time?

BIOLOGY

Most of the life science information you need is contained in the blue and tan sheets in the colored packet you have received. However, there are other items to mention:

- The most widespread dune plant was described in the beginning of the geology section.
- When marsh plants die, they decompose (rot) partially and are covered with similar vegetation from later years. As these deposits of rotting plants build up, they compress the lower layers into a dense material called peat. If the ocean rises and covers it, and the sand scours off the grasses on top, the surface becomes very slippery. Mr. P has a short story about peat. By the way, the Irish discovered hundreds of years ago that they could dig up the peat in Irish bogs and marshes, dry it, and burn it in stoves (like woodstoves) to heat their houses. They call it "turf," but it's the same stuff!
- A boar is the wild variety of a common barnyard animal, although boars tend to be rather ferocious and dangerous. They are hunted in various areas of the world.
- Speaking of hunting, what would hunters be shooting at (offshore) in a way that would bring shotgun shells floating in onto the beach? Hunters are not supposed to drop their shell casings into the water, by the way, and many don't. It is obvious, however, that some still do.
- A plaice is a type of fish—common around here—that gets its name from one aspect of its shape. The "pla" of plaice comes from the Latin "plat" and Greek "platy." What is the more common name for this fish?
- Speaking of edible creatures that live in the water, there are other tasty species hereabouts. You can see evidence, bobbing around on the water, of lots of spots where people are trying to "obtain" one of these creatures, which Mr. P. likes to call benthic seagulls, because they eat rotting things that sink to the bottom the way seagulls often scavenge on land. They are really, however, arthropods. Mainers sometime refer to them as "spiders" because they are fairly closely related.

PHYSICAL SCIENCE

Your teacher will present information about the Seabrook Station Nuclear Power Plant on the southwest side of the Hampton-Seabrook estuary. In the early part of our walk, we will walk right on top of the massive cooling tunnels from the plant. Why does a nuclear plant need cooling tunnels?

MATH

Remember the following:

- Number of degrees in a circle
- The primary compass directions
- The names for the several shapes of polyhedra (plural of polyhedron)
- The formula for finding area
- The number of minutes in an hour. (Don't laugh at that one. You'd be surprised how many adults forget this when they're figuring out durations of time.)
- How a meter compares to a yard. (We use both metric and U.S. units of measurement in your worksheets.)
- The number of feet in a yard

LANGUAGE ARTS

- Who wrote, "The Lord in his wisdom made the fly, and then forgot to tell us why?" (Nash, 1942, p. 214)
- And also, "I think that I shall never see,
  A billboard lovely as a tree,
  Indeed, unless the billboards fall,
  I'll never see a tree at all." (Nash, 1933, p. 31)
- Do you remember what is necessary to write a complete sentence?

SOCIAL STUDIES

- The Hampton River bridge does have an official name. Look for a plaque.
- Hampton Harbor does not have many large commercial fishing boats. It does, however, have large, clean fishing boats that cater to tourists. These are usually called party boats, because they carry large parties (groups) of people out on day-long or half-day fishing trips. There are smaller fishing boats and some lobster boats that operate from Hampton Harbor.

At the New Hampshire Marine Memorial, a serious activity will take place. Please listen respectfully.

- When you are talking about the branches of the military, USA does not stand for United States of America. What does it mean?
- How about USN? This is especially relevant here.
- R usually stands for "Reserve," meaning part-time service members who are called to active duty when necessary.
- MM means "merchant marine," referring to sailors and officers on commercial freight-carrying ships. They are not really in the armed forces, but during times of war, they are attacked and have to defend themselves. Many merchant ships are lost in wars.
- AAF refers to a military branch that started out as a part of another, older service branch and was separated after WWII.

- Pease Air Force Base was built in Newington and Portsmouth in the 1950s and originally named Portsmouth AFB. It was soon re-named for Captain Han Pease of Plymouth who was a bomber pilot in the Pacific in WWII.
- Listen carefully to the legend of Thorvald Ericson, who might have visited this area about 1,000 years ago. The story tells about an encounter with Indians, a resulting death and a funeral.
- There used to be many more US Coast Guard stations along our shorelines. Many have been closed for different reasons. The station at the north end of North Beach was a large three-story red and white building that was used until it was removed in the mid-1960s. When little kids (including Mr. P) hung out on the beach here, it was very exciting to see the Guardsmen take out their amphibious vehicle (traditionally called a "duck") through a beach access that no longer exists, although you can easily see where it was. The crew would drive the duck out into the water for awhile, then put it away for a few weeks. They only did this a handful of times per summer, so it was a rare treat.
- You will find several groups of small, usually brown-shingled shacks or houses along a few stretches of beach. There used to be scores and scores of them up and down the New Hampshire coast. These were "fish houses" or "fish shacks" that local fishermen used for cleaning and drying their catch and to store their equipment. As long as the buildings were used for fishing purposes, they were not taxed. Gradually, some folks gave up fishing and started to clean out their fish houses, remodel them, and live in them. At this point, the local towns started taxing them as homes, and many people gave them up. Most of the houses have been torn down, but there are a few left, being used as homes or summer cottages. Ask your teacher about their recollection of the fish houses in the early 1960s.
- In September 1942, a mine exploded underwater in Portsmouth Harbor. Mines are underwater explosives meant to protect certain areas from attack by ship. No one ever found out for sure what had caused the explosion, but there is a theory, which is unproven, so it remains a mystery. At Little Boar's Head, you will hear the story about a German U-Boat and a submarine net.
- Alvin T. Fuller was a member of a very wealthy family from Massachusetts. He was Governor of the Bay State quite a few years ago, and he owned a thriving Cadillac and Oldsmobile dealership in Boston. His family spends much of their time at the sprawling family estate just north of Little Boar's Head in North Hampton. The largest home no longer exists. It used to be at the far south end of the expansive lawn you need to measure. When the owner of the home died, the descendants did not want to pay the taxes on it, so they dismantled it about 1960.
- The first direct trans-Atlantic telegraph cable was completed in 1874. It left North America at Rye Beach, just south of Straw's point. It actually ran right through a section of drowned forest. The Cable

House still exists, just a few hundred feet inland, but it is now a private home.

- People use snowshoes in the winter. Horses used to use "bog shoes" on the marsh.
- During World War II, when German and Japanese submarines cruised up and down the coasts of the US, there were hundreds of towers built as part of the war effort. What could someone do from these towers that could not be accomplished as well from ground level? A great hint is that there were huge coastal artillery guns installed at Fort Dearborn at Odiorne Point.

GEOGRAPHY

Use your maps often. They will help you keep track of where you are and where you're going. There are various geographical terms that are mentioned in your worksheets that you can figure out as we get to them IF YOU PAY ATTENTION TO WHERE WE ARE.

- You should all know that if you look at a map of the New England coast, there is a large peninsula called Cape Cod that sticks out from the main part of Massachusetts. When you look to the south and southeast from here on a clear day, and you see a peninsula sticking out, some people (all tourists) think they're seeing Cape Cod. They're not. It's too far away. They're seeing Cape Ann, which is where Gloucester and Rockport are located.

ADDITIONAL CURRICULUM ACTIVITIES

In Chapter 5, we provided additional curriculum activities for elementary, middle, and secondary grade levels and for all subjects. In Chapter 6, we provided additional activities for elementary and secondary grade levels as well as open-ended activities that encourage divergent thinking and allow students to choose their topic and pursue it to the best of their ability. Similar divergent activities are found in Chapter 7. Because much of Chapter 8 is dedicated to examples of how to adapt the curriculum to different grade levels for all subjects, it is these divergent, open-ended assignments that I address in this section. Assignments that are open-ended allow students to work to their potential regardless of grade level. Specific criteria or rubrics can be designed by teachers at the elementary, middle, and high school levels, requiring students to work to their ability. These more creative assignments can be problem solving or theme-based and are an effective way to integrate two or more subjects in an interdisciplinary approach. The interdisciplinary approach is a critical curriculum pathway that is not only relevant in preparing students for real-world applications, it also necessitates the self-affirming alternative assessment as a way to evaluate student products. For these reasons, the open-ended assignments that promote creative and divergent thinking are a vital way to balance the curriculum approaches for students in the outdoor classroom.

ORIENTATION FOR PARENTS, STUDENTS, AND STAFF

Letters to Parents

Communication with parents is vital to the success of an Outdoor Education Program. This communication needs to be early and thorough. First, parents need to know the answers to all of the "who, what, where, and when" questions of the trip. A good letter will often be the beginning of this cooperation and participation, and a well-prepared letter that addresses parent concerns will minimize redundancy in the form of questions and/or complaints that could come from a lack of information. At the very least, you will want passive partnership and cooperation on the part of the parents. At best, you could create active participation from parents in the form of group leaders.

The following is an actual letter to parents artifact that explains who is going, what students are going to do, where they will be, and when they will arrive at specific destinations. The letter for the Phoenix seacoast backpacking trip follows:

> Dear Parents:
> To help to keep you informed of all of the paperwork we have given (or will soon give) to students about our seacoast trip, we have assembled the following list:
> - A tent/stove/cooler note (Fri 5/23)
> - A medical form and permission slip combination (Wed 5/21)
> - An equipment list (March and Wed 5/21)
> - A parent participation note, asking who can join us and when (Wed 5/21)
> - An itinerary (Wed 5/21)
> - A student behavioral contract (Wed 5/28)

Please fill out the contract, the medical form/permission slip, and if you are available for any time at all, the parent participation slip. Then gather them all, along with the fee (see hardship note below), and send the whole bundle back to us by Monday, June 2, one week before the trip.

In one of our earlier notes home, we indicated that the cost for this activity would be $20 (see hardship note below, please). This fee will pay for transportation, materials (folders, tidal shore book, and others), and a few miscellaneous items (ice refill, Seacoast Science Center admission at Odiorne). As with any ORMS field trip, if the cost is a hardship for a family, just send a confidential note to one of us, and we'll take care of the fee. No student will be left behind for lack of funds.

Thanks for your help as we've put this experience into place. We'll have a great time. Quite a few parents have already indicated that they will be joining us for part or the entire journey. If you discover at the last minute that you're able to come, just show up! We'll be glad to have you with us.

Dear Parents:

Your student has assumed the responsibility for bringing one or more of the following items for use with tent partner(s) and/or cook group members.

- A tent/stove/cooler note (Fri 5/23)
- Tent: Please set it up at home with your child during this week to confirm that you have all necessary parts, then send it to school Friday morning (6/4). Later that day we will have students set up the tents themselves on our back field to show that they know how to do this. Tents will then stay at school for loading into vehicles the following Thursday morning (6/10).
- Cook stove: Please show your child how to use the stove between now and the time of trip, then send it to school on Thursday morning (6/10) with a full tank (sufficient for two meals). Each cook group will have an adult in attendance during all operations with the stove.
- Cooler: Each cook group is allowed to bring one cooler for perishable foods. Please send it in Thursday morning (6/10) with ice or other coolant. We will be able to replenish the ice supply Thursday evening, if necessary.

If you would like to contribute a piece of firewood for our evening campfire, please send that along, too, on the morning of the trip. We will check with the Rye Fire Department for a permit.

This week would also be a good time to start pulling together the clothing and equipment necessary for this expedition, so students don't have to run around too much that last week, driving you all crazy trying to find things. Students received a complete equipment list several weeks ago, and we have included one here for you.

As always, thanks for your assistance. We couldn't do this without major parent help.

Equipment List

Along with the letter to parents should be an equipment list of important items that students need to gather before the trip. These recommendations should be thorough and should "err on the side of caution." The following is the list that we used:

Phoenix seacoast backpack equipment list (daytime)

Clothing/equipment/food to be carried in backpack while hiking:

- Shorts
- Short-sleeve shirt
- Sneakers or running shoes
- Socks, with spare pair
- Underwear, with spare pair
- Long-sleeve shirt or sweatshirt or sweater or fleece jacket
- Rain jacket that really repels water (also acts as windbreaker)
- Long pants; rain pants or wind pants if available
- Winter hat
- Sandals for tide pools (Tevas, etc.)
- Sunscreen and insect repellent
- Tissues (a few)
- Sunglasses
- Ball cap or similar hat
- Worksheets and compass from teachers; pencils/pens of your own
- Food and drink for one day at a time
- Small plastic bag for your trash, two 1-gallon-size food storage bags for wet clothing water (at least one liter)
- Band-aids
- Camera (Optional)

If the weather permits us to stow a few items with the overnight gear, we'll let you know that before we start out.

Overnight clothing/equipment/food to be stowed in vehicle for transport to Abenaqui Country Club:

- Clean pairs of clothing above
- Towel
- Soap; any other necessary personal items (perhaps comb, brush, deodorant) washcloth

- Toothbrush and toothpaste
- Flashlight with spare battery and bulb
- Sleeping bag
- Sleeping pad
- Small pillow if you want (you can make pillow from clothing; I'll show you), stuffed bear, moose, penguin, iguana (mandatory for parent chaperones)
- A small amount of duct tape
- *Tent rain fly, and all necessary stakes, poles, ropes, etc.; plastic ground cloth
- *Camp stove or backpacking stove, with full tank of gas and any necessary equipment
- *Cookware and utensils, can opener; soap and sponge to clean dishes; another small plastic trash bag
- *Food for (1) evening meal, (2) breakfast, (3) lunch second day

Starred items will be discussed in more detail during the next few weeks. All necessary medications will be coordinated by nurse, teachers, parents, students. Leave valuables at home!

Optional: tennis ball or similar, frisbee, but not lacrosse sticks, baseball bats, hockey sticks, etc.

PLEASE LABEL ALL EQUIPMENT AND CLOTHING.

DO NOT BRING: Generator (someone asked us this last year); knife, except butter knife type, unless you are an adult; matches or other fire-starter, unless you are an adult; and music of any type. We want kids to be together, not isolated.

Cell phones and a first aid kit should always be on hand for teachers on any outdoor classroom experience in case of emergency.

Permission Slip and Medical Release

The permission slip and medical release form should always be pre-approved by the school district's legal officer.

GENERAL HEALTH INFORMATION/MEDICAL RELEASE

PLEASE BE AS OPEN AS POSSIBLE ABOUT YOUR STUDENT'S MEDICAL NEEDS AND RESPOND TO THE FOLLOWING, ELABORATING WHERE NECESSARY. THIS FORM IS CONFIDENTIAL AND IS SEEN ONLY BY THOSE WHO WILL BE RESPONSIBLE FOR YOUR CHILD WHILE AWAY FROM SCHOOL.

1. Student name: _____

2. Parent(s) name: _____

3. Home phone: _____ Business phone: _____

4. Does your child have any:

Medication allergies?_____ If yes, explain:_____

Food allergies?_____If yes, explain:_____

Other allergies?_____ If yes, explain:_____

5. Does your child have any special diet requirements?_____

If yes, be specific: _____

6. Please provide date of last tetanus booster: _____

7. Medications needed on trip:

Name of medication:_____ Dosage: _____

Times to be administered:_____As needed:_____

Reason for medication:_____

8. Phoenix teachers have my permission to administer Tylenol to my child
   at my child's request in case of illness: Yes _____ No _____

It is policy that no medications will be dispensed unless they are in the
original marked container. Medications must be given to the teacher by
the parent prior to departure and not packed in luggage.
   In the event of a medical emergency, I/we give permission to the
supervising teacher to secure proper treatment for my/our child. (Every
attempt will be made to contact you prior to such a decision.)

Parent Signature: _____Date: _____

Permission Slip

I/we give my/our student, _____,
permission to participate in the Seacoast Hike on May 20 through May 21.
I/we recognize that there are possible hazards (for example: rough terrain,
cold and/or wet weather) associated with the trip. I/we expect that the
teachers and trip leaders will take reasonable precautions to ensure the
safety of my/our student.

Please list phone numbers where you may be reached in case of emergency throughout the period of the morning of May 20, 2002 through approximately 5:00 p.m. on May 21, 2002:

Parent Signature:_____Date: _____

Leader's Itinerary

Responsible leaders are necessary for the success of an outdoor classroom expedition. These leaders become responsible for the small groups of students from the beginning to the end of the outing. They take attendance, monitor academic work in the field, and generally keep the group functioning as a team. Good group leaders can be recruited from dependable parents, community leaders, school board members, school administrators, fellow teachers, student teachers, teaching interns, university volunteers, and trusted older students.

First, each leader needs a trail map that shows distances and elevations. They also need to be oriented to the curriculum objectives and the "who, what, where, and when" questions of the trip. This orientation could be accomplished in the form of a leader's itinerary. The leader's itinerary is a chronological sequence of events with notes about what the leader might expect in terms of student questions and concerns. This enables the leader to anticipate and troubleshoot any problems that might arise, ranging from backpack and equipment difficulties to curriculum activities and sights not to be missed. Informed leaders are critical to get the groups from one point to another intact and functioning as a team. Once the groups have arrived at these points, the overall expedition leaders can address curriculum issues with the whole group, thus reinforcing the group leaders.

The following is the leader's confirmation form and itinerary that is used for the ORMS sixth grade seacoast trip.

Dear Parent:

Your son/daughter has suggested to us that you might be able to accompany us on the upcoming seacoast trip (date). To help with our planning, please indicate your availability, sign below, and we will accept this as confirmation you will be joining us.

Please send the complete form to school by Thursday, June 3. This will allow us time to set up volunteer responsibilities. If you need any information, feel free to contact us. If you would like to volunteer, please sign up below.

Thanks for your enthusiastic support!

The Phoenix Team

I, _____ will be accompanying

the Phoenix Team on their Seacoast Trip as follows: _____

_____ 1. Crazy as the teachers—on the whole trip: 6/10 6:30 a.m. to
6/11 5:30 p.m.!

_____ 2. Single day commitment—State which day: _____

_____ 3. Single day commitment—Two days, no nights, I like my sleep!

_____ 4. Night only, can sleep through the job on Tuesday!

_____ 5. Other: _____

Parent Signature: _____ Date: _____

The following is the Phoenix seacoast backpack itinerary.

Prior to Trip:

Thursday, June 3: Due date for paperwork: permission slip, medical forms, etc.

Friday, June 4: Tents to school to be set up and checked. They will stay at ORMS.

All other equipment (sleeping bags, coolers, stoves, etc.) arrives Thursday, June 10.

Day 1: Thursday, June 10

6:15–6:30 a.m.	Arrive ORMS to load gear into vehicles, kids into buses
7:15 a.m.	Leave ORMS
8:30 a.m.	Start hike at NH/MA state line, after pit stop at Hampton Beach
10:30 a.m.	Arrive Seashell - Hampton Beach
12:45 p.m.	Arrive Hampton North Beach at Comfort Station - lunch, tide pools
2:00 p.m.	Leave North Beach
3:30 p.m.	North Hampton Beach
4:00 p.m.	Little Boar's Head
5:00 p.m.	Abenaqui Country Club—Tenting Area
5:00-7:00 p.m.	Set up, eat, clean up
7:15-8:30 p.m.	Campfire on beach (conditions permitting)
9:00 p.m.	Prepare for bedtime
9:30 p.m.	Lights out!

Day 2: Friday, June 11

6:00 a.m.	Wake up
6–7:30 a.m.	Eat, clean up, dismantle camp
7:30 a.m.	Police the area, inspect
8:00 a.m.	Resume northward trek with smiling faces
10:00 a.m.	Group Photo on Mysterious Wood Structure, north side Straw's Point
11:30 a.m.	Rye Harbor State Park (probable lunch)
1:30 p.m.	Concord Point
2:00 p.m.	Wallis Sands
3:00 p.m.	Arrive south end of Odiorne Point SP
3:00-4:30 p.m.	Visit Seacoast Science Center at Odiorne (tentative)
4:30 p.m.	Prepare to board buses
5:00 p.m.	Leave Odiorne to Return to ORMS
5:30-6:00 p.m.	Arrive ORMS

THE ONLY DEFINITE TIME IS 6:30 a.m. THURSDAY. ALL OTHERS ARE APPROXIMATE, SUBJECT TO WEATHER AND OTHER FACTORS.

The following is the addenda for parents who were unable to attend the Seacoast backpack trip parent meeting:

1. For payment: checks payable to ORMS

2. We are looking for shuttle drivers and cargo vehicle/drivers.

   Cargo vehicles and drivers are needed to carry gear (tents, stoves, sleeping bags, etc.) to Abenaqui Thursday morning (unless you want to drive the vehicle to work for the day and bring it to Abenaqui at 5:00 p.m., which we have had people do in the past) and leave the vehicle for us to open up at 5:00 p.m. The next morning we will need to reload and drive the vehicle to Odiorne (or back to Durham for unloading at 5:30 p.m.).

   Shuttle drivers are needed because we have parents who will have cars at the beach and will need to be driven from the car drop point (Abenaqui) to the walk start point to join students Thursday a.m. A sim-

ilar need will exist on Friday a.m. The time commitment here is fairly
brief (2–3 hours).

If you are able to help out in any of these ways, please let us know. Thanks.

PROGRAM EVALUATION

Every outdoor classroom expedition and program can benefit from being
evaluated. I designed a comprehensive evaluation plan for the Outdoor
Education Program at the ORMS for Professor Roland Kimball, chairman
of the Education Department at the UNH for a graduate course in Program
Evaluation and School Administration. The following is a summary of that
program evaluation.

ORMS Outdoor Education Program Evaluation

An evaluation of the Outdoor Education Program had been completed in several areas. The curriculum assignments were graded as the students did background preparations, recorded observations, and wrote conclusions about
each trip. The academic achievement of individual students and group work
were documented by their teachers. Program accomplishments were reported publicly to students of education from UNH and Brandeis University, in
local newspapers, and in other published articles. Documentation of program
effectiveness consisted of slide presentations, print montages, news captioned
pictures and articles, parent testimonials, student journals, a school board
award, students narratives, student and professional newspaper articles, and
presentations of the program goals and activities.

Assessment of Goals/Activities

The validity of the program's effectiveness was determined by gathering
comments from teachers, parents, students, principals, and teacher education program director Mike Andrew.

Expert Opinion

Dwight Webb, professor in counseling, participated in a 2-day overnight
backpacking trip and later published the following article in *The Humanist
Educator* (American Personnel and Guidance Association, 1980).

Outdoor Science Adventure

As part of the science curriculum, a unique outdoor education program is being offered to all 150 seventh-grade boys and girls at the Oyster River Middle School in Durham, New Hampshire. Jim Jelmberg, a middle school science teacher, conceived this idea 6 years ago and now, along with 17 staff members and with support from parents, combines science with self-concept. These overnight programs include backpacking, rappelling, and cross-country skiing, as initiative adventures which enable students to transport themselves to varied natural habitats from New Hampshire's seacoast to its White Mountains.

Two Assumptions:

Jelmberg's outdoor education is based on two assumptions. First, the program provides a positive bonding for students, teachers, and parents. Three goals in this first assumption are instruction, adventure, and mutual understanding. Instruction in the "outdoor classroom" attempts to integrate life, earth, and physical science activities. Students and parents are briefed with background information before each trip, observations are recorded during the expedition, and conclusions are written afterward. The adventure component takes place when the students transport themselves, and their own gear, across wilderness terrain. These adventure initiatives, particularly rock climbing, instill confidence, trust, and self-reliance that become so important to students who face more subtle, but continuing academic and social challenges. From the outset students are assured that they do not have to be athletic; all they have to do is to try.

The third goal is reached when students, teachers, parents, and administrators work together outside of the school building. While hiking, cooking, and investigating their natural environment, the whole person becomes observable, roles are less fixed, and this leads to increased mutual understanding. Student groups, with teachers and parent leaders, are heterogeneously balanced and formed randomly from all sections of a grade level. These smaller groups work together in all problem solving, from rappelling rock faces and mending broken backpacks to meal and shelter preparation. Cooperation, sharing, and mutual help become essential as students experience different habitats, seasons, and initiatives. All of this working together serves to strengthen peer relationships between community and school.

The second assumption is founded in the program goal that students will experience success, and that their concepts of self will be more positive as will their attitudes about their natural environment and academic assignments.

Teacher and Student Responses

To give the readers another example of how these expeditions can be adjusted and modified to a different grade level, below are both teacher and student responses to a reporter for *The Transcript*, a New Hampshire seacoast newspaper, after the completion of the first trip for sixth graders.

"This is the first year that we have involved sixth graders in the Outdoor Education Program," commented science teacher and originator of the program, Jim Jelmberg. "As anticipated, they did very well with both the curriculum activities and with the hiking itself." Each student group worked very well together as a team," Jelmberg said, "and had the backup of parents who went along on the trips and were active participants." Jelmberg said the trip was adjusted to sixth graders and their group hike was several miles shorter than the former seventh grade hike.

Science teacher, John Parsons said, "Special thanks should go to members of the Abenaqui Golf Club in Rye for letting groups camp on their grounds and for generously providing facilities."

One enthusiastic student who took part in the trip was Dan Wittner. According to Wittner, "It was fun hiking along the beach. Camping was great fun. We got to choose who we wanted to camp with. We cooked our own meals on a Coleman stove and learned cooperation." Wittner added, "You should have tasted our macaroni and cheese."

Reflecting back on the trip, sixth grader Kristen Limber said, "I learned all about the ice age and where the rocks came from. The trip was fun, and we got ten minutes to go swimming at Wallis Sands Beach." However, it was great to get to Odiorne Point and take off my backpack. Next time I'm traveling lighter."

Sea-Fever

"I must go down to the seas again, for
the call of the running tide
Is a wild call and a clear call that may
not be denied;
And all I ask is a windy day with the
white clouds flying,
And the flung spray and the blown
spume, and the sea gulls crying."

—*John Masefield*

REFERENCES

Masefield, J. (1962). Sea fever. In *Poems* (p. 20). New York: MacMillan.

Nash, O. (1933). Song of the open road. In L. Smith & I. Ebeustadt (Eds.), *I would-n't have missed it* (p. 31). Boston: Little, Brown.

Nash, O. (1942). The fly. In L. Smith & I. Ebeustadt (Eds.), *I wouldn't have missed it* (p. 214). Boston: Little, Brown.

9

OUTDOOR EDUCATION AT THE UNIVERSITY LEVEL OF LEARNING

Jon McLaren

It also follows that all thinking involves a risk. Certainty cannot be guaranteed in advanced. The invasion of the unknown is of the nature of an adventure.

—Dewey (1944)

All my life people have asked the question, directly or indirectly, "Why in the hell do you climb mountains?"
I can't explain this to other people. I love the physical exertions. I love the wind. I love the storms. I love the fresh air. I love the companionship in the outdoors. I love the reality. I love the change. I love the rejuvenating spirit. I love to feel oneness with nature. I'm hungry; I enjoy eating. I get thirsty; I enjoy the clear water. I enjoy being warm when it's cold outside. All those simple things are extremely enjoyable because, gosh, you're feeling them, you're living them, your senses are really feeling. I can't explain it.

—Petzoldt (1976)

Outdoor education programs have rapidly expanded, almost unchecked, for the past 20 years on college campuses. This has been a good thing for creativity, program development, and integrating of experiential education models into varying aspects of college campuses.

There are so many diverse programs performing countless duties that analyzing them, even a few specific institutions, would prove ineffective toward the goals of this chapter and the book. This chapter accomplishes two things: (a) explaining the more popular program models used for experiential education in higher education, and (b) detailing the University of Maryland's program model to serve as a resource guide.

Outdoor education programs are as diverse as the professors, administrators, and students who oversee them. These programs on college campuses most often fall into one of three program models: clubs, academic units, or recreation programs.

CLUBS

One of the earliest forms of organized outdoor education was through the emergence of outing clubs on college campuses in the early 20th century. Two of the more famous clubs, the Dartmouth Outing Club and the Hoofers from UW-Madison are still active today. Clubs are the most prolific and diverse types of outdoor education form on campuses today. Universities are very good at encouraging students with similar interests to form and maintain clubs. It is, after all, great for campus marketing to show that list of 400 student clubs to prospective students.

Student-run outdoor clubs can be found on almost all U.S. college and university campuses in the United States. Student clubs range from small hiking clubs, to clubs that take international expeditions. These clubs get funding from membership dues, student government allocations, and/or departmental dollars. Clubs most often embody the old outdoor education tradition of "common adventure." Common adventure models can best be described as friends getting together to do a certain activity. There is usually no leader, group gear is shared, and everybody chips in for food and gas. Although some clubs maintain this common adventure model, others are more structured with elected officers (president, vice president, etc.), hold regular meetings, maintain an inventory of equipment, and publish a semester calendar of programs. Although the structure and programming of most clubs is casual, others are formal and para-professional. At many campuses, a structured outdoor club is the official outdoor program for the campus community. When this is the case, more oversight is given to the club to ensure consistent programming.

The University of Maryland has several outdoor clubs. They include the mountain biking, surfing, and Terrapin Trail Club. The Trail Club holds weekly meetings, elects officers, manages its own inventory, and runs its own trips. The Trail Club is completely independent from the Outdoor Recreation Program. The two compliment each other quite well—offering a vast array of trips between the two. Often overshadowed by academic programs, our outdoor recreation centers and student-run clubs provide an important outlet for those wanting to keep outdoor activities purely recreational.

Because of the varied programs and populations served, clubs often suffer from a lack of oversight. It is common to find trips are led by untrained and ill-equipped students. Although many steadfastly hold to this common adventure model, I feel standardization holds the key to evolving programs both big and small into better managed organizations that will be able to serve students more effectively.

ACADEMIC UNITS

Almost as common as having an outdoor club is finding a canoeing or rock climbing physical education (PE) course in a school's catalog. Similarly, academic outdoor education programs run the gamut from activity class offerings to undergraduate and graduate degrees. Although most universities will have some type of outdoor skills course; few have the expertise in teaching the most crucial aspect of outdoor education within the academic context— outdoor leadership.

I think that outdoor education's true calling is in academia—it is here where true learning can occur. This is not to say that a PE climbing class is not valuable, it is a vital offering. Activity classes alone leave a void where other tenets of outdoor education and leadership could fill them. Often lacking in outdoor education courses are the fundamental tenets to outdoor leadership and social change—empowerment, environmental awareness, civic engagement, and critical thinking skills.

Although activity courses are usually found in PE departments, outdoor education course offerings and entire programs are housed within a variety of academic departments. Colorado State University's Natural Resources Management Program houses its outdoor classes; Southern Illinois University at Carbondale has a Recreation Department within the College of Education that offers an outdoor recreation major and an administration master's degree. Outdoor education majors often prepare students for work in the municipal parks and recreation fields. This diverse housing of outdoor education programs brings a wide array of skills and backgrounds into the classrooms for the students to benefit from. There are a number of places to find descriptions and comparisons of academic programs. There are a tremendous amount of quality programs; I would like to mention a few here.

Garrett College, in western Maryland, runs a 2-year associate's degree program called the Adventuresports Institute. Over the years, this program has maintained a level of professionalism and forward-thinking that is hard to come by. This program not only aims to teach students; but also to train them as guides. The Adventuresports Institute mission statement follows:

> The mission of the Adventuresports Institute® is to expand opportunities to experience the manifold benefits of safe participation in adventure recreation; to educate and credential a workforce of skilled and environmentally sensitive professionals who can occupy positions of responsibility within the field of adventure recreation; and to support aspirations for economic development through the adventure industry. (www.adventuresportsi.org)

The Adventuresports Institute has partnered with Frostburg State University for those students who wish to transfer to complete a bachelor's degree in parks and recreation. Additionally, plans are underway to construct an Adventuresports Institute training facility.

Prescott College is widely known as having one of the strongest outdoor education bachelor's and master's degree programs. Prescott's mission states the following:

> It is the mission of Prescott College to educate students of diverse ages and backgrounds to understand, thrive in, and enhance our world community and environment. We regard learning as a continuing process and strive to provide an education that will enable students to live productive lives while achieving a balance between self-fulfillment and service to others. Students are encouraged to think critically and act ethically with sensitivity to both the human community and the biosphere. Our philosophy stresses experiential learning and self-direction within an interdisciplinary curriculum. (www.prescott.edu)

With true interdisciplinary course offerings, a fundamental commitment to experiential education and coursework that emphasizes out of classroom learning, Prescott has become a model for all programs. Prescott College not only balances academics and adventure, they are interwoven together as one.

OUTDOOR RECREATION PROGRAMS

The third way outdoor education manifests itself on college campuses is through outdoor recreation programs. Outdoor recreation programs are almost always housed in campus recreation departments through the division of student affairs/student life or they are run out of athletic departments. Outdoor recreation programs are highly structured and run by one or more full-time professional staff members. A common misconception among students and professionals alike is that outdoor recreation professionals need a degree in such a field. Although outdoor recreation professionals require technical expertise in one or more areas, these hard skills transfer to only a small part of the administrative job. Coursework or majors in communication, psychology, business, and education prepare students more holistically for an administrative job. Field experience and certifications are an excellent way to compliment one's academic work.

Outdoor recreation programs across the country will all have one or more of the following components: student staff, equipment rental center, rock climbing facility, challenge course, bike shop, and adventure trip program.

Student Staff

Most often, the core of any outdoor program are the student staff members who serve a variety of roles. Students might be volunteer or paid staff, depending on the organizational structure of the individual program. Maryland's outdoor program is run by 60 to 80 paid student staff each year. The program employs three full-time staff members (director, challenge course coordinator, and business manager) to hire, train, and supervise students and to provide direction to the organization.

Staff positions at Maryland include rental desk agent, bike shop mechanics, trip leader, climbing wall staff, and challenge course facilitator. In addition, each program area has student supervisors.

Equipment Rental Center

Collegiate rental centers are often very similar to one another. The largest variables are the size of the center and the inventory. Most centers will have the following equipment for rent: tents, sleeping bags, stoves, and backpacks. Programs in specific geographic areas will often have specialized equipment for rent, such as skis and snowboards, rafts, winter camping, mountaineering equipment, and mountain bikes. In addition to offering rental equipment to the university community, rental centers will have books and maps for customers to use. Maryland's outdoor center is 5,000 square feet, and includes the following rooms: equipment storage, bike shop, two offices, bathroom, and rental/resource center that also serves as a meeting room.

Rock Climbing Facility

Rock climbing walls are becoming a standard fixture on college campuses. With a variety of installation techniques and endless design possibilities, climbing wall vendors have a wall to suit any budget. The standard operating plans for collegiate climbing walls include having student staff belay for climbers and give belay tests. Schools require that students pass a safety test in order to belay. A rock climbing facility greatly increases the responsibility of the program risk manager, as numerous waivers and inspections need to be properly documented and stored. Properly trained student staff, detailed inspection reports, and keeping up with trends in the industry will enable a professional to enjoy and expand climbing wall programs.

Challenge Course

The challenge course is perhaps the most likely aspect of outdoor education to make a direct connection with the academic side of campus. Year after year, more college campuses are seeing the benefit of a challenge course. Traditionally, schools with off-campus land might host the course off-site. Recently, schools have constructed challenge courses on the main campus. Both the University of Wisconsin-Eau Claire and the University of Maryland have courses that are showcased on campus.

Consisting of both low and high elements, the challenge course is utilized by various teams, classes, and student groups on campus and various businesses, schools, and nonprofits from off-campus. The University of Maryland has a high course and extensive low course in the same facility at our outdoor rock climbing facility. The facility is directly behind the Campus Recreation Center, one of the showcase buildings on campus. The challenge course employees 25 students, each of whom have completed a semester-long training program. Fiscal year 2005 saw 59 groups on the course and gross revenue of more than $100,000. Maryland is finding the challenge course to be a consistent revenue-generating program in addition to providing a valuable service to the local community.

Bike Shop

A growing number of schools with outdoor recreation centers are adding a campus bike shop. A campus bike shop helps promote bike commuting, physical fitness, and can help generate revenue for local bike shops. The University of Maryland's bike shop is a true experiential education laboratory. Paid student bike mechanics oversee the shop, while customers learn for themselves how to fix their own bikes. The shop is free of charge, does not sell parts, and customers work on their own bikes. It is common to find an experienced cyclist working on his or her own bike while a staff member is showing someone basic maintenance for their bike. Keeping the grassroots feeling alive, the shop offers a large "free parts" cabinet where used, but still working, parts are for the taking. In addition to teaching customers about their bikes, bike shop staff maintains the rental inventory of mountain bikes.

Adventure Trip Program

The adventure trip program can be the most time-consuming of all outdoor education components. The most important part of a trip program is the trip leaders; these students need to be matched with the mission and vision of the program. In addition, their skills need to be developed to fulfill the needs of the program. Although many students who apply to be guides will have valuable outdoor experience, few will be ready as outdoor leaders. For consistency and risk management's sake, Maryland usually accepts into its trip leader program students who have more leadership experience and maturity than technical experience. The proper trip leader training program will give students all the technical expertise they need while advancing their leadership and management skills. The University of Maryland employs 25 trip leaders, each of whom complete 1 year of training prior to leading trips.

Compared with other programs, the trip program serves a small number of students. About 200 students go on trips throughout the year. Day trips include rock climbing, caving, hiking, white water rafting, and sea kayaking. Overnight trips include backpacking, sea kayaking, canoe camping, and climbing/caving combination trips.

A successful model for integration academics and adventure has been the emergence of wilderness orientation programs. Often a joint venture between the outdoor recreation program and another academic or orientation department, wilderness orientation programs strive to ease the transition of first-year students to a college campus by (a) creating a safe atmosphere where lasting friendships can be made, (b) integrating academics and adventure by using faculty and staff leaders on the trip, and (c) expos-

CAMPUS RECREATION SERVICES

ing students to outdoor recreation as a healthy lifestyle activity. Maryland's wilderness orientation program is Terrapin Expeditions for New and Transfer Students (TENTS). TENTS trips average 3 to 6 days in length and offer a variety of outdoor opportunities.

UNIVERSITY OF MARYLAND TRIP PROGRAM

It is my firm belief that no book or manual is able to act as a comprehensive training tool. What follows is an overview of the Maryland trip leader training (TLT) program; reading this material will not make one a qualified guide. Farideh Sadeghin, Kate Ver Ploeg, and Emily Axelbaum assisted in compiling the following resources.

Trip Philosophy and Goals

The trip program was created in 1997 to give the students, faculty, and staff of the University of Maryland an opportunity to participate in outdoor recreation trips. Outdoor Recreation Center trips seek to provide the students, faculty, and staff of the University of Maryland with adventure-based, experiential education programs. The program is committed to providing low-cost opportunities to participate in and experience the natural environment. The program is dedicated to preserving the environment and will promote the responsible use of natural areas. The program strives to accomplish the following:

1. Teach people basic outdoor skills.
2. Enhance environmental awareness.
3. Introduce people to "Adventure."
4. Develop student staff into fully functioning outdoor leaders in a variety of skill-based areas.

There is an immense amount of knowledge that can be learned through trip leading. This material is merely the tip of the iceberg, and is catered to the program at the University of Maryland. Information you will learn, but is not in this resource includes:

- Wilderness medicine (Wilderness first and [WFA]//wukderbess furst resoibder [WFR]) Swift Water Rescue
- Stove repair

- Top rope set-ups
- Leave no trace (LNT)
- Map/compass

Expectations

Staff

All trip leaders are expected to be able to do the following:
- Set up top-ropes and lead a climbing trip.
- Lead a 3-day backpacking trip.
- Lead caving day trips.

Every trip leader should then choose two other activities in which to specialize and inform the ORC Director in the fall of Year 2 training. Each trip leader will then pursue more extensive and in-depth knowledge for each of these two chosen activities. This is accomplished through personal adventures and outside reading. The goal is to become a skilled specialist in each activity. To become "head trip leader," trip leaders must log personal adventure hours and complete the requirements listed on the specific activity sheets located in the staff binders in the ORC.

Activities to specialize in include:

- Sea Kayaking
- Snowboarding
- Mountain Biking
- Road Biking

Other expectations include:

- Arriving prepared and on time to trip meetings and trips.
- Attending all mandatory staff meetings and functions, unless ORC Director is notified in advance of a valid excuse.
- RESPECT. It's mandatory. Treat all participants, other trip leaders, and folks encountered along the way with appropriate language and actions.
- Alcohol, drugs, and tobacco products = not allowed

Program

Trip leaders can expect to gain a thorough understanding of wilderness travel skills and outdoor leadership, as well as a solid training in the introductory basics of backpacking, climbing, sea kayaking, caving, and LNT.

Trip leaders will have access to the ORC library resources and outdoor equipment for use on personal trips. Ultimately, the ORC and its trip leader training program are here for your development. The more you put into it, the more you'll get out of it.

Staff Evolution

Year 1: Training

Fall: Endurance Trekh—2 days
　　　Climbing—1 day
　　　Backpacking—3 days
　　　Sea Kayaking—3 days
　　　Caving—1 day

Spring: Wilderness First Responder—9 days
　　　Spring Break Trip—6 days
　　　Backpacking II—3 days
　　　Sea Kayaking II—2 days
　　　Climbing II—1 day
　　　Driver Training
　　　Personal Adventures

Year 2: Training: Assistant Trip Leader

Fall: August Canada training—12 days
　　　Assistant trip leader on participant trips
　　　Advanced rock set-ups
　　　Driver training

Spring: WFR—9 days in June (if not in Year 1)
　　　Assistant trip leader on participant trips
　　　Spring break trip

PERSONAL ADVENTURES—In sun, rain, snow, and every other season.

Year 3: Beyond . . .

　　　Lead ORC participant trips
　　　Head leaders plan and lead TLT trips with Jon

Games for the Field

Climbing

Do you have a participant who is super good and needs more of a challenge? Have him or her try climbing blindfolded!

Caving

Zen Counting. Have everyone turn off their headlamps and sit completely in the dark. Someone starts counting with "1." Then someone else says "2," and so on. The point, however, is to reach 20 without anyone saying the same number at the same time. Therefore, if two people say "10," at the same time, then you must start over. It's tricky especially because nobody can see who will speak next!

Backpacking

Try something new on the trail! You'll need a roll of masking tape and a pen. Think of different people for participants and other trip leaders to be, write it on the tape, and stick it on the person's backpack. For example, you could make someone "Elvis." Everyone sees that that person is Elvis and treats them like that, giving them hints while hiking. The object is to guess who you are! Don't limit yourself to famous people. You can use characteristics as well. Other good ideas are: emits horrible gas, can't stop hiccuping, has third eye, or is pregnant with an alien baby.

Be creative and make up you own games for the trail and trips!

THE FOUNDATION

The exhilaration of outdoor adventures comes from the unpredictability of the wilderness. One of the reasons why we keep heading back out on the trail is because of those unexpected moments of natural awe—a bear sighting, a spectacular sunrise, a shooting star. In the woods, we see what we look like without a daily shower or a clean outfit. We realize the edge of our endurance when we must hike all day in the rain, test out the mettle of our leadership when overtaken by a thunderstorm on a ridge, or find our creativity when confronted with a broken sleeping bag on a cold night. Each adventure is unique in its memorable highlights and learning experiences.

However, although the unpredictable keeps us coming back for more, the success of our trips is largely dependent on our possession of solid skills, our respect for the environment we work in, and our cohesion as a group as we travel.

Outdoor Leadership

A few thoughts on leadership.

> Leadership is not magnetic personality—that can just as well be a glib tongue. It is not "making friends and influencing people"—that is flattery. Leadership is lifting a person's vision to higher sights, the raising of a person's performance to a higher standard, the building of a personality beyond its normal limitations. (Ducker 2003, p. 121)

> A leader is best when people barely know he exists, not so good when people obey and acclaim him, worse when they despise him. . . . But of a good leader who talks little when his work is done, his aim fulfilled, they will say, "We did it ourselves." (Tzu, 2006, p. 94)

> I start with the premise that the function of leadership is to produce more leaders, not more followers. (Nader, 2000, p. 341)

> *Webster's II Dictionary* defines leader as: "To show the way . . . "

Outdoor leadership takes it outside. We use the natural environment to foster a new knowledge and appreciation of ourselves, each other, and our natural world. By facilitating a better understanding and appreciation of the natural world and the individual, we seek to inspire our participants to new levels of environmental activism, outdoor activity, and self-challenge. We can inspire people by teaching them how to paddle, cheering them on along the trail, or pointing out a wildflower. We try to promote and provide positive outdoor experiences for every participant we take into the woods. Whether it is a day hike or a month-long course, leadership remains one of the biggest factors in determining the success of a trip and the impact we have on participants.

> Twenty years from now you will be more disappointed by the things that you didn't do than by the ones you did do.
> So throw off the bowlines. Sail away from the safe harbor.
> Catch the trade winds in your sails.
> Explore. Dream. Discover.
> —Mark Twain

SKILLS

As trip leaders, you will directly affect the experience each participant has by how you design, plan, and execute the trip. The skills an outdoor leader must possess are multiple and various. They can be simplified into three traditional categories: hard skills, soft skills, and meta skills (Priest & Gass, 1997).

Hard skills are those that are easily trained and easily assessed, such as technical ability, backcountry medical knowledge, and leave no trace skills.

Soft skills are more difficult to train and assess than hard skills. They focus more on working with people in the field, including activity or trip organization, instruction, and facilitation skills.

Meta skills connect and integrate the hard and soft skills, making the outdoor leader effective at exhibiting all skills. Meta skills include communication, a flexible leadership style, critical problem solving and decision making, judgment, and ethical thinking.

Important: No set of skills is more valued than the other two. A successful outdoor leader must possess skills from all three.

UNCLE JONNY'S FOUR RULES TO LIVE BY:

1. Show up.
2. Pay attention.
3. Do your best.
4. Don't sweat the outcome.

John Graham (1997), a seasoned mountaineer and author of *Outdoor Leadership*, has collected a list of what people expect from leaders. People expect good leaders to:

1. Be good at planning and organizing.
2. Possess self-confidence.
3. Be technically confident (this includes first aid, route finding, and weather knowledge).
4. Be caring of others.
5. Make good decisions.
6. Be trustworthy.
7. Communicate well.
8. Inspire others to be at their best.
9. Build and maintain morale.

10. Be good teachers.
11. Be able to deal with different people.
12. Be good at conflict resolution.
13. Build and guide teams.
14. Anticipate problems and deal with them proactively.

Outdoor leadership is learned through practice by getting out there and doing it. However, a responsible leader never heads out ill-prepared. Although ultimately you must discover and develop your own personal leadership style, there is a wealth of knowledge to be gained from others' trials and errors. If you're interested in learning more, check out the books and other resources in the Outdoor Recreation Center. Here are a few suggested readings to get you started:

- Outdoor Leadership by John Graham
- Soft Paths
- All *Leave No Trace* materials. *Leave No Trace* (LNT) information can be found at www.lnt.org

- *Secrets of Warmth*
- *Wilderness First Responder* (WFR) books
- *Everyday Wisdom: 1001 Expert Tips for Hikers*
- *FLOW: Psychology of Peak Performance*

Plan Ahead and Prepare

In other words, all the work we do as trip leaders before the pre-trip meeting.

- Know the area regulations, order the permits, and check the weather.
- Double check the med-kits, bring extra clothing and extra food, and pack matches or a lighter.
- In the backcountry, keep groups as small as possible; avoid high use seasons.
- Repackage food to minimize waste (and cut down on weight).
- Bring a map and compass.

Travel and Camp on Durable Surfaces

- Durable surfaces are established trails and campsites, rock, gravel, dry grasses, or snow.

- Always walk single file through on-trail puddles and mud, rather than widening the original trail or creating a new one.
- Camp at least 200 feet from lakes and streams.
- Find a campsite; don't make one. And keep it small, where there's little vegetation.
- In the backcountry:
  - ✓ Disperse use to prevent the creation of campsites and trails.
  - ✓ Avoid places where impacts are just beginning so that re-growth can take place.

Dispose of Waste Properly

Pack it in, and pack it out—food, litter, toilet paper, and hygiene products.

- Do a sweep of each campsite and rest stop before you leave.
- Pooping: Dig a cat-hole 6–8-inches deep (about height of a trowel blade), at least 200 feet from water, camp, and trails. Cover when finished. Do not use trowel to do anything except dig the original hole.
- Dishes: Eat or pack out all food particles. Carry water 200 feet away from streams or lakes, use small amounts of biodegradable soap. Scatter strained dishwater.

(Questions about the Partner Poop? Contact Jamison Williams or Kurt Pfund).

Leave What you Find

Self-explanatory. Look, don't touch. No architecture.

Minimize the Use of Campfire Impact

Don't have them. Unless there is an obvious, designated fire-ring.

- Keep fires small. Use sticks with a diameter no bigger than that of your wrist.
- Burn all wood and coals to ash, put out campfires completely, then scatter cool ashes.
- In an emergency, use a fire pan under mounded dirt so that you may scatter dirt and ashes together.

Respect Wildlife

- Do not approach or disturb wildlife. Observe from a distance.
- Do not feed wildlife. It exposes animals to chemicals and foods that they are not accustomed to.
- Store food appropriately either in a van or by bear-hanging it.

Be Considerate of Other Visitors

- If in a large group, make way for smaller groups to pass on trails.
- When taking a rest break keep bikes/packs/persons on the sides of the trail.
- Keep voices down to prevent disturbing other people and wildlife.

Note: These are general and basic guidelines. Each environment that you travel through has specific LNT requirements. For example:

1. Sea kayaking: You can pee below the high tide line, but you should dig your cat hole above high tide. If you're on a popular island, you should pack it out.
2. Caving: Pack out all human waste.

Expedition Behavior

Unfortunately, too many rules of expedition behavior remain unspoken. Some leaders seem to assume that their team members already have strong and generous characters like their own. But judging from a few of the campers we've encountered, more rules ought to be spelled out. Here are 10 of them (Tomb, 1994).

> RULE #1—Get the hell out of bed.
> Suppose your tent mates get up early to fetch water and fire up the stove while you lie comatose in your sleeping bag. As they run an extensive equipment check, coil ropes and fix your breakfast, they hear you start to snore. . . . They will devise cruel punishments for you. . . . Had you gotten out of bed, nobody would have had to suffer.

> RULE #2—Do not be cheerful before breakfast.
> Some people wake up perky and happy as fluffy bunny rabbits. They put stress on those who wake up mean as rabid wolverines. Exhortations such as "Rise and shine, sugar!" and "Greet the dawn, pumpkin!" have been known to provoke pungent expletives from rabid wolverine types. . . . The best early morning behavior is simple: Be quiet.

RULE #3—Do not complain.

About anything. Ever. It's 10 below zero, visibility is 4 inches and wind-driven hailstones are embedding themselves in your face like shotgun pellets. Must you mention it? Do you think your friends haven't noticed the weather? Make a suggestion. Tell a joke. Lead a prayer. Do NOT lodge a complaint! If you can't carry your weight, get a motor home.

RULE #4—Learn to cook at least one thing right.

If you don't like to cook, say so. Offer to wash dishes and prepare the one thing you do know how to cook, even if it's only tea. Remember that talented camp cooks sometimes get invited to join major expeditions in Nepal, all expenses paid.

RULE # 5—Either: (a) Shampoo, or (b) Do not remove your hat for any reason.

After a week or so on the trail, without shampooing, hair forms angry little clumps and wads. If you can't shampoo, pull a wool hat down over your ears and leave it there, night and day, for the entire expedition.

RULE # 6—Do not ask if anybody's seen your stuff.

Experienced adventurers have systems for organizing their gear. They very rarely leave it strewn around camp or lying back on the trail. One of the most damning things you can do is ask your teammate if they've seen the tent poles you thought you packed 20 miles ago. Should you ever leave the tent poles 20 miles away, do not ask if anybody's seem them. Simply announce, with a good-natured chuckle, that you are about to set off in the dark on a 40-mile hike to retrieve them, and that you are sorry. It's unprofessional to lose your spoon or your toothbrush. If something like that happens, don't mention it to anyone.

RULE # 7—Never ask where you are.

If you want to know where you are, look at the map. Try to figure it out yourself. If you're still confused, feel free to discuss the identity of landmarks around you and how they correspond to the cartography. If you (a) suspect that a mistake has been made, and (b) have experience in interpreting topographical maps, and (c) are certain that your group leader is a novice or on drugs, speak up. Otherwise, follow the group like a sheep.

RULE # 8—Always carry more than your fair share.

When the trip is over, would you rather be remembered as a rock or a wimp? . . .When an argument begins, take the extra weight yourself. Then shake your head and gaze with pity upon the slothful one. . . . On the trail that day, during a break, load the tenderfoot's pack with 20 pounds of gravel.

RULE # 9—Do not get sunburned.

Sunburn is not only painful and unattractive, but it's also an obvious sign of inexperience. Most green horns wait too long before applying sunscreen. Once you've burned on an expedition, you may not have a chance to get out of the sun. Then the burn gets burned, skin peels, away, blisters sprout on the already swollen lips. Anyway, you get the idea. Wear zinc oxide.

RULE #10—Do not get killed.

Suppose you make the summit of K2 solo, chain-smoking Gitanes and carrying the complete works of Hemingway in hardcover. Pretty macho, huh? Suppose now that you take a vertical detour down a cre- vasse and never make it back to camp. Would you still qualify as a hero? And would it matter? . . . The worst thing to have on your outdoor resume is a list of the possible locations of your body. Source: http://www.radford.edu/~recparks/Wilderness/expedition.htm

Keep up expedition morale with trail games, time takers, and conversation. When participants are puffing up the hill, or kayaking against the wind, or waiting to climb, keeping them entertained and engaged will go a long way towards enhancing their enjoyment of the trip.

Questions are super quick and easy starters. The easiest way to get indi- viduals to open up is to ask them about themselves.

1. If you could travel anywhere in the world, where would you go and why?
2. Tell me a funny story from your past.
3. What would you love to be doing in 10 years?
4. Favorites, and why: animal, candy bar, holiday . . .
5. What was your best-ever Halloween costume?
6. And the general interest questions: major; siblings and pets; career aspirations; hobbies; how do you like Maryland and why did you choose it?
7. How did you decide to sign up for this trip? Have you ever done this before? How did you become interested in outdoor activities?

THE TRAININGS: IN-DEPTH

Year 1 Development

Year 1 trip leader trainings are meant to give new trip leaders basic knowl- edge and experience in leadership and outdoor activities. Year 1 trainings are not meant to be comprehensive enough to make full trip leaders out of those who attend them. They are intended to give all new ORC trip leaders a similar background from which they may then go forth to gain the further experience and certifications that build a trip leader. The trip leader training program is founded on the belief that no training program is good enough by itself to be truly effective; you will also need to get out there and learn through your own experiences, building hard skills and realizing leadership styles.

Soft Skills

The following are "soft skill" components of TLTs:

- Leadership styles: Trip leaders will be able to identify a variety of leadership styles. They will be able to explain which styles they possess without being restricted to one.
- Goals: Trip leaders will be able to identify the importance of goals in general, goal setting, and goal assessing throughout the trip process.
- Facilitation: Trip leaders will be able to identify the various components of facilitation and explain their importance.
- Group dynamics: Trip leaders will be able to discuss the evolution of a group and explain the importance of knowing this information.
- Ice breakers/initiative: Trip leaders will be exposed to a variety of icebreakers and teambuilding activities, while learning the importance of these for trips.
- Conflict resolution: Trip leaders will be equipped with the skills necessary to deal with difficult interpersonal situations.

Hard Skills

The following basic skills are necessary on most ORC trips. After completing the training year, trip leaders should personally possess these skills and be able to teach them to others.

Semester 1. TLTs should focus on learning these skills and becoming proficient in them. These skills should be covered as the need for each arises and then practiced with each successive trip. By the end of Semester 1, each TLT should have mastered THE FOLLOWING:

- General LNT principles including campsite selection, campfires, backcountry hygiene, waste management, washing dishes, etc.

- How to set up all types of ORC rental and trip tents.
- How to use the ORC trip and rental stoves.
- How to purify water (using both water filters and polar pure).
- Basic backcountry cooking.
- How to set up a bear bag system.
- How to get warm and stay warm.
- Knowledge from the book, *How to Shit in the Woods*.
- How to size and pack a backpack.
- How to set up a top-rope climb with natural anchors.

If more experience and/or instruction is necessary, trip leader trainees should inform the TLT coordinator and specific skill trainings and sessions will be organized.

Semester 2. Each TLT should plan to present a mini demonstration/class on at least one of these basic outdoor skills. The goal is to practice the "soft" skill of teaching "hard skills" to a group. Trip leaders may be asked for advice, and trainees should offer feedback to each presenter on the quality and creativity of each lesson.

Individual Trip Run-Downs

Endurance Trek

Pre-training. TLTs should look up the "10 essentials" and prepare a day pack with everything they need for a 2-day, 1-night trek. No tents, stoves, sleeping bags, or tarps. TLTs should expect the following:

- To be challenged.
- To be surprised.
- To have fun.
- To expand their knowledge of outdoor skills.

This training will cover:

- Survival skills: staying warm, sleeping without a tent or sleeping bag, what to do in case of an emergency, being prepared for anything.
- Map and compass skills.
- Assessing hazards and risks.

POISON IVY! "Leaves of three, let it be. Four or more, eat some more."

- Basic outdoor/trip skills including LNT and pooping in the woods.
- Team building, communication, and group dynamics.
- Hiking and decision making on little sleep.

RISK = PROBABILITY x CONSEQUENCES

Climbing Training

Pretraining. **Before the trip, TLTs need to complete the following:**

- Know how to tie a water knot, figure 8 knot on a bite, figure 8 follow through, super 8 knot, bowline, double bowline, water knot, and a girth hitch.
- Have a University of Maryland climbing wall belay certification.
- Be familiar with climbing and belaying.
- Know the LNT principles for climbing.

TLTs can expect the following:

- To learn about climbing and top rope set-up with natural anchors.
- To become familiar with climbing equipment and safety.
- To learn about ORC climbing trips.
- Not to actually climb.

This training will cover:

- Types of rope, rope construction, and rope maintenance.
- Types of webbing, carabineers, and harnesses.
- Top-rope system set-up: GREAS.
- Knot usage.
- Route selection.
- Climbing safety—assessing hazards and risks.
- How to check/test a top rope set-up.
- How to explain the top rope set-up and the climbing process.
- Practice, practice, practice—build confidence in set-ups.
- How ORC climbing trips are run.

Backpacking Training

Pre-training. TLTs should know how to set up the ORC trip tents and use the trip stoves. TLTs can expect the following:

- To learn the basics of backpacking.
- To hike uphill carrying a heavy pack.
- To practice LNT.

This training will cover:

- How to fit a pack.
- How to pack a pack.
- Tent set-up.
- Stove safety.
- The secrets of staying warm.
- The concept of layering.
- Water purification.
- LNT, specifically regarding campsites and waste disposal.
- Different activities and games that can be used on trips.

Green Glass Door

What you need: Nothing!

To Play: Tell people that in a room in a far away land there is a green glass door. On the other side of this door lies the most magical land. In order to enter into this utopia, you must bring the right gift. Only certain things may pass through the door. For instance, you can bring a tree, but you can't bring a leaf. Or you can bring the zoo but not a walrus. Basically, you can bring anything that has double letters in the word. It's really fun when participants get super frustrated and angry. Heh Heh Heh. Being a trip leader is the best.

Moon Society

What you need: A stick.

To Play: Grab your stick and light the end on fire a bit, blowing on it until you have a nice, glowing red end. Explain the society: "*The moon society started hundreds of years ago. It is a very polite and courteous society. All you have to do to become a member is to draw a moon using this stick, like so.*"

Then you draw a moon any way you would like. Pass the stick on to your fellow trip leader, who thanks you, and proceeds to draw a moon herself. She then offers it to the next person. Only polite people are allowed into the moon society. Everyone else can try until they figure it out.

The Game

Objective: Not to think of the game.

How to Play: The game starts with a 15-minute period in which the participants try to forget about the game. After 15 minutes, the first person to think of the game, even just for a second, loses and must announce his or her loss to the rest of the group whether it is by phone, email, text message, IM, or simply stating he or she has lost. The game then starts over with another 15-minute period for people to clear their mind of the game.

Helpful Hints to Winning: Stop yourself from subconsciously associating anything with the game.

Sea Kayak Training

Pretraining. TLTs should complete the following before leaving for this training trip:

- Demonstrate a wet-exit to an ORC trip leader
- Read about the LNT principles for sea kayaking.
- Know how to stay warm and dry.
- Know how to use ORC trip tents and stoves.

TLTs can expect the following:

- To learn about and gain experience sea kayaking.
- To experience cold water for extended periods of time.
- To learn about sea kayak equipment, safety, and LNT.

This training will cover:

- Equipment introduction and use.
- How to paddle a sea kayak.
- Paddle strokes.
- Boat control.
- Basic water safety (when and where to paddle under certain conditions).
- Risk management and assessment.
- Group management (on the water).
- Rescue techniques.
- Reading water charts/navigation.
- Shooting bearings/open water crossings.
- Landings on shore.

- Camping while sea kayaking.
- Tandem kayak use and care.
- Sea kayaking LNT.
- Post-trip equipment cleaning and storage.

Caving Training

Pretraining. TLTs should familiarize themselves with the LNT principles for caving—they will be covered in more depth on the trip.
TLTs can expect the following:

- To challenge themselves (with a new activity/skill in an uncomfortable environment for some).
- To explore a cave.
- To learn about caving equipment and safety.
- To learn more caving LNT principles.
- To learn about leading ORC caving trips.

This training will cover the following:

- What to bring—equipment, survival gear.
- How caves are formed.
- LNT.
- Caving safety and risk management.
- What to do with a group on an ORC caving trip: appropriate activities.
- How to manage a group in a cave.
- How to handle fears in the cave.
- Ways that leaders can make participants feel safer and more comfortable if they're scared of the dark, heights, or the unknown.
- Facilitation.

Thousands of tired, nerve-shaken, over-civilized people are beginning to find out that going to the mountain is going home; that wildness is necessity; that mountain parks and reservations are useful not only as fountains of timber and irrigating rivers, but as fountains of life. (John Muir, Founder of the Sierra Club)

Winter Backpacking Training

Pretraining. TLTs should prepare as if they themselves were leading the trip. This means grabbing extra gear, food, essentials, and so on.
TLTs can expect the following:

- To become more experienced with LNT practice.
- To learn about backcountry cooking.
- To learn about hypothermia and construct a hypo-wrap.

This training will cover the following:

- What to bring for a winter expedition—clothing and food.
- The concepts of layering and calories, calories, calories.
- Backcountry oven use.
- Backcountry nutrition.
- The signs, symptoms, and treatment of hypothermia.
- How to set up a hypo-wrap.
- The art of snowshoeing (depends upon snow).

Driving Training

Pretraining. TLTs should come prepared to learn about van and truck maintenance and use.

TLTs can expect the following:

- A van/truck orientation.
- To become familiar with the requirements to become an approved driver.
- To learn the necessary and required van/truck preparations.
- To practice trailer attachment.
- To discuss safe driving techniques.

This training will cover the following:

- Trailer attachment, driving, and back up procedures.
- Tips for safe driving on highway and back roads.
- Accidents/vehicle trouble.
- Getting gas.
- Passenger control.
- Night and long trip driving protocol.
- Van pick-up: when and how.

After the training, each TLT must schedule an individual driving time with Jon. This will consist of 30 minutes of on-road practice in which the TLT will demonstrate that he or she knows basic procedures and can safely handle the vehicle.

Year 2 Development

Year 2 trip leaders will work as assistant trip leaders. They will work with experienced trip leaders to learn the paperwork procedures and on-the-trail facilitation techniques through both observation and practice.

Through trip planning, trip shadowing, additional trainings, personal adventures, and other experiences, Year 2 trip leaders should become very comfortable with the elements of trip leading that are universal on ORC trips.

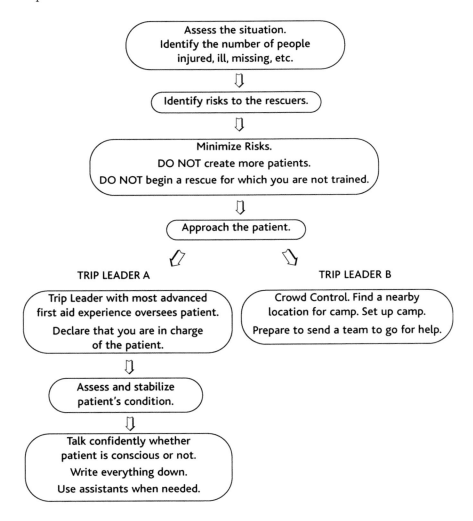

Figure 9.1. Emergency Response Flow Chart (Leaders A and B)

Trip Leaders can expect the following:

- Trip planning/paperwork.
- To help lead pre-trip meetings.
- To know and lead icebreakers, group initiatives, and games to play on trips.
- To teach LNT principles to people who may be very unfamiliar with wilderness ethics.
- To teach camping skills to participants.
- Risk and hazard assessment, the decision-making process.
- Group management and people skills.
- Conflict resolution and problem solving.
- Understanding different leadership styles and further development of your own.
- Evaluation of your performance on a trip and the overall success of a trip. Identifying and working on areas that need improvement.

TIPS & TRICKS

❖ Keep copies of Emergency Action Plan (EAP), directions, and emergency contact list in front pocket of each Med-Kit. Each vehicle has a Med-Kit.

THE TRIP

Remember: an outline checklist of all pre-trip and trip procedures can be found in the bulletin board folders in the ORC.

The following section offers tips and suggestions for planning and making sure your trip runs smoothly. This section will not cover every criterion that you must fulfill. For that, follow the guidelines established on the trip leader check-list forms.

Trip Planning

Proper Prior Planning Prevents Piss Poor Performance.

—Paul Petzoldt

Once assigned a certain trip, it is the responsibility of the trip leaders to plan every aspect of the trip. This should be done *at least* seven days before the pre-trip (that's at least **14 days before the trip**).

Trip File

Trip files are kept on every trip we run. In them, you can find EAPs, pre-trip and trip itineraries, equipment and food lists, maps and directions (**NOT from MapQuest**), and other pertinent information. Use these as helpful guides, not as ready-to-copy itineraries. **All EAP phone numbers and addresses must be checked to make sure that they are current.**

TIPS & TRICKS
❖ **Grab road atlases for where you'll be driving, in addition to your directions.**

Remember:

- Advance notice is required for some places with reservations and permits.
- Alternative and evacuation plans/routes in event of emergency.
- The van.
- P2 (pre-pre) meeting with Jon.
    - ✓ Bring pre-trip packet, directions, emergency contact sheet.
    - ✓ Bring QUESTIONS! Just ask.
    - ✓ Discuss petty cash.
    - ✓ Schedule post-trip meeting—bring your calendars.

Pre-Trip Gear Inspection

- Inspect, stock, and check-out Med-Kits that you are taking on your trip.
- Check that tents are complete and in good condition.
- Check cleanliness and working zippers of sleeping bags, poly-pro, fleece, gore-tex, etc.
- Check cleanliness of water bottles and cook kits.
- Fire up all stoves.
- Inspect all ropes and climbing gear.
- Check all life jackets and throw ropes.

- Check all canoes and kayaks for structural damage and foot pedals.
- For biking trips, make sure that bikes have been inspected and tuned up by bike mechanics in the shop.

Pre-Trip Meeting

Your participants are nervous, uncertain, anxious, and looking to you for guidance. This is *the time to take* a *strong, directive leadership role.* Be organized, prepared, friendly, and animated. This meeting potentially sets the tone for the whole trip.

- Call participants to remind them about the pre-trip meeting and things they need to bring (towel/bathing suit, emergency information they forgot when they signed up).
- Frontloading: It's crucial to have packing lists and itinerary hand-outs that participants can look over while you wait for everyone to arrive.
- *Know what you're going to say and who's going to say it.*
    - ✓ Intros
    - ✓ Risks
    - ✓ LNT
    - ✓ Expectations
    - ✓ Itinerary: Decide on *departure time*
    - ✓ Food: Decide *cook/tent groups (two to three people)*
    - ✓ Equipment and packing
    - ✓ Questions, questions, questions
- Ice breaker; make it fun, energetic, and enthusiastic. This is the first time people are meeting their fellow trip mates. The goal is to get them to relax and get to know their future tent mates.

TIPS & TRICKS

❖ Use the challenge course or climbing wall for your pre-trip meeting!

Sample Packing Lists

Backpacking

- ✓ Backpacking stoves/fuel
- ✓ Cook kits, fry pans, serving spoon *

- ✓ Matches *
- ✓ Tents and ground tarps *
- ✓ Sleeping bag, sleeping pad *
- ✓ Backpacks - Fit to participants
- ✓ Headlamp *
- ✓ Rain Gear *
- ✓ Fleece jacket and pants *
- ✓ Polypro top and bottom *
- ✓ Water bottles (at least 3 liters)
- ✓ Water filter and Polarguards
- ✓ Trowel and TP *
- ✓ Bear bag rope
- ✓ Trash bags *

Optional:
- ✓ Camera *
- ✓ Frisbee *
- ✓ Hackey sack *
- ✓ Cards *

Not Provided:
- ✓ Warm hat
- ✓ Gloves
- ✓ Non-cotton pants
- ✓ Underwear
- ✓ Socks
- ✓ Camp shoes
- ✓ Utensils/bowl/mug
- ✓ FOOD
- ✓ Toiletries
- ✓ Bandanna
- ✓ Chapstick
- ✓ Sunscreen, sunglasses, sun hat
- ✓ Money for car ride
- ✓ Bathing suit
- ✓ Towel/pack towel
- ✓ Sandals/shoes that **will get wet**

Sea Kayaking

Starred backpacking items, plus:
- ✓ Coleman stoves/fuel
- ✓ Wet suit, booties
- ✓ Spray skirt, life jacket, paddling jacket
- ✓ Paddle, kayak
- ✓ Dry bag
- ✓ Water bottles (at least two)
- ✓ Orange jug—Water (can be filled at base camp)

Food Suggestions

Breakfast

- Instant pancake mix
- Instant oatmeal packets
- Bagels with cheese or peanut butter
- Nutri-grain bars
- Instant coffee or tea
- Butter

Lunch (Anytime between breakfast and dinner)

The key is easy, no-cook.
- Tuna (in no-drain packets)
- Bagels with cheese or peanut butter
- Hard fruit that won't get mashed in your pack (apples and oranges)
- Dried fruit
- Energy bars
- Snickers—the original energy bar
    - ✓ GORP—"Good Ol' Raisins and Peanuts." Add in dry cereal (Cheerios and Chex work well), M&Ms, other nuts, craisins, etc.
- Sardines
- Carrots

Dinners

- Ramen noodles—add in pre-cut fresh veggies, cheese, and potato flakes for *Ramen Supreme*

- Lipton pasta/rice packets
- Pizza bagels
- Velveeta shells and cheese
- Couscous—for a variation, try adding in dried fruit, nuts, and curry
- Burritos or quesadillas
- Stir-fry
- Stew—veggies, cumin, soy sauce, potato flakes for heartiness

---

TIPS & TRICKS

❖ Re-package food into Ziploc bags to cut down on bulk
❖ Waterproof all sleeping bags and backpacks by lining inside of stuff sack backpack with trash bags

---

Equipment (Gear Check-Out)

The following is a guide to help make this a quick, organized process. Gear can be distributed to participants either at the pre-trip meeting or right before the trip leaves. **Know that this process takes a while.**

- Before handing out gear, participants must sign the equipment liability form. Make sure to remind participants that they will be held financially responsible for each item on their contract.
- Each participant and trip leader should fill out a trip equipment form complete with all the gear that they are using from the ORC.
- Inform the participants that the equipment is due back at the end of the trip. No equipment should be taken home after the trip. *Bring clothing to wear home from ORC.*
- Trip participants can take their gear with them after the pre-trip meeting, or the gear can be left in the trip cage, clearly marked.
- If the trip is cancelled and participants have equipment, they will have until the upcoming Monday to return gear. Inform them that a late fee will be assessed after this time.

When to Call McLaren

- Any incident involving the vehicles.
  - ✓ Accidents
  - ✓ Breaking down

     ✓ Stalls
- Anytime you contact emergency personnel.
- Anytime someone is transported to a hospital.
- Any suspected head or spinal injury.

Remember: The cell phone is not to be used as a security blanket. It is not a substitute for quality trip planning, precautions, or good judgment on the trip. We hope to never use it.

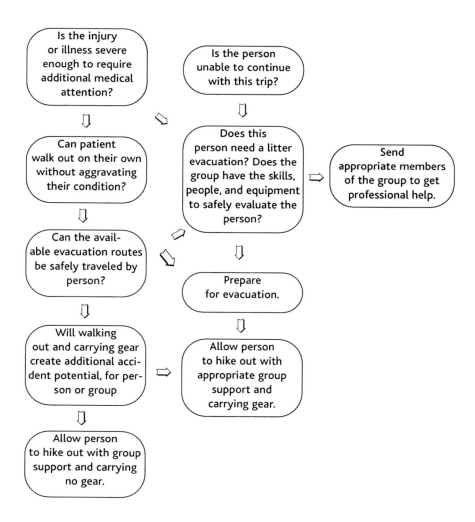

Figure 9.2. Evacuation Plan Flow Chart

Running the Trip

Don't forget:

- All participant forms.
- Cell phone (coordinate with other trips during same days).
- Motorola talkabouts (coordinate with other trips).
- Petty cash (from Jon).
- Participant evaluations and pens (to fill out on the way home).
- Remind participants to have money available for food, etc.

Cell Phone Use

1. The cell phone will be taken in the outdoor recreation vehicle every time it leaves the ORC.
2. The cell phone will only be used for emergency purposes.

Itinerary—It's Important

"Structure gives you freedom," as a wise woman once said.
Having a detailed itinerary gives you the freedom to be flexible if the group's needs and desires change. You can relax knowing that you have it all dialed.

POST-TRIP

Debriefs/Processing

As trip leaders, we can affect a more meaningful trip for our participants if we offer some kind of opportunity for processing and reflection. Debriefing is usually done verbally through a discussion facilitated by the trip leaders. Numerous issues should be considered.

Setting. Processing should be done when all participants can focus on the task. Give yourself enough time to process. Sitting in a circle usually facilitates good discussion. Make sure you're in an area where there are not a lot of distractions.

Physical Presence. Be a role model during the processing session. Maintain eye contact with speakers. Sit somewhere that allows you to see everyone in the group. Your demeanor at this time will set the tone for the entire session. Make sure that you are sitting upright and acknowledge people's responses.

Silence. Don't worry about moments of silence. Give the group time to think. You can always rephrase questions in order to elicit different responses.

The final debriefing should be held at the end of the trip. Do it **before** getting back to campus, before people scatter to clean gear and before they start thinking about all the homework they have waiting for them. A debrief can also be done at the end of each night before going to bed.

> If future generations are to remember us with gratitude rather than contempt, we must leave them more than the miracles of technology. We must leave them a glimpse of the world as it was in the beginning, not just after we got through with it.
>
> —President Lyndon B. Johnson

SAMPLE DEBRIEF QUESTIONS

WHAT?

- If you could send someone a snapshot of one moment on this trip, what would it be?
- One new thing I learned was . . .
- What was your favorite meal on the trip?
- Close your eyes—what sound comes to mind that would characterize *the trip?*
- Everyone say one word to characterize the trip.
- Tell a rose and a thorn from the day/trip.

SO WHAT?

- What were your high and low points of the day?
- What kind of challenges do you feel were overcome by yourself and the group today?
- If you could write a letter to yourself today, what would you say?
- How has this trip affected your concept of the outdoors and nature?
- Today was unlike any day before in my life because . . .

NOW WHAT?

- In a year, what do you most want to remember about these few days?
- Have you discovered anything new about yourself while being in the wilderness?
- What is one significant thing the trip has changed for you?
- If you could have brought one more person on this trip, who would it have been and why?
- Are there any challenges you feel you still need to work toward achieving and how will you continue to work toward them?
- Where do you think this is leading you in terms of values and judgments, and how have your fellow participants helped in your growing process?
- How well did the group work together today? Did everyone feel satisfied by our performance today? Can we change anything?
- What is a personal challenge that you foresee in the upcoming semester?

Use your imagination! Facilitate debriefs in a way that works best for you and the group.

Gear Check-In

- Check gear in carefully (set up tents; wash dishes; clean boats; Gore-Tex/wet gear hung to dry; dirty and washable gear put in laundry cart). No gear may go home with participants unless absolutely necessary. They will be charged late fees if not returned by Monday.
- Med-Kits checked in and restocked.
- Tents and dishes put away within 3 days.
- Trip leader evaluations completed within 1 week.
- Post-trip meeting with director within 2 weeks.
- Put all paperwork in the trip folder. Include any helpful information for future trip leaders. Place folder in black basket beneath the trip leaders bulletin board.

REFERENCES

Graham, J. (1997). *Outdoor leadership: Technique, common sense & self-confidence.* Seattle, WA: The Mountaineers.

Muir, J. (1992). *John Muir: The eight wilderness discovery books.* Chatham, IL: Diadem Books.

Nader, R. (2000). *The Ralph Nader reader.* Carmichael, CA: Seven Stories Press.

Petzoldt, P. (1976). *Petzoldt's Teton trails: A hiking guide to the Teton Range with stories, history, and personal experiences.* Salt Lake City, UT: Wasach Publishing.

Priest, S., & Gass, M.T. (1997). *Effective leadership in adventure programming.* Champaign, IL: Human Kinetics.

Tomb, H. (1994). *Cool of the wild: An extremist's guide to adventure sports.* Chicago: Contemporary Books.

Tzu, L. (1996). *Tao teh ching.* Acton, CA: Shambhala Press.

III

MYTHS AND LEGENDS

10

MYTHS AND LEGENDS IN OUTDOOR EDUCATION

Greg S. Goodman

James R. Jelmberg

My Heart Leaps Up
"My heart leaps up when I behold
A rainbow in the sky:
So was it when my life began;
So it is now I am a man;
So be it when I shall grow old . . ."

—William Wordsworth

Greg Goodman, Peter Ordway,
Ash Hallett

GENE ROSE,
AUTHOR, SIERRA HISTORIAN

We'd like to introduce this last section of this book with a few words of history and inspiration from outdoor writer and naturalist, Gene Rose. Gene is a prolific and gifted writer, and he is the author of several great books of Sierra history including *Magic Yosemite Winters* (1999), *San Joaquin — A River Betrayed* (2000), *Giants Among the Forests* (2004), *Sierra Centennial, High Odyssey* (1974), and *Reflections of Shaver Lake* (1987). He shares his mentors with us here.

Of the California's towering Sierra Nevada, the great naturalist John Muir said it best when he described the range as the most sublime mountains he had known. The grandeur of Yosemite, the size and longevity of the fabled Sequoia, the serenity of Lake Tahoe, and the majesty of Mount Whitney have lent validity to Muir's assessment.

With its great natural diversity, the Sierra boasts the biggest trees, the deepest canyon, and the highest peak within the 48 states. It is a land of superlatives, a land rich in both human and natural history. It is also a land of legend and lore, boasting a human and natural history of staggering proportions. The great Gold Rush, the pony express, the transcontinental railroad highlight the Golden State.

What Muir said indirectly is that the Sierra Nevada represents one of the foremost settings for outdoor education. And it was Muir, the naturalist, wanderer, inventor, and mountaineer, who led the way to this high classroom. En route, the transplanted Scotsman left a trail of service and altruism that has made Muir California's most revered and venerated citizen. Today, long after Muir has left the scene, his great Range of Light stands as one of the higher institutions of learning—a great natural classroom—and one without walls.

The foundation for his classroom has lengthy dimensions. A century ago, when the resource raiders were indiscriminately logging, mining and burning the mountains of the west, Muir saw the carnage and reacted. Something had to be done to protect the mountains. After some thought, he recognized that education was the key to protecting his mountain world. Persuasion would be more effective than coercion. His plan called for replacing the dark shroud of ignorance using education and enlightenment to his Range of Light classroom.

In 1901, as the first president of the Sierra Club, Muir took the young and struggling club to the Yosemite high country for its first group outing. He also brought along several of his friends, experts and teachers in the emerging field of natural science. As for Muir, he taught geology in the field—in the canyon and on the mountainside—where it should be taught.

For 3 weeks his charges looked, listened, and studied the flora and fauna in high country. The outing worked its magic. When the club's members returned home, they were recharged and committed to the cause of conservation. With that initial outing, the Sierra Nevada had become a natural classroom, an open-air laboratory for learning. Muir's lectures—and love of nature—had paid off.

In the following years, the annual outings became the club's rallying point. The high trips moved to Kings Canyon the following years. The school bell rang on other high classrooms. Mount Whitney, Mount Rainier, and the Canadian Rockies heeded the teacher's call, and the students came running. Every other summer the "High Trips" would return to their Yosemite classroom. The wanna-be mountaineers learned not only natural science, but the legends and lore of the mountains as well.

Muir's students also learned their personal obligation to the American earth—and to future generations. From these early programs the clubbers learned that they had a personal responsibility to protect the best of the American earth. Thus, the outdoor classroom, the mountain campsite, had become a prime spot to gain recruits and converts.

Often, Muir's lectern was a mountain summit or a streamside boulder or forest stump. His courses spanned the natural world. Muir's specialty, "Studies in the Sierra," while emphasizing geology or glaciology, recognized the importance of engaging nature in the field. He had numerous "TAs" (teaching assistants)—nature, in all her grand and glorious dimensions. Among other benefits, the outing gave the club motivation and mission.

For his efforts, Muir would be recognized as the "father of the national parks" and California's most venerated citizen. Over the years, he brought some of America's next generation of conservationists into the fold. Many of the foremost names of the American environmental movement were nurtured and in these field classes.

His beloved Yosemite emerged as the "Great University of the Outdoors." Even after he had crossed the ultimate divide, the Club's "High Trips" continued to grow in size and subject—until they became too large and unwieldy. By that time, Muir's message, his philosophies had taken root.

Stephen Mather, who would become the first director of the National Park Service, heard Muir's lecture-turned-sermon during the Club's 1912 outing in the Mount Whitney area. He took the lecture to heart—every American has a moral responsibility to protect the nation's most scenic and significant lands.

Later, Mather, while touring several of the first national parks, was appalled by the deplorable conditions at such locations as Yellowstone, Yosemite and Grand Canyon. Mather wrote a hot letter to the U.S. Department of Interior—only to be offered the job of redressing the problems. He hesitated at first, but then took the challenge. From this series of events emerged "The best idea this country ever had—the National Park Service."

Mather also recognized the need for outdoor education and interpretive nature programs in building the park service. One of his first efforts centered on what was essentially a public relations campaign to make Americans aware of their great natural treasures. Following Muir's lead, Mather believed that if he could get Americans to the struggling parks, making them aware of their significance, he might gain the political support necessary for their protection.

With his own funds, Mather launched his grand vision. He hired a gifted writer, Robert Yard, to help advance the establishment of a National Park System. Yard also recognized the importance of outdoor education and interpretive programs.

On one early tour of Kings Canyon, Yard spoke to the potential of outdoor education in furthering the Mather's agenda. "Crossing the pass we found another complicated basin with many lakes on the south. What a glacial laboratory this one area will make some day! The summer classes of all the universities of America may study here at once and scarcely see each other."

As the national parks grew under Mather's leadership, he often turned to the Sierra Club for support. The club became his handmaid and lobbying arm. Every Sierra Club member and park visitor became a messenger—or a missionary—in the great crusade to protect the best of the American earth.

In launching his great crusade for the National Parks, often hailed as "the best idea this country ever had," Mather realized the importance of education. Even after his premature death, his vision was perpetuated in the Yosemite Field School, setting the foundation for an interpretation program that would eventually touch all the various units of the National Park System, one that now embraces more than 380 units.

Outdoor education would serve an important role in educating the pubic to the preservation mandates of the park service—and protecting the nation's most unique lands. Countless individuals have been touched by the magic and majesty of the western parks. The "graduates" from nature's school are among the nations foremost stewards and conservationists.

Environmental icon Joseph N. "Little Joe" LeConte, who succeeded Muir as Sierra Club president, had it both ways. He was an educator of the highest level. During the school year, LeConte served as professor of mechanical engineering at the University of California. Summer time found him in the High Sierra organizing the outing program. Year after year, LeConte served the cause of preservation, providing the insight and motivation in advancing park protection to Kings Canyon. By the time he exited the scene, Little Joe had also become one of the giants of the American preservation movement.

The advocates of outdoor education herald from many other directions and callings. The famed naturalist Louis Aggassiz said it quite succinctly when he urged his disciples to "study nature, not books." Naturally, his favorite classroom was the outdoors, which was also his curricula.

A young and aspiring photographer became a Sierra Club member and an ardent participant in the outing program. Ansel Adams found inspiration and poignant images among its ridges and rills. Eventually, he left the Sierra Club and became a sparkplug for the Wilderness Society. His close friend and associate, David Brower, went on to become one of the foremost environmentalists of the late 1900s and early 2000s, forming Friends of the Earth and then, Earth Isle Institute.

We should not forget those countless unsung heroes who helped make the Sierra Nevada the great education center of the outdoors. Although it often appears that the great crusade was a male-centric movement, such was not the case. The pioneers in petticoats played a significant role in advancing outdoor education and the conservation cause.

Botanists such as Alice Eastwood and Enid Michael were at the forefront in advancing and identifying the flora of the Sierra. Every trip to the mountains became a field trip to new frontiers. Unfortunately, much of Eastwood's work was lost in the 1906 San Francisco earthquake, but enough remains to validate her commitment to botany and outdoor education.

Michael served as the first woman ranger naturalist at Yosemite, 1920-1942, imparting an appreciation for nature among countless park visitors. A trained botanist and ornithologist, she authored more than 500 articles on Yosemite flora and flyers—more even than John Muir.

Julia Shinn, the wife of Charles Shinn, the first supervisor of the Sierra National Forest, emerged as the mother figure for the early forest rangers. Both she and her husband were ardent Sierra stewards with a long history of dedication to conservation.

Her friend, Lena Redington, wife of Paul Redington, another Forest Service pioneer, carried the Sierra Club banner even higher. Marion Randall Parsons picked up the torch and ran with it long after her husband had died.

Author Mary Austin discovered the mountain magic from her Owens Valley home of Independence. Her backyard Sierra served as her motivational classroom, highlighted by her eloquent book, The Land of Little Rain.

Susan Thew, another Sierra stalwart, pledged her time and money to the conservation crusade that helped establish Kings Canyon as a national park.

To a person, regardless of gender or age, all of these crusaders, once anointed by the spirit of the Sierra, have become teachers and advocates of conservation or preservation, instilled by way of field trips or outdoor studies.

Collectively, these earth stewards discovered that the mountain spine of California was more than a pile of rocks. Whether it was an outdoor classroom or a natural cathedral, most of those anointed recognized that the setting was special and unique. As such, it was conducive to outdoor instruction. Frequently, they discovered that it was a classroom where the students could be motivated to an even higher level,

In the days before World War II, a variety of outdoor schools or mountain summer schools flourished at many areas in the Sierra. The University of California had its summer campus at Lake Tahoe. Stanford turned to Fallen Leaf Lake. Fresno State College maintained a campus at Huntington Lake, introducing a large number of young people to the out of doors and natural sciences.

With the dawning of the environmental movement in the 1960s, outdoor recreation and education received a big boost. One of the great western pioneers included the late Paul Petzold of Tetons and Wyoming. A veteran of the famed Tenth Mountain Division of World War II, Petzold taught what many considered the ultimate subject, that is, survival.

Outdoor education programs often go to extremes. They span the spectrum of human knowledge. Yes, there are such diverse subjects as basket weaving, botany and survival training, but they offer fringe benefits of personal growth and development.

"Knowing you can survive a hostile environment or an adversity is a great personal attribute. In addition, there are often social and psychological benefits attached to outdoor education classes," Petzold said.

Today, his Outward Bound also uses the Sierra, the Tetons, and other natural areas for field classes—if not a proving ground. Such courses subject young people to some of the most rigorous and demanding survival training in the nation.

By its very nature, outdoor education is education outside the school—and outside the box. Besides traditional subjects, almost every program incorporates some measure of natural science or history.

Boy Scouts, Girls Scouts, and the YMCA have their summer camps with a wide range of recreation and educational programs. Even church, health, and municipal camps incorporated some measure of natural science in their schedules.

By one Forest Service estimate there were more than 70 different outdoor camps in the Sierra Nevada. Each one provides some form of outdoor education.

The Yosemite Institute campus at Crane Flat in Yosemite National Park offers youngsters from urban schools the opportunity to experience Yosemite and the Sierra. Over the past 30 years, approximately 40,000 students have had the opportunity to discover the wonders of outdoor education. Yes, Dick and Jane can read tree rings and identify the flora and fauna of their mountain world. They learned how in an outdoor classroom.

Nature's great laboratory of learning has countless campuses and classrooms. Some formal, others informal, all tied to the concept of outdoor education. By its very setting, the outdoor classroom often serves as a break or change from the confines of the traditional classroom. Students recognize these classes are special or extra-curricula events that merit their attention.

Today in Muir's spiritual home, Yosemite Valley, park visitors can learn to climb a rock in a commercial program sponsored by the park concessionaire, or attend any one of a dozen different and free interpretive walks conducted by National Park Service rangers.

The Sierra is a mountain world of awe and wonder. In many ways, the mountain range is a gigantic outdoor learning center. In today's vernacular, outdoor education is "virtual reality" at another level.

Almost every visit to the mountains is a learning experience. The connection or linkage between outdoor education and environmental stewardship is evident. Even municipal youth or church camps usually provide some instruction into natural science. The connection between church, youth, and municipal camps often rely on outdoor education to compliment their main objectives. Health-related camps, such as the asthma camp, advance other forms of education and enlightenment in their programs.

In many ways, the outdoor classroom is the portal to higher education of another calling. Such experiences call on us to be the best that we can be. The trail to the outdoor classroom is often long and lasting; it beckons us onward and upward, underscoring the need to pursue a lifetime of learning.

Through the years, I have seen the pilgrimage to the peaks of the Sierra take on greater numbers. Young or old, structured or not, the migration to the outdoor classroom goes on, pushing the seasons, seeking the wisdom and enlightenment that goes with education.

The venerated John Muir once discovered that when he looked at one part of the great puzzle he saw it hitched to everything else. Only on the grand campus did the facts of life reveal themselves.

The late Karl Sharsmith, famed Alpine botanist of the Yosemite high country and a professor of botany at San Jose State College, looms as another great teacher. The legendary mountain man was a walking encyclopedia of Sierra flora. An early graduate of the Yosemite Field School, Sharsmith was part of the Park Service effort to advance outdoor education through interpretive programs. For nearly 50 summers, the High Sierra was his classroom. Whether it was on the slopes of 13,000-foot Mount Dana or the ice of the Lyell Glacier, Karl's ultimate classroom was outdoors and up—and the air conditioning was always on.

Today, the effort goes forward on new frontiers: The Yosemite Institute, the seminars of the Sequoia Natural History Association, the proliferation of field classes, nature seminars. Such classes show up almost routinely. The newest campus of the University of California at Merced, an hour's drive from Yosemite, has already set the foundation for an expanded outdoor education program with the National Park Service.

By their very nature, outdoor classes are out of the ordinary. I have often marveled at the reaction of young students as they view the architecture of a wildflower with a simple hand lens. Such experiences go a long way in opening up a new world of interest and wonder.

My own world has been shaped by such experiences. Botany, geology, glaciology and more. Now, after more than 70 years of basking in the Sierra's embrace, hiking its trails and pursuing its magic, I see John Muir's mountains not as the Range of Light, but perhaps the great Range of Life and Learning, bestowing its magic motivation on those who touch its side.

Tom Bonaccorsi,
original ORMS OEP Leader

A few years back, as a guest instructor at the University of California, I led a class on the literature of the Sierra Nevada. Although the classroom setting under the towering Campanille was fine, it could not compare with the ambiance of a weekend session under the towering peaks. Reading John Muir's (1992) *The Mountains of California* or Clarence King's (1997) *Mountaineering in the Sierra Nevada* takes on special significance when read by flashlight around a roaring campfire.

Now I am involved with Elderhostel, encouraging seniors to pursue life-long learning—and using the wilderness as an outdoor classroom as their outdoor class. "Mind or muscle. Use or lose," has become my byword.

Young or old, adolescent or chronologically enhanced, nature's classrooms provide unlimited opportunities for personal growth and development. Such onsite or empirical experiences open many doors to higher education.

I once pondered why the famed explorer Ponce de Leon could not find the fabled fountain of youth. Undoubtedly, he needed a little more outdoor education or navigational training. In all likelihood, the famed nineteenth century adventurer could not find the trailhead to the Sierra. Go west, Ponce. The fountain of youth is not in the swamplands of the South. Try the outdoor classrooms of the Sierra!

DAN GARVEY, PRESIDENT OF
PRESCOTT COLLEGE, PRESCOTT, ARIZONA

1. *Thirty years ago we/you began our quest in outdoor education. Little did we/you know that we/you were at the beginning of a burgeoning effort that would lead to a range of activities today from university instructor workshops to orientation activities for Fortune 500 company employees. When you started, did you ever think outdoor education would become so widespread?*

    Thirty years ago I wasn't thinking of the broad and varied applications possible. I was aware that outdoor programs were available for the elite in our society (prep-school students) and the most needy (programs for at-risk youth) but I had no idea these methods would be inhaled by our culture to the extent now available.

2. *How did you become interested in the outdoors?*

    Two starting points for me: (1) I loved the outdoors and all things connected to it so that when I was taken rock climbing in Yosemite in 1966 I knew I had a new recreational outlet available, and (2) I witnessed the power of OE [outdoor education] when I worked in a residential treatment center for boys. I began taking students into the wilderness and I found I could create powerful learning experience for the boys that were unavailable in a more traditional institutional setting.

3. *When did you begin to connect your outdoor calling as a way to work with schools and kids?*

    Gandhi once said that "he found the things that were in the very corners of his life suddenly became his life." That was my experience with OE. I don't remember ever having a job were I didn't use OE in some form or fashion. I have often thought that I'd find a more effective teaching methodology and I'd gravitate toward that approach but I remain convinced that experiential education is the most transformational approach available.

4. *Who and what have been your biggest influences in outdoor education?*

    My students/clients have been my biggest influences because they have helped me understand my own limitations and strengths.

5. *What has been the most adventuresome activity that you have done with your students?*

    Sailing around the world with Semester at Sea has been the most vulnerable activity I've ever done. The unanticipated problems that occur when you have responsibility for 650 college students going in and out of 11 different countries is staggering and always leaves me exhausted by the end of the voyage. Strictly focused on more traditional OE activities, I'd say some of the late winter/early spring trips into the White Mountains stand out because the weather was unpredictable and extreme.

6. *What has been the best learning activity that you have done with your students?*

I don't have a clear image of the best or even the top 10. I tend to believe or hope that I got as much out of every experience as I could based on my preparation and experience. Some activities remain very identifiable because something profound or theatrical might have happened on

Greg Goodman, original
ORMS OEP Leader

these experiences. As I reflect back, I'm not sure they were any more powerful although they may be more memorable.

7. *Is there anything you would like to add to this interview for the Myths and Legends chapter?*

Only that the best is yet to come. Our industry has been trying to justify the power of EE [experiential education] for decades; today, there is no doubt that experiential education is the most powerful form of instruction. An acknowledgment of the power of EE will undoubtedly encourage more educators to seek these techniques for their students. Those of us who see ourselves as outdoor instructors might not recognize the extent of growth within the broader field of experiential education but this growth is occurring.

GARY R. SELLS, DIRECTOR, SCOUT ISLAND EDUCATION CENTER, FRESNO COUNTY OFFICE OF EDUCATION, FRESNO, CALIFORNIA

I am an enthusiastic, but unintentional, outdoor educator. That sounds like being a devoted, but disinterested, dentist! Well, with the honesty out of the way and my credibility in pieces, I should point out that my enthusiasm for the out-of-doors is a product of my gene pool. Having been born in rural Tennessee and raised by generations of farmers, herders, and an honest mule trader or two, I was nurtured to love being outside, smelling the unique aromas of the seasons and forever fascinated by the miracle that lightning bugs never needed to change their batteries. Oh me, oh my. How wonderful to have been a child in the country and, even more wonderful, how incredible the impact our childhood memories have on our yearnings and passions when we reach adulthood (I am still working on that title).

I have been blessed, in the truest and most sincere definition of that word, to have made a livelihood in the public schools of California. Having been a high school science teacher, district office administrator, high school and elementary site administrator, university research director, and now, and NOW, the best of ALL . . . a director of an outdoor education center located along a river. You see now, blessed is not a too strong nor too theologically charged word to describe my professional journey from the red clay of the mid-South to the sunny San Joaquin Valley in central California. Amen and pass the nets, buckets and bug spray!

John Parsons, original
ORMS OEP Leader

The Fresno County Office of Education saw fit to make two confluent and bold decisions in 2001 and 2002 to purchase 150 acres of property in the San Joaquin River bottom. Eyebrow-raising to say the least! The intent of the superintendent and governing board was to make the emphatic declaration that children, teachers and adults of all ages in Fresno County deserve to have their very own environmental preserve and unique classroom. Amen and re-elect 'em all!

The 75-acre, historic Scout Island (formerly the area's Boy Scout camp site and later a privately held game preserve) and 75 additional acres of beautiful farm and ranching property across the river in Madera County now "belong" to education, educators, and generations-to-come of central Californians. Needing a Tennessee-bred director, I became that "unintentional" outdoor educator aforementioned. What a wonderful (truly, full of wonder for me) experience I am having. And, what a wonderful, I know I'm gushing, opportunity to relive my childhood love for the aromas, the sights and sounds of being out in creation.

The Scout Island Education Center works with the 35 school districts in our county and is open, without charge, to 180,000 students to plant seeds of environmentalism, environmental literacy, and, most important, create a memory or two. At the Island, teachers and their students can take docent-led field trips, participate in teacher-directed lessons, enjoy instruction from the staff of Fresno County Office of Education's Leadership Academy (in-class and/or high-low ropes experiences) or register to come to the site and just enjoy sharpening observation skills, develop creative writing, sketch images of critters and vegetation, sing and/or sharpen their poise and confidence through public speaking at the site's two amphitheaters or—just walk about and fall in love again with one's unique memories of having been a child in rural Tennessee.

I invite you to visit our Web site at www.scoutisland.org and perhaps come visit us some day. We dish out a goodly portion of central California diversity, seasoned with a pinch of southern hospitality. It would be my delight to host you on a tour of this beautiful treasure; if you don't mind consorting with an unintentional outdoor kinda guy.

JED WILLIAMSON, PRESIDENT,
STERLING COLLEGE, STERLING, VERMONT,
AND MOUNT EVEREST CLIMBER

1. *How did you first become interested in the outdoors and have a calling for the outdoors?*

I was fortunate in that I grew up on a 60-acre game farm 80 miles north of New York City. It was rural at the time. My father decided that if he was going to have to be engaged in the rat race, he might as well also be involved in the human race and decided to raise us kids in a rural setting. Out my back door I was able to fish and yes, even hunt, at an early age. The second piece, pretty interesting, was that only a few miles away lived a fairly well-known person at the time, Lowell Thomas. He was a news broadcaster. He loved kids, and he loved the outdoors; skiing in particular. His broadcasts came from all over the world, but he had a studio right there just a few miles from where we lived. He had a ski hill and [he would] call us kids up on the weekends when there was snow. He would get us on the phone and say, "Ski on over here and as soon as you get the hill packed out, I will have Irving start up the rope tow." We had cable bindings in those days and we would go over there and pack out the hill and then ski. That was growing up in the 1940s and early 1950s.

That really got me going. When I arrived at the University of New Hampshire in 1958 as a transfer student, I signed up for an Outing Club trip for climbing the first weekend. I never looked back. I climbed just about every weekend. At the end of my third year, I was in Pinkham Notch and just had come down from doing a climb with my partner. We were eating dinner at Porky Gulch, the AMC [Appalachian Mountain Club] hut there. This guy was mouthing off about British Columbia and how he was going to go there next summer. My buddy and I said we would like to join him. He said, "Okay, meet me at the hotel in Golden on July 20." This 6-week expedition to the Selkirks was my first.

2. *When did you begin to connect your outdoor calling as a way to work with schools and kids?*

Right after I graduated I started teaching high school English and my motto was, "There has got to be a better way." I started to think about how I could bring some outdoor short-term experiential approaches to literature. That is when I came up with the ideas like taking the kids out on a cold rainy day to little setups all around the school perimeter for them to try to build a fire. I gave them three matches. If anyone got a fire going, of course I put it out. Then we discussed Jack London's To Build a Fire. It was direct, personal experience before discussion ensued. I continue that today. I am teaching the book Touching a Void here at Sterling College. I begin by taking them for a 2-hour crawl downhill. Then we set up a belay situation where they hold another classmate until they can't hold them anymore. That approach has been part of my whole career.

I worked for Outward Bound (OB) for a number of years. That was after coming out of the Army—the government contract I couldn't refuse. The motto OB used at the time was, "It is For Us to Ignite the Flame and Others to Keep it Alive." I decided that it is better for us to try and work on ways to keep the flame alive. That is when I started thinking about how I could bring something into teacher education. In the early 1970s, I co-designed a 15-month master of arts in teaching program for the Department of Education at the University of New Hampshire [UNH]. We called it "Live, Learn, and Teach." In addition to learning the usual skill needed, such as classroom management techniques, participants were provided with the road map for designing experiential curricula. I did this work for 9 years, and I must say it is the career piece that gives me the greatest pride. I'm pleased that the program is still going today.

3. *That was a great innovation that you did at UNH in the master's program. Who and what have been your biggest influences in outdoor education, who were your mentors?*

I kind of gave you a couple of them. I would say Lowell Thomas in getting us all going in skiing. I would say my mother and father because of growing up on the game farm taking care of critters and large gardens. Then there were my peers in the Outing Club at UNH. They were a real enthusiastic group of folks. Another individual name would be Bill Putnam, the fellow who led the expedition to the Selkirks. With us was Ben Ferris, a close friend of Bill's who was a medical doctor at the Harvard School of Public Health. In 1950, he started an annual journal called *Accidents in North American Mountaineering*. In 1974, he and Bill turned the editorship over to me and I've been doing it ever since.

Those are a few names, but there are certainly many other mentors in my life. Right now I have a hundred of them right here at Sterling College in the form of undergraduate students who teach me stuff every day.

4. *What has been the most adventuresome activity that you have done with your students?*

I never like to just pick one. Our orientation here is called "Sense of Place." First-year students spend the first couple of weeks doing a variety of activities that are designed to provide an in-depth orientation to our surroundings. It culminates in a night compass course over the Lowell Mountains just north of the campus. This is a really interesting exercise. This year it rained from the moment we left until the moment we got to the vans. We don't intervene. We are at the back of the group for any risk management issues that may come up. We also have a winter expedition, four days and three nights in the Lowell Mountains again, that all the first-years do. I also get to climb with them. The first year I was here I designed and then built, with students, a three-sided climbing wall with a roof on it. That is our gym.

5. *Where is Sterling located?*

It is affectionately known as the Northeast Kingdom. We are northwest of St. Johnsbury; about 20 minutes from Canada.

6. *What do you think has been the best learning activity with your students?*

Jim Jelmberg,
Director ORMS OEP

I think everything from our academic courses to "bounder," which is learning everything from how to use tools to canoeing, hiking, and skiing. Bounder is a regular afternoon activity. There would also be things that a couple of colleagues and I would teach a course called, "Triumph of the Human Spirit," which is a literature course. We would think of experiential things to do that would tie into the literature that we were reading. I gave the example from "Touching the Void." So what would *you* do if you were teaching the book Endurance? How could you provide students with some experience that would give them an idea of what is involved in spending a year and a half isolated in the Antarctic? We think up activities that get them cold fast.

7. *Is there anything that you would like to add?*

You know, I have had a lot of fun in this educational journey, which I call the expedition of a lifetime. A quick anecdote. When I was working for Outward Bound and the students were out on solo for 3 days, I always thought of things to do that would give them something to talk about when we came back together again. I would go to their various camps and turn on a tape recording of a Bach cello partita for 3 or 4 minutes and then sneak away. Then when doing the debriefing, I would wait and see who would be the first kid to say, "I heard a lot of music while I was on the solo." That is fun at nobody's expense. I think that is the big thing. We must keep all the potential activities we could do in some kind of perspective so that the fun we are having is at no student's expense and, most importantly, that there would be some kind of helpful thing for them in the process.

DEB FREED, CLARION, PENNSYLVANIA,
A BACKYARD DABBLER

It was not until late in my adult life that I even recognized my connection with the outdoors. I should have seen it coming for there were signs along the way. For the most part, my childhood provided an unfettered opportunity to explore the acres of farmland and bordering streams and a river near my home. I attended summer camp at a sprawling site where even the long walks between the dining hall and platform tents were mini adventures. Our family vacations were often tours to historic places balanced with lakeside cottages. One trip took us on a 6-week bus trip from Ohio to Texas to California and back. My fifth-grade teacher enrolled the entire class in Junior Audubon. At the time I was a reluctant member, preferring to play softball and marbles rather than learn about birds during recess. That introduction to birds would resurface later in life. My degree in mathematics and employment in computer science and then later in social service did not connect me with the outdoor world. Spending time in a natural setting was a weekend thing. Once I had established a career and family, however, vacations gravitated to our national parks, wildlife refuges and scenic train adventures. In the out-of-doors was where I wanted to be. In furnishing our home, I surrounded it with artwork from local artists, ranging from carvings and photographs of birds to posters of the nearby forest, watercolors of roadside flowers, and oils of outside landscapes. In hindsight, it could not be more obvious that I love the outdoors and all it entails.

In my 30s I became involved with Girl Scouting and was attracted to their outdoor programs. I learned a lot about self-sufficiency, problem solving, and adapting to unplanned situations. Hands-on experiences taught me resourcefulness and instilled a level of self-confidence. I joined the local Audubon chapter and instantly signed up for every field trip I could. Day-long birding events were ones that passed all too quickly. Disappointed when the day was ending, we patiently waited at dusk for the short-eared owls to hunt the open field until we lost all daylight. Our family moved from a house in town to one bordering a hemlock stand on the south side of a ridge above the river. Having more than just a weekend peek at nature filled a void that had been empty since my childhood days of rambling and playing outside.

I love both the familiar cycles in nature and the unexpected discoveries. Some days I find beauty in the grand sights of a sunset, stars, clouds, and waves of tall grasses. Other days I thrill at the delicate purple strands in the spring beauty flower or the prints of the predators' wings in the snow. Every day is delightfully enhanced with the backyard birds at my feeders. Special days during migration fill the edges of the yard with warblers and unusual species like the Marsh Wren attracted to the waterfall above our goldfish pond. Nothing can compare, however, to the first-ever sighting, known as life bird, like the Snowy Owl in a Pennsylvania cornfield! The great surprise in unexpected discovery can happen anywhere. In November, at a roadside rest along the interstate, we crunched over millions of hickory nuts. Our quick collection yielded two cups of the precious meats!

Although I own several field guides and subscribe to several periodicals on nature, I still consider myself a dabbler. From one year to the next I have to refresh my wildflower and birding identification skills, especially recognizing birdsongs. I am not driven to keep a life list of birds or travel to see special species; however, I would take a walk with a naturalist any day of the week. I am comfortable with that level of engagement. It doesn't drive me or my family crazy. In daily walks with my golden retriever, I have fun following snow tracks and figuring out who was chasing what. I like using all my senses; smelling the trailing arbutus flower; tasting teaberry; feeling pine needles; listening to the wind and watching the birds. I enjoy watching a chickadee take a snow bath or looking up in the sky to see a squadron of common nighthawks on approach with their broad white wing bars looking like landing lights. I can even calmly step over a black rat snake basking in the sun across my path and not flinch at seeing it climb a tree. My contacts with nature have given me so much pleasure. In the midst of schedules and responsibilities I appreciate the total "in-the-moment" feeling whenever I venture outdoors. Either with others or by myself I will continue to dabble in nature.

MYTHS AND LEGENDS
TIM CHURCHARD: LECTURER AND COACH, UNIVERSITY OF NEW HAMPSHIRE, DURHAM

1. *Thirty years ago we began our quest in outdoor education. Little did we know that we were at the beginning of a burgeoning effort that would lead to a range of activities today from university instructor workshops to orientation activities for Fortune 500 company employees. When you started, did you ever think outdoor education would become so widespread?*

No. I never even heard the term *outdoor education*. When we started we had a bunch of kids that were at risk, and the only thing they really had in common was (and we discovered this through testing) low self-esteem. They were all kids who had been in the juvenile detention system, problem kids. So we said, "What can we do to address their self-esteem?" Certainly, everything in the classroom should address self-esteem, but we wanted something more dynamic. So we decided to get involved with a ropes course because we had gone to a ropes course with Keith King and Tommy Herbert. Concord High School was one of the few schools that had a ropes course at the time. We had some training in that, we got a grant, and we built a ropes course in Rochester. Then we naturally went from that to rock climbing and got some instruction in that. We went out west and climbed in Colorado with Rick Medrick and got a lot of instruction in teaching climbing. I remember Keith King saying, "There are two kinds of climbers, one are people who are crag rats and just like to climb, and the other are people who use the rock for teaching, as a metaphor." We fell into the latter category because that kept us from having to climb some of these dangerous climbs that people do. We actually ended up using places like Cathedral Ledge and White Horse with these kids. We saw what it did.

We started giving our students a self-esteem test before and after, and their self-esteem skyrocketed. But we also realized that if you didn't follow it up with a lot of success that it wasn't going to continue, and it may even drop lower than before because the expectations go up. We then get very much involved. Someone gave us the book *Schools Without Failure* by William Glasser (1975). We went to workshops with William Glasser in Portland, Maine and we started really seeing how the lack of failure was the thing that gradually elevates self-esteem instead of spiking it like the rock climbing did. We incorporated all that in with the academics. Every kid that came had a history of failure to that school. We told them that we were throwing away their records. We weren't accepting their records from the school. They were starting from zero with us. It was in their hands as to where they were going to go with that.

[Jim: It was a demonstration of trust to them.]

Yes, yes, and we weren't going to make any judgments about what they had done in the past. We had some tough customers. We stuck with that and everything we did we geared toward self-esteem, and we developed a community service program. I thought that had probably more of an impact than the outdoor program where we had these kids who were, basically, takers in their life, and we gave them the opportunity to give back. They were getting credit. We got by the school committee with granting high school credit for community service hours. We were granting them social studies credits in community service. We had them helping people and doing things for other people and raising money for charity. The program involved academics, social service, and outdoor programs. I think where we got the most bang was we had a system of certified belayers. It was our own system, but we had hats made for them that said "Certified Belayers" on them. If they passed all the tests, we could trust them to belay other people. We were bringing other school groups and they would do the belaying. They had never been trusted like that before. What I've always found out, is that if you give people real responsibility, they act responsibly. What I said was, "If you screw this up, some of you could be killed or get hurt badly." They never screwed it up. Never. They became very responsible and they became caretakers of the younger students who came in the school, and they started working with elementary kids and started feeling that responsibility. In that sense that's where a lot of the power was—in giving them real responsibility. In the outdoor programs that's real responsibility. If you are out in the winter, and it goes below zero, and you're in the White Mountains, you got some real responsibility for your own self and other people who depend on you. So that is where we addressed the long-term self-esteem, and then we added the rock climbing experiences, the climbing of Mt. Chocorua in the winter and staying at Zealand Hut in the winter. What we really got onto there was the effect it had on their self-esteem.

[Jim: That was great Tim! It seems as though you started off with the adventure part, the rock climbing part, and that's an intense experience that builds confidence, but in order to sustain this for the long run, you brought in the conceptual approach from Glasser and the academic approach as well.]

Yeah, we started getting into "You're not going to fail." We started really defining teaching as a partnership with students, and "We're not going to fail here," and "Here's what we need to do." It's not going to work all the time. We certainly had some kids who didn't make it, but we had some spectacular things done and accomplishments by kids. That wasn't always measured by graduating either. It was measured by their becoming real contributing citizens instead of takers.

[Jim: Yeah, sounds like John Dewey.]

I don't know if you remember, but it was about 5 years ago now, where the firemen from Rochester went into the house that was burning and rescued two infants. Their mother was outside and the infants were left in. These guys went in, crawling in on their hands and knees, not knowing whether the building was going to fall down or what. These men were interviewed all over the country for saving these kids. They had to feel their way through, because the kids weren't even crying by that point. They felt their way through the house on their hands and knees, crawling, full of smoke, and they got the infants out. They resuscitated them and got them to the hospital and the kids are thriving today. One of those was one of our kids we had dealt with through school. He had been in all kinds of trouble as a kid, but now he's a hero. He's a good kid anyway. I'm glad we didn't look at his past records.

[Jim: Right, and he's someone, as you say, who's taken on real responsibility and who's done it well and thrived on it.]

Absolutely, and he thrived on the outdoor program and the community service program. I would advise you, that if you had the time to get a hold of him, he's a fireman right over there in Rochester, Dominick Belleou. He was a character too, big personality. We knew he was going to do well, we just didn't know what it would be. We were pretty sure it wasn't going to be academic. He's done very well for himself. One of the things I like talking with you about, anyway, is the art of teaching versus the science of it. You have known when to let go and when to reign in, and not do one consistently, all the time. I was just telling this fellow here that the movie *Million Dollar Baby* has a great quote. The boxing coach tells the manager, "There's a part of every great fighter who doesn't listen to his coach, and that's what makes him a great fighter." There are kids that are going to do whatever you say. Well, that's going to get boring, and it robs some creativity. The teachers need to know when they need to back off and let this kid create his own thing within some structure, and you need to know when to put yourself into it or stay out of it.

2. *How did you become interested in the outdoors?*

When I was a kid growing up in Saugus, I would go out in the morning, in the summers when we weren't going to school, and my mother would say, "Do you want a sandwich or not? I'll see you tonight." I was out all day and I was always in the woods. There was a brook that we hung around, and I was always at the brook. There was a pond that we fished and swam in the summer and played hockey on in the winter. I was in the fields or the woods. To me the outdoors is spiritual. My feeling is that everyone has a spiritual need, and for me that satisfies that. I moved up here to the woods because there were just too many people where I grew up. There are no more woods there. I need the woods, and I need the fields and all that. Now for me to do something in terms of education, I said "You gotta be kidding me, I can go rock climbing, I can do this as part of a job and take kids overnight?" The only problem I have is I hate sleeping on the ground. I never sleep well and I only sleep two or three hours and that's it. So I got myself a hammock and that works.

3. *When did you begin to connect your outdoor calling as a way to work with schools and kids?*

It was working with these troubled kids when I did it. I came up from Massachusetts. I had been teaching down there for about 10 years and I came up here for this alternative program. I had to find something creative to do with them because they weren't making it in traditional classrooms. We had to create a real nontraditional classroom. We talked with some of the old mentors in the field, Karl Rhonke, Keith King, people like that, Rick Medrick. I love Keith King's phrase about using rock as a teaching tool and the mountains and the rivers. To me it was the real responsibility. If you don't do this right, someone's going to get hurt badly, and I never saw it fail.

4. *Who and what have been your biggest influences in outdoor education?*

Bill Cuff has been my biggest influence in outdoor education. He started with me, and I may know as much if not maybe more in different areas of that. That's not where it is. It's the ability to connect it and create meaning from it. I just learned so much from him. He was better than anyone else, better than any of the gurus that write books. He can make the connections and really use that as a tool and a metaphor for life that kids we were working with needed. He was the biggest influence. Keith King was a very big influence. I did my first rapell with Keith King. You never forget that. I thought I was going into the jaws of death. [Laughter] I did my first white water canoeing with Keith King. In fact, the hike that you were talking about along the New Hampshire coast, I did that with a group of kids and Keith King, and I stayed over at that friary. Oh yeah! I did the whole thing.

[Jim: It must have been Peter Ordway that got you started, because he was connected with Keith.]

He must have been, because we did it with Keith and Peter wasn't a part of that particular hike.

[Jim: Peter got me interested in doing that with kids and he got me organized and set up for it. I did it with a group of kids from the Somersworth Middle School. Peter didn't come on the trip, but he did get me started thinking about and planning it. I talked with him when we started our program.]

I got it from Keith or Keith got it from him, or something. It's interesting that you did that same experience that I did. I found that to be a really meaningful experience for the kids. Keith did that whole program at Keene State College. It was called "Living in Vigorous Environments" and we spent a lot of time with that. We went across country with that group out to one of the Experiential Education Conferences out in Mankato, Minnesota. It was Jim Schoel and Paul Radcliffe that were the real influences on me at Project Adventure. Paul's retired; he's sailing Winnapasake. There's a big, old sailboat that he built. He can build anything and he lives on that pretty much. He was associated with Dan Garvey when he was up at Ossipee.

5. *What has been the most adventuresome activity that you have done with your students?*

I went out to Calgary, Alberta, and was going to work with a woman who worked with emotionally disturbed kids. When I got to meet the guy who was my boss, there were two other guys along with myself and this woman. She had two other guys because she had 20 kids and we were going to do a glacial hike in the Kutanai Wilderness in British Columbia. We were going to be up there for, I think, 10 days. We were going to climb a glacier, climb a mountain, and we were going to do some rock climbing and river running in this 10-day period. One guy I worked with was a French Canadian kid from Quebec, and he was a guide on the Rivera Rouge in Quebec, which is a wild river. He was out there to be the river guide, and the guy that was the mountaineering hot shot was a Scottish guy who had immigrated to Canada and led the Canadian expedition to Mt. Everest. So he had climbed Mt. Everest. Those are pretty heavy guys and the kids were fantastic. The thing that made it the most significant experience I had done with kids was there were a lot of grizzlies. We had to really be thorough with these kids about food, how to take care of the food and not to take it in the tents with you. A kid woke me up one night and I looked out of the tent and saw a cub tearing apart a backpack, and it was into the candy. It was a bear cub, and I'm thinking, "I'm smart enough to know that if there's a bear cub here there's a mother fairly close." I didn't want the kids to wake up, so I just lay there and watched. I found out later that the other two guys were doing the same thing. I watched this bear cub tear this whole thing apart and pick out what it wanted and then they finally left. After that happened we were contacted, on foot, by a ranger. He said that we needed to leave because there had been a couple of attacks and they were looking for bears to sedate and get out of there. We still had two more nights to sleep on our way out of there. So that was probably the most adventuresome one with kids.

6. *What has been the best learning activity that you have done with your students?*

I think it happened around community service. We had a day when all the ones that they worked with came together. We had some kids who were reading to shut-ins. We had some kids who were working in the library; we had a peer-tutoring program where they were tutoring younger kids in the elementary school. We had a day where they could all bring them to the ropes course. They were all certified belayers at that time and they brought them to the ropes course and took them through. We were just there and I was watching and we didn't do a thing. To me, the best example was the learning that went on there. It was like a win–win–win situation. The learning for us was about how right we were in trusting these kids. The learning that those kids had was that they discovered some of their own power and their own worth in terms of what they were doing for these younger kids. There were, literally, stars in their eyes. The mentors that they had been working with knew that a year ago some of these kids were in a juvenile detention system and were just a drain on society, and they turned things around by just feeling better about themselves. So that really stands out to me.

7. *An important feature of the program that we did with the kids at the Oyster River Middle School was the integration of adventure and academics. We would hike or ski into an adventuresome habitat like the NH Seacoast as an expedition, and we would gather information in the outdoor classroom. How do you feel about the possibilities of integrating academics with adventure?*

They're endless. One of the things that you do, a lot more than I, is the whole sailing thing. The crew has got to do something to get from Point A to Point B. Sometimes you can't even go because of the fog or bad weather. When you anchor at night you're almost naturally always sitting in an oval, which is supposedly the best possible configuration you could get for discussion. I've never used it with kids. I've used it with some corporate groups and it works magic. So I think the possibilities are endless and, I think, you can just think of more things to do. Where I'm working now, I have a lot of environmental education graduate students. One of the things they have to come up with in class is a learning module. Some of the things they're coming up with involve using nature as a classroom.

A kid was talking yesterday about a "bog walk," and the kid had pictures of carnivorous plants around here. He's talking about getting a high-speed camera to catch this carnivorous plant trapping some kind of bug. You start thinking like that and the possibilities are absolutely endless. Every time I take the kids into the outdoor classroom, whether it's the seacoast or up here to college woods or back at school, I would have a certain amount of activities planned and while I was planning those I would think up more; but while the kids were out there with me working, I would always come away with more ideas of what to do the next time. I think you're right. It's just a very stimulating place to be and it stimulates the idea of developing curriculum when you're out there. It's a very rich, rich environment.

8. *Is there anything you would like to add to this interview for the Myths and Legends chapter?*

Yes, there is something that I always have to add. It's my mantra. I go over this so much that the kids are sick of hearing me say it in my Experiential Ed. class. When someone is a facilitator in the outdoors, and especially in adventure, it increases the power that teachers already have because the students feel more vulnerable. What I find is that the kids I'm dealing with in college haven't spent a lot of time playing in the woods. So it's an unfamiliar area to them and they feel very vulnerable. I think that we have to really pay attention to the teachers we are developing now to properly manage the power that they have. They can get a group or a kid in the outdoors to do anything, just about anything, and that isn't always educational. It's so seductive for a teacher to be able to have that kind of control. It's almost irresistible. I tell them all the time that you can get the group to do what you want. What I really believe that the teacher needs to do is take the group or the learner where they need to go, not where you need them to go, because it starts to feed your own ego. I see that as a problem. I see it happening way too much. I think we need to be in it for the right reasons, not because we need to have power ourselves because of our own insecurity. I see that as an issue. So that's my addition.

DWIGHT WEBB, COUNSELOR EDUCATOR, UNIVERSITY OF NEW HAMPSHIRE

Dwight Webb has been leading trips in the Sierra or in the White Mountains for the past fifty years. An inspiration to many aspiring counselors as a professor at UNH, Dwight is probably best known for his love of life and his devotion to the beauty of the planet. Ever generous of spirit, Dwight shares his inspiration: his dad and this lovely place called Earth.

I have this memory of crying uncontrollably and being completely devastated at age 9 when my dad took my brother to Caramba, and didn't take me. I wanted to be seen as the big strong and capable boy that I was not. All he said was . . . "maybe next year."

Caramba was Nirvana, the illusive fountain head, the Garden of Eden, and the castle on the hill all rolled into one. It held all the mystique and lore of unknown adventure and although not designated as such, it was a "rite of passage." To be invited was to "carry my own weight" and to be seen as on the threshold of manhood. Complaining of a heavy pack on this 11-mile wilderness fishing and camping trip deep into the San Jacinto Mountains was not within the norms of trek members. Even though I didn't know what the word norms meant then, at some level I just knew! It was the summer of 1943, I was 10, and true to his word, Dad told me to make my pack ready and attach it to the frame he had made for me. I was being treated like a young man, and I knew what would be expected of me.

Five hours into the trip, I asked, "What's a cache, Dad?" "Take a look over here son," he said as he lifted the lids off two icebox-size containers covered with galvanized sheet metal. Inside were blankets, flour, cornmeal, beef jerky, salt, sugar, dried milk, condiments, soap and other necessities, such as a big canvas tarp, all of which he had hauled up with pack animals years earlier when he built this hidden treasure now lying between two fallen trees and low growing shrubs.

We made camp a mile or so farther on into Caramba, and we slept under at least a million stars at almost 10,000 feet. When the sun came up, Dad was gone. My Uncle Bob, his brother Lee, and my brother Loren said we would fish this day, and "Dad got an early start," I caught my first fish that day and when we all gathered around the campfire, we tallied up. Loren had about 10 trout, my uncle Bob and his brother Lee about the same. Dad had 35 trout—all keepers! When I asked him how he did it, he said "You have to sneak up on them son. Fish can see you, and they can hear you. You have to think like a fish!" He showed me by taking his pole and baited hook and literally crawled on his belly to the stream by the camp, dropping his invitation for dinner to the trout below the embankment and pulled in 36. In the back-country in those days, he didn't pay much attention to the daily limit, and at that time, I don't remember anything like "catch and release."

There is no way I could ever forget the trip to Caramba; like the duck to his mother, I was imprinted. It launched me into a life of hiking and camping in the outdoors for the next half century. My dad was a great outdoorsman and I thought he was probably one of the great fishermen of all time. I'm 73 now and I still think it! Powerful images not forgotten over the 63-year span are fresh and still bring a smile to my face as I think of that boy I was.

Fishing with Dad in later years, I remember that he would always yell out, "Meat on the table" when he caught one. We either ate them or preserved them to eat another day.

My dad had a great frontier spirit. He grew up on a dirt farm in Oklahoma, being born in 1908, the year that territory became a state. He knew how to salt pork, jerk beef, can fish, and otherwise keep foods from spoiling. These survival skills were simply a part of his culture.

Another nice memory I remember from a fishing trip to Lake Henshaw was when he cooked a roast beef and vegetables in a big cast iron pot that he placed over coals in the ground, covered this with gunnysacks, and then shoveled dirt over while it did it's magic for about 3 or 4 hours. Delicious! The visual memory in writing this is as rich and tasty as was the food back then.

In the 1960s, I led wilderness trips for teenage boys with my friend Phil Cassaroli. We took three trips each summer, with up to 15 boys in each for six summers, in a program we called *Expedition Golden*. I'd like to think that some of the 200 or more boys were likewise the recipients of imprinting on the wonders of adventure in the natural world.

Arriving in New Hampshire in 1967, I was blessed to make friends with and be invited to join Peter Ordway and Ash Hallett, the founding fathers of what became known as the Ordway–Hallett Raiders. This was a loose conglomeration of rascals and no-good bums like Greg Goodman and others too outrageous to mention. For some 39 years now, we have hiked the White Mountains of New Hampshire, and on a couple of occasions extended our reach to Mt. Katahdin, and even over the waters to the Pennine Way, the backbone of England. With the help of the Raiders, other friends and my four sons, in 1987 we built Fort Dwight, a fine cabin on the Kancamagus which remains the headquarters of this band of brothers distinguished for their good cheer and rowdy singing in said cabin's rafters. Thankfully Peter and Ash's sons, Jon and Michael, were also imprinted (sort of like a soul tattoo) by their fathers, and the likes of good uncles such as the aforementioned professor Greg Goodman of Clarion University and professor emeritus James Jelmberg of UNH, both mentors extraordinaire with continuing passion for the great outdoors. I am honored to be a co-recipient of the dedication of this book, but offer this advice in advance. Reading is good, but hit the road Jack and Jackie, nothing quite like it for soothing the soul.

ABOUT THE EDITORS

Greg S. Goodman has been an outdoor education teacher and school psychologist for the past 30+ years. His joy continues to be spending a day in the outdoors and living in awe of nature's beauty. Although a glass of wine or a haute meal can entice, they are ascribed the most meaning after a cold-soaking, ass-kicking day in the woods. "Here's to it and to it again. If we don't get to it to do it, we won't get to it to do it again!" (Ashton Hallett).

As I think about my roots in this outdoor education stuff, I really have to go back in time several decades to when my great friend and mentor, Peter Ordway, first led me on a traverse of New Hampshire's White

Mountain Presidential range. For those unfamiliar with the Appalachian Trail and this particular stretch of its 2,000 plus miles, this is one of the most spectacular hikes in the world. Rambling up and down over peaks named for Adams, Washington, Madison, Jefferson, and Monroe, this trek at more than 4,000 feet includes wonderful views, and it gives the hiker a feeling of expansiveness unrivaled in most New England landscapes. Being above treeline for most of the way, the walker can, on a clear day, look about and drink in some of the best to be had in New Hampshire hiking.

Peter Ordway, my high school outing club leader, brought eight of his favorite charges along for an early summer, end-of-the-year backpacking experience in 1968. As a novice in this group, I had little idea of what to expect, but with Peter, I knew we would be well entertained. Peter was the high school student's dream teacher. Brilliant and entertaining, Peter was one who never wanted to surrender his youth. In the days of the late 1960s and early 1970s, boundaries were loosely defined, and we all enjoyed the romping prankster-ism of the period. On this 4-day adventure, the hiking and hilarity of endorphin-soaked minds was not only intoxicating, it was positively addicting. For me, it was rebirthing . . . beginning and connecting with nature as I had never before dreamed. Scouting in my youth was a meeting on Wednesday nights and talk of badges. Backpacking with Peter was full immersion in the wonderment of earth's beauty. Hooked, I was.

Continuing our trips into the mountains through the winter, Peter convinced me that I should try a 26-day stint at the Colorado Outward Bound School. In the summer of 1970, I enrolled in C-28 and spent 26 days confronting my sense of self and learning more than I ever imagined possible. From the first moment off the bus, we were handed gear I'd never seen before and given a shout to get up and go! Off to a gorge for a Tyrolean traverse, and the adventure continued for 25 more days. Howie Hoffman was our leader, and we were well served with his tenacious appetite for the rigor. Having come through Outward Bound with his own unique experiences, Howie was charged with a sense of purpose that was unforgettable. On Howie's initial course, his leader was killed by a loose rock. From Howie's leadership, I was totally transformed.

Raised as a Jewish boy by a mother who never recovered from the loss of her only other child, my mother's gift to me was an acute fear of water, heights, and/or anything that could possibly lead to my demise. The seed of fear was planted deeply, and Outward Bound was this demon's exorcist! For the rest of my life, I would continue to use this metaphor as my strength to combat any fear or doubt. The feeling was never totally absent, but the courage to battle and conquer was always affirmed. "To serve to strive and not to yield" is Outward Bound's motto, and it has been my salvation.

Coming from Outward Bound, I became a man on a mission. For the next 20 years, I taught Outward Bound adaptive programs in schools and mental health centers. During these years I enjoyed the opportunity to meet and to work with many incredibly invigorating and exciting individuals: Peter Ordway, David Enegess, Regon Unsoeld, Jed Williamson, Dwight Webb, Lance Lee, Karl Rohnke, Bob Lentz, Keith King, and many more. From students to co-workers, we forged fabulous friendships on the rivers, cliffs, and mountains we ventured to visit. To this day, I continue many of the relationships that began on those trips. For Peter Ordway and the others who helped me along the road, my gratitude is immeasurable.

In the song Ramblin' Boy, the last verse sums it up for me:

> "Now if when we die, we go somewhere,
> I'll bet you a dollar, he's a-ramblin' there."

As I think back on all of those endorphin-filled, exhausting, and wonderful days, I appreciate the real value of how much I gave because of the incredibly rich reward I've gleaned. In nature is the preservation (Porter), and in each other is soulful sustenance for our existence on the planet. Giving the gift of just one day in the mountains (or on the water) could transform a life and awaken a spirit that could change another's world. What greater good could a teacher imagine?

Jim Jelmberg, formerly a freestyle ski coach at Waterville Valley Ski Resort in New Hampshire, comes to outdoor education by way of years of middle school and college teaching and a life-long love of the outdoors. As a 7-year-old, I hiked daily through the woods with friends to swim and dive from the high jagged cliffs of the abandoned granite quarries where my grandfather and uncles had worked, a mile from my home in Rockport, Massachusetts.

My outdoor adventures include working as a construction worker and ski patrolman through college and later as a ski instructor, including teaching in the Italian Alps in Cervinia. My biggest adventures include glacier skiing in the Italian and Swiss Alps on the Plateau Rosa under the Matterhorn and skiing the most difficult runs at Tuckerman's Ravine, New Hampshire's steepest and most extreme ski Mecca. Tuckerman's is a rite of passage for the most serious skiers in the northeast. Characterized by avalanches, forbidding rocks, and no ski lifts, the unique nature of this place is defined by its great beauty and great danger. To ski this Ravine is the ultimate in preparation and problem solving, because falling is not an option in many of the runs.

I am eager to reflect on these experiences and to help others with what I have learned: to balance my outdoor philosophy and my life's work, teaching. Consistent with my mind, body, and spirit approach to life, I believe that learning should be an adventure that should appeal to the whole child, not just to the cognitive domain. It was this integration of learning and adventure that prompted me to design and direct the schoolwide Outdoor Education Program at the Oyster River Middle School in Durham, New Hampshire, the inspiration for this book. The ideas of this program were disseminated in presentations ranging from teacher workshops in New Hampshire and Massachusetts to seminars at the University of New Hampshire and Brandeis University.

My philosophy of education tells me that the outdoor classroom is an adventuresome avenue for providing equal opportunities to all students for both academic and personal growth. Hiking, skiing, and rappelling seem like formidable challenges to many kids, similar to some of the academic courses they face, and success with these outdoor challenges can build confidence for academic and personal success. I believe the outdoor advice of "taking just one step at a time" can be a metaphor that works for both adventure and academic challenges. This metaphor can be made very clear to our kids in exciting and highly motivating outdoor environments.

To provide peer support for the challenges of hiking and curriculum problem solving, students help to choose diverse and gender equitable student groups that become microcosms of democratic decision making. This democratic process produces valuable teamwork, trust, and lasting friendships. When I ask my college students what they remember about their kindergarten through Grade 12 school years, they almost never say anything about what they learned academically. When I run into my former middle school students, however, they remember the outdoor expeditions they experienced years ago. They recall what they did, what curriculum they learned, and how much fun they had. This is the power of the outdoor classroom.

This duality with academics and adventure is a consistent theme in my life. While recently designing and coordinating a master's degree program in middle school education at Notre Dame College, I also finished my quest to climb all 48 of the 4000-foot mountain peaks in New Hampshire, becoming a member of the Appalachian Mountain Club's Four-Thousand Footer Club. I now teach in the 5-year Master's Degree Program in Teacher Education at the University of New Hampshire and enjoy hiking, ski racing, and sailing with my wife Johanne, a retired schoolteacher. She is the teacher from whom I have learned the most.

REFERENCES

Glasser, W. (1975). *Schools without failure*. New York: Harper Paperbacks.

King, C. (1997). *Mountaineering in the Sierra Nevada*. Yosemite National Park, CA: Yosemite Association.

Muir, J. (1992). *John Muir: The eight wilderness discovery books*. Chatham, IL: Diadem Books.

Rose, G. (1974). *High odyssey: The first solo winter assault of Mt. Whitney and the Muir Trail area, from the diary of Orland Bartholomew and photographs taken by him*. Friday Harbor, WA: Howell Press.

Rose, G. (1987). *Reflections of Shaver Lake*. Fresno, CA: Word Dancer Press.

Rose, G. (1999). *Magic Yosemite winters*. Truckee, CA: Coldstream Press.

Rose, G. (2000). *The San Joaquin: A river betrayed*. Clovis, CA: Word Dancer Press.

Rose, G. (2005). *Giants among the forests: A history of the Sequoia National Forest*. Tollhouse, FL: Interpretive Association.

Wordsworth, W. (1798). My heart leaps up. In G. Leggett (Ed.), *12 poets* (p. 101). New York: Holt, Rinehart and Winston.

AUTHOR INDEX

A

Altenbaugh, R.J., 49, *68*
Andrade-Duncan, 51, *68*
Apple, M.W., 60, *68*

B

Baker, J.A., 46, 64, *68*
Bandura, A., 11, *14*
Barrett, J., 102, *120*
Bates, M., 51, 54, *68*
Benard, B., 60, *68*
Bialeschki, M.D., 30, *42*
Blanchard, S., 17, *26*
Bomotti, S., 60, *68*
Bourdieu, P., 48, 49, 51, *68*
Breunig, M., 37, 41, *42, 43*
Bridge, K.A., 31, *42*
Bridger, R., 46, 64, *68*
Brown, V.B., 36, *42*
Bruner, J., 52, *68*

C

Cairnes, B.D., 65, *68*
Cairnes, R.B., 65, *68*
Camp Kehonka, 36, *42*
Carey, K., 20, 24, *27*
Cashel, C., 41, *43*
Chase, M., 51, 54, *68*
Cheng, C-L., 7, *14*
Chung, A., 51, 54, *68*
Cole, D., 7, 12, 13, *14*
Comer, J.P., 50, *68*
Coxford, A.F., 53, *68*

D

Dagenais, R., 52, *68*
Damasio, A., 6, *14*
Dewey, J., 7, 14, 22, *26*, 128, *133*
Dieser, R.B., 35, 36, *42*
Dosch, D., 52, *68*
Duval, L., 32, 34, *42*

SUBJECT INDEX

DATE DUE

Demco, Inc. 38-293

Printed in the United States
200494BV00002B/36/A